CONSTITUTING FAMILIES:
A STUDY IN GOVERNANCE

ARSP BEIHEFT 57

ARCHIV FÜR RECHTS- UND SOZIALPHILOSOPHIE

ARCHIVES DE PHILOSOPHIE DU DROIT ET DE PHILOSOPHIE SOCIALE

ARCHIVES FOR PHILOSOPHY OF LAW AND SOCIAL PHILOSOPHY

ARCHIVO DE FILOSOFÍA JURÍDICA Y SOCIAL

FRANZ STEINER VERLAG STUTTGART
1994

CONSTITUTING FAMILIES: A STUDY IN GOVERNANCE

UNITED KINGDOM ASSOCIATION
FOR LEGAL AND SOCIAL PHILOSOPHY

NINETEENTH ANNUAL CONFERENCE
AT CARDIFF. APRIL, 1993

EDITED BY
DEREK MORGAN & GILLIAN DOUGLAS

FRANZ STEINER VERLAG STUTTGART
1994

Die Deutsche Bibliothek - CIP-Einheitsaufnahme
[Archiv für Rechts- und Sozialphilosophie / Beiheft]
Archiv für Rechts und Sozialphilosophie : ARSP = Archives de philosophie du droit et de philosophie sociale. Beiheft. -
Stuttgart : Steiner
Früher Schriftenreihe
Fortlaufende Beil. zu: Archiv für Rechts- und Sozialphilosophie
NE: Archives de philosophie du droit et de philosophie sociale / Beiheft; ARSP / Beiheft
57. United Kingdom Association for Legal and Social Philosophy: ... Annual conference / United Kingdom Association for Legal and Social Philosophy.
19. Constituting families. - 1994
United Kingdom Association for Legal and Social Philosophy:
... Annual conference / United Kingdom Association for Legal and Social Philosophy. - Stuttgart : Steiner
(Archiv für Rechts- und Sozialphilosophie : Beiheft ; ...)
Früher Schriftenreihe
19. Constituting families. - 1994
Constituting families : a study in governance ; at Cardiff, April 1993 / ed. by Derek Morgan & Gillian Douglas. - Stuttgart : Steiner, 1994
(... Annual conference / United Kingdom Association for Legal and Social Philosophy ; 19) (Archives for philosophy of law and social philosophy : Beiheft ; 57)
ISBN 3-515-06481-8
NE: Morgan, Derek [Hrsg.]

 Dieses Buches wurde auf alterungsbeständigem Papier gedruckt. Druck: Druckerei Proff, Eurasburg.
Printed in Germany

Contents

List of Contributors

Brenda Almond; Professor of Philosophy, School of Philosophy, The University, Hull, HU6 7RX

Bob Brecher, School of Historical & Critical Studies, University of Brighton, 10-11 Pavillion Parade, Brighton, BN2 1RA

Ruth Chadwick, Professor of Moral Philosophy, Centre for Professional Ethics, University of Central Lancashire, Preston PR1 2HE

Gillian Douglas, Senior Lecturer, Cardiff Law School, PO Box 427, Cardiff, CF1 1XD

John Eekelaar, Fellow of Pembroke College, Oxford; Reader in Law, University of Oxford, OXI IDW

Michael Freeman, Professor of English Law, Faculty of Laws, University College London, Bentham House, 4-8 Endsleigh Square, London WC1 OEG

John Haldane, Reader in Moral Philosophy, Department of Moral Philosophy, The University, St Andrews, Fife, Scotland, KY16 9AL

Sandra Marshall, Department of Philosophy, University of Stirling, Stirling, Scotland, FK9 4LA

Derek Morgan, Senior Research Fellow, School of Law, Glasgow University, Glasgow, Scotland, G12 8QQ

Kenneth Norrie, Senior Lecturer, School of Law, The Stenhouse Building, Strathclyde University, 173 Cathedral Street, Glasgow, Scotland, G4 0RQ

Katherine O'Donovan, Professor of Family Law and Legal Theory, Rutherford College, University of Kent, Canterbury, Kent, CT2 7NP.

Derek Morgan and Gillian Douglas

The Constitution of the Family: Three Waves for Plato

> 'The complexities of family life are no longer capable of being reduced to simple certainties.'[1]
>
> 'There is no such thing as society; there are only individuals, and families.'[2]

1. Introduction

A thematic division of the essays in this volume would fall into two parts; in the first they treat of philosophical questions of contemporary family life, particularly the contested question of justice. In Part II they address the policy of family law and, particularly, the concepts of rights and responsibilities within families.[3] Essays in that Part are concerned with what Eekelaar identifies as rights discourse as a mode of ethical reasoning and questions arising from the adequacy of that conception as a basis for identifying the best or proper interests of family members. Taken together, the essays examine what – building on Katherine O'Donovan's plea for an extended conversation involving moral arguments in family law – we may call a constitutional colloquy in the moral economy of the family;[4] in that way a study of families may be seen increasingly to be a study in governance and government.

The essays deal variously with relations between the state and the individual and the way in which the state permits, acknowledges or facilitates families. Freeman, O'Donovan, Chadwick and Brecher concentrate their attentions on the nature and status of marriage and its alternatives or dissonances, while Eekelaar and Almond introduce to the debate the nature and circumstances of parenthood. Marshall and Morgan and Norrie and

1 Law Commission, *The Grounds for Divorce, Report No. 192*, (London, HMSO, 1990), para. 3.6

2 Margaret Thatcher, *Woman's Own*, 31 October 1987, p.10; and see Margaret Thatcher, *The Downing Street Years*, (London, Harper Collins, 1993)

3 Two recent essays which address some of these questions are William Duncan, 'The Constitutional Protection of Parental Rights: Discussion of the Advantages and Disadvantages of According Fundamental Status to Parental Rights and Duties', and Lucy Smith, 'Children, Parents and the European Human Rights Convention', both in John Eekelaar and Petar Sarcevic (eds.), *Parenthood in Modern Society: Legal and Social Issues for the Twenty First Century*, (Dordrecht, Martinus Nijhoff, 1993), at 431–46 and 447–62 respectively

4 To use that notion of moral economy once famously identified by E P Thompson, 'The Moral Economy of the English Crowd in the Eighteenth Century' *Past and Present*, 50, 1971 76 at 79. In an early article on surrogacy, Derek Morgan developed this notion in an examination of what he there called the 'architecture of contemporary life.' The general observations on that theme, there specifically applied to surrogacy, are relevant for a consideration of general issues here; see 'Making Motherhood Male: Surrogacy and the Moral Economy of Women' *J of Law and Society* 12, 1985, 219–38

ARSP-Beiheft 57. Derek Morgan & Gillian Douglas (eds.)

Haldane complement that from their different perspectives, in examining the issue of autonomy over decision making at the more specific levels of reproductive choices and of medical treatment decisions of and for children.

Haldane, in a paper written in response to Norrie, provides a critical survey of so much of the preceding discussion as may be equated with an attack on the family. 'The case for the family' Haldane writes;

with which I have been concerned is based upon its roles as a central factor in the moral formation of young persons, and as a continuing locus of their deepest concerns. This case is not refuted by such claims as that there is often abuse within families or that the institution itself may be used for other ends whose value is open to question. ... let not the pursuit of perfection blind us to the value of what we have already.[5]

While there is much divergence from that view, each essay takes as its starting point the injunction laid upon family lawyers that those '... who remain technicians cannot contribute to the current debate currently raging about the family.'[6] As Pamela Symes has appropriately observed of the agenda of the critical legal studies approach to family law;

which items appear on that agenda and how we approach them will very largely be determined by two things: our theory of human nature and probably, more importantly, our view of what we consider to be the appropriate concerns of the lawyer.[7]

And what is the role of law in this world of renegotiated domestic arrangements? Linda Nielsen, following Mary Ann Glendon,[8] has captured well the dynamic which these essays seek to explore:

Family law today centres on the economic conditions of the family – the law of family property – which institutes a series of community rules. This consists of an interaction between four elements; the family, property, the law, and ideology. The more specific grounds for community rules are to be discovered partly in social conditions in the family and partly drawn from an ideological base in order to fashion any economic conclusions.[9]

Ruth Chadwick, more explicitly than other contributors, analyses this latter question. She suggests that the dispute between individualism and collectivism (variously addressed by Freeman, O'Donovan, Brecher, Eekelaar, Almond and Chadwick herself), and the family as a possible site for its resolution or mediation, represents not only a possible model for family law, but itself adds another dimension to the tension or opposition between individual and communitarian values.[10]

5 John Haldane, 'Children, Families, Autonomy and the State', Chapter 9, below.

6 Michael Freeman, 'Towards a Critical Theory of Family Law' *Current Legal Problems* 38, 1985, 153 at 155

7 Pamela Symes, 'Property, Power and Dependence: Critical Family Law' *Journal of Law and Society* 14, 1987, 199 at 199

8 Mary Ann Glendon, *The New Family and the New Property*, (Toronto, Butterworths, 1981) and Glendon, *The Transformation of Family Law: State, Law and the Family in the United States and Western Europe,* (Chicago, Chicago University Press, 1989)

9 Linda Nielsen, *Familie Formueretten; Skilsmisse og Skifte*, (Copenhagen, GEC GAD, 1993), 497

10 In her paper, and those of other contributors, that opposition is stylised into the various approaches of John Rawls, *A Theory of Justice,* (Oxford, Oxford University Press, 1971), Susan Moller Okin, *Justice, Gender and the Family*, (New York, Basic Books, 1989) and Alistair MacIntyre, *After Virtue*, (London, Duckworth, 1981). A valuable acknowledged contribution to the literature is Will Kymlicka, 'Rethinking the Family' *Philosophy & Public Affairs*, 20, 1991, 77–97

As becomes evident, the contributors to this volume do not speak in one voice on either concern identified by Symes; they record a polyphonic chorus to the central dramatic of the 'family.' Nor would they necessarily share a common understanding of the proper role and authority of law and lawyers. But where they would be in agreement is in their concern to identify and analyse the many contemporary roles and functions which the state has laid upon the family,[11] and the way in which philosophical descriptions and evaluations of human natures reflects and refracts, measures and mediates, those concerns. Together, the essays address three different understandings of 'constitution'; i) how are families made up? ii) how are families made? iii) what rights, interests, duties and expectations exist between members of the family and the wider society? These questions provoke both legal and philosophical answers, although as Katherine O'Donovan argues in her essay in this volume, there has been a tendency of late to drift away from, to deny, explicit moral reasoning in family law and policy in favour of vague and unspecified notions of common sense.

2. The Family: Not Waving, But Drowning?

The family has long been a troubling site for political philosophy, largely because it has been seen as a distraction from public responsibilities. Plato had an neat expedient for resoloving this; he abolished the family. Although he recognised that his proposals might be problematic he felt fortified in this project by having '... escaped one wave without drowning, [viz] and dealt with the regulations about women.'[12] In her essay here, Ruth Chadwick echoes another, perhaps more compelling, reason why the family continues to be the site of continuing concern; it is itself a locus for the dispute between rival political philosophies such as individualism and communitarianism. 'Given the lack of resolution to this debate, it is not surprising that the question of what values should inform family law is problematic.'[13]

The evocation of the family as the private haven to which we return from the stresses and strains of the public sphere is part of its myth.[14] It has been assumed to follow that the rules which govern relations in the public domain are unnecessary and undesirable

11 For one of many valuable contributions to historical perspectives of this relationship see R Dingwall and J M Eekelaar, 'Families and the State: An Historical Perspective on the Public Regulation of Private Conduct' *Law & Policy*, 1988, 341–61, exploring debates on English social policy for children in the nineteenth and twentieth centuries. There is a characteristically compelling review of 'Politics, family, state' at chapter 3 (57–82) in D H J Morgan's *The Family; Politics and Social Theory*, (London, Routledge & Kegan Paul, 1985).

12 Plato, *The Republic*, (Harmondsworth, Penguin ed., 1955; rev. ed. 1987; trans. Desmond Lee), Book V, part.2. A contributor to the *Boston Quarterly Review* in 1859 lamented that 'The family, in its old sense, is disappearing from our land, and not only our free institutions are threatened but the very existence of our society is endangered.' (quoted in Anthony Giddens, *Sociology*, (Cambridge, Polity Press, 2ed., 1993), 421).

13 Ruth Chadwick, 'Moral Reasoning in Family Law – A Response to Katherine O'Donovan', Chapter 4, below

14 As Douglas has observed elsewhere, 'a debunking of the myth of the 'family' is urgently required', Gillian Douglas, 'Family Law under the Thatcher Government' *Journal of Law and Society*, 17, 1990, 411 at 425 n.6

in the family, that to impose such rules is for the state to 'interfere' in people's privacy and autonomy. The extent to which this assumption has led to, or facilitated, inequality within family relationships has been explored by several commentators in the past[15] and the need to rethink the position and role of the family in the light of gender inequality has been notably propounded by Susan Moller Okin,[16] whose arguments are discussed and criticised by Michael Freeman, in his Austin lecture, and Katherine O'Donovan.[17]

It is not that families as such are declining, there is little demographic evidence to support that, rather that the family as the aristocratic nobility have known it is under seige. This society, almost unique in the political calendar of late twentieth century, post modern, European societies of the west, has been poorly studied, and the contribution which it makes to the private and political agendas perhaps little understood.[18] But beyond that it enters the frame usually through the activities of a limited number of families; and often is captured through the lenses trained on a number of members of one family. The family in the 1990s is not so much in the firing line,[19] it is one of the pieces of armoury with which political and philosophical deabte is conducted.

Thus, it has become fashionable, especially in conservative party rhetoric for party consumption, to identify social liberalism as the motor for British decline, by which is ususally meant moral decline, and the idyll of the compleat family as in large part the remedy for many of these perceived ills. For that argument, liberalism, or excessive permissive liberalism is responsible for and identified with personal permissiveness, lax educational practices, rising crime and the decline of family cohesion. Political concern has, accordingly, turned from the form to the substance; the concern of the last years has been less, for example, with marriage and its alternative forms of cohabitation, but more with 'moral' aspects of responsibility in relationships.

The 'back to basics' idea announced at the 1993 Conservative Party Conference has caught in its trail a voluble debate about single mothers and their housing and other state benefits, juvenile and youth offenders, responsibilites and the Criminal Justice Act 1993, children left at home by themselves (the 'home alone' stories of Christmas 1993), the fiscal responsibilites of fathers and the Child Support Act 1991. The family has been

15 Ranging from, in relation to adults; – the unequal distribution of power between husbands and wives in the allocation of household income (see, J Pahl, *Money and Marriage,* (Basingstoke, Macmillan, 1989)); – unequal sharing of childcare and household chores (see, Ann Oakley, *Subject Women*, (London, Fontana, 1982 ed., 163–86, and *The Sociology of Housework*, (Oxford, Martin Robertson, 1974) passim, for the classic exposition); – domestic violence (R Dobash and R Dobash, *Women, Violence and Social Change,* (London, Routledge, 1992); – unequal effects of breakdown of the marriage or relationship (L Weitzman, *The Divorce Revolution; The Unexpected Social and Economic Consequences for Women and Children in America*, (New York, Free Press, 1985)); and in relation to children, child abuse and neglect, see, eg., Michael Freeman, *The Rights and Wrongs of Children*, (London, Frances Pinter, 1983)

16 *Justice, Gender and the Family,* (New York, Basic Books, 1989)

17 See below for a resume of these important arguments

18 A fleeting glimpse of its extraordinary tenacity and influence was discerned in the ferocious exchanges, marshalled behind the campaigning rhetoric of Lady Saltoun of Abernathy, in the House of Lords debates on the Human Fertilisation and Embryology Bill 1990. See, House of Lords, *Official Report,* 7 December 1990, cols 1089–91.

19 To recall the metaphor used by J Coussins and A Coote, *The Family in the Firing Line,* (London, NCCL/CPAG, 1981)

handmaiden to constitutional precedents (Government Minister Tim Yeo forced to resign office by his local constituency following revelations of a child born of an adulterous realtionship) and pall-bearer to constitutional presidents (Austrian president 'Must Choose between Love and Duty' *The Independent* 24 January 1994).

And in the few months since these papers were delivered at the Association for Legal and Social Philosophy Annual conference in Cardiff in April 1993, the Lord Chancellor has published proposals for divorce law reform, the government is consulting about the age of consent for lawful homosexual relationships, a 59 year old British woman has given birth to children following infertility treatment in the Italian clinic of Dr Antinori Severino, and the French government announced immediately a legislative prohibition on such treatments for post-menopausal women. A young German woman, pronounced brain stem dead has been mechanically ventilated for the (supposed) benefit of her 19 week old unborn fetus (it died) and the Human Fertilisation & Embryology Authority has issued a Consultation Paper – *Donated Ovarian Tissue in Embryo Research & Assisted Conception* – in part to gauge public reaction to the proposal to use eggs from aborted female fetuses in assisted conception services.

Children have been abducted from one of their parents by the other (who was subsequently imprisoned for contempt of court); an American Court has ordered the return of a two year old child to her biological parents notwithstanding that she had been placed for adoption a few weeks after her birth and appeared to regard her carers as her "parents."[20] Kimberly Mays was inadvertently given to the 'wrong' parents in the maternity hospital; fourteen years later when her biological parents applied for custody, what was particularly newsworthy was that she was regarded as of an age to resist the claim herself.[21] And in *Hecht* v *Superior Court for the State of California for the County of Los Angeles*[22] the California Court of Appeal, Second District, had to consider the novel issue of 'deep freeze families.' Arguing that now deceased Kane's frozen sperm should not be released by the clinic to impregnate his partner, Deborah Hecht, despite his request to that effect in his will, his adult children from a previous marriage argued that destroying the sperm would 'help guard the family unit' in two different ways. First, that it would prevent the birth of children who would never know their father and "never even have the slightest hope of being raised in a traditional family." Second, such an order would "prevent the disruption of existing families by after born children." They failed.[23]

The social consequences of changes, developments and movements within Europe will have their effects on family and individual life;[24] the opt-out from the Social Chapter

20 *The Times*, 3 August 1993, the 'Baby Jessica' case;

21 *The Guardian*, 19 August, 1993.

22 (1993) WL 209685 (Cal. App. 2 Dist.), June 17 1993

23 And for a similar French case see the judgment of the Tribunal de Grande Instance de Toulouse 11 May 1993 in the case of *Pires* v *Centre Hospitalier Regional de la Grave*. On the question of future generations see, John O'Neill, 'Future Generations: Present Harms' *Philosophy*, 68, 1993, 35–51. The question of access to children born following assisted conception has been considered by the European Court of Human Rights in *Application No. 16944/90 against the Netherlands*, digested in (1993) 1 *Med Law Rev* 404)

24 Some of these are considered in the various essays collected in John Eekelaar and Petar Sarcevic (eds.), *Parenthood in Modern Society: Legal and Social Issues for the Twenty First Century*, (Dordrecht, Martinus Nijhoff, 1993)

of the Treaty of Maastrict is important[25] as is the potential addition of new, especially Scandinavian, members of the Community.[26] But perhaps the most lasting effects on families, in many ways, will be outside law and family policy altogether – in the outcome and the example of the ritualised barbarity to which Bosnia has been allowed to succumb.

Two vignettes capture something of the nature of the contemporary debate about family values and British society. First, a woman who is not, it appears, herself thoroughgoingly heterosexual, refused the offer of free tickets to see a production of Shakespeare's *Romeo and Juliet* on behalf of her schoolchildren because, it was reported, she felt the play celebrated nothing but heterosexual love. For this she was pilloried, the Secretary of State for Education was petitioned by the Local Education Authority to undo all the government's recent policy on local management of schools when the school's governors and parents lent unyielding support to the teacher, and the circumstances of her appointment were called into question. It developed into a naked question of power and authority, choice and responsibility, worthy of the best medieval morality play.[27]

But perhaps most disturbing was the abduction, torture and killing of two years old James Bulger and the subsequent trial of his 11 year old assailants. We live increasingly in the surveillance society and the global village, in which we are watched over in the bank, the store, the petrol station, the telephone booth; day and night surveillance is facilitated by the possibilities of chip technology. Information about our movements, our tastes, pleasures and purchases can be transmitted almost instantaneously from one side of the globe to the other. In this society, the abduction – particularly perhaps the all too visible abduction preserved on shopping centre video cameras, so-called security cameras, – and the killing of James Bulger, demonstrated that even in these panoptic places, societies in which our every move is watched, clocked, date coded and recorded, precious losses can occur if people do not take care.

'The work of the family lawyer regularly provides evidence of the human capacity to exploit, abuse and oppress those weaker than ourselves, but such frailty should not be viewed in isolation from the culture, the structure within which we function.'[28] Without directly addressing that case, it nonetheless stands as a metaphor for what these essays are trying to explore; value, worth, meaning, citizenship, justice. Each can have a debased or counterfeit hue, a lustre which looks appealing but which on examination turns out be synthetic. As these essays demonstrate, the evidence of injustice can take varied and subtle forms, and no one conception of human nature is likely to satisfy a desire to explain or defend it.

Finally, the Tony Bland case[29] shows that it is not only in relation to children that family interests and family views about what should happen to individual members may be regarded as important.[30] The ageing revolution means that decision making questions

25 See Ruth Nielsen and Erica Szyszczak, *The Social Dimension of the European Community*, (Copenhagen, Handelshojsholen Forlag, 2 ed., 1993)

26 See Svien Andersen and Kjell Eliassen, *Making Policy in Europe: The Europeification of National Policy-Making*, (London, Sage, 1993)

27 The arguments and the sequeale are variously reported in the British press in January 1994.

28 Symes, *op. cit.*, 199

29 *Airedale National Health Service Trust* v *Bland* [1993] 1 All ER 821

30 On this generally see the excellent survey by Andrew Grubb, 'Treatment Decisions: Keeping it in the Family' in Andrew Grubb, (ed.), *Choices and Decisions in Health Care*, (Chichester, John Wiley & Sons, 1993), 37–96

and the ethics of deciding for others will continue to assume an increasingly important and controversial role in contemporary social policy.[31] It will be an area of personal and political moment as much as the more familiar areas with which social policy and the family have been concerned.[32] It also provides a good example of the language of the moral in family law and the role of the state.

Speaking in 1978, Margaret Thatcher identified what was to become the theme of perhaps one of the Conservative Government's most lasting policy credos;

> We know the immense sacrifices which people will make for the care of their near and dear ... Once you give people the idea that all this can be done by the state ... then you will begin to deprive human beings of one of the essential ingredients of humanity – personal moral responsibility.[33]

This became translated into Government policy, which by 1981 read;[34] '... the primary sources of support and care are informal and voluntary ... Care in the community must increasingly mean care by the community.' This policy illustrates neatly Brecher's characterisation of the conservative government programme of 'community care' which is

> ... [in] 'returning' people to 'the community'; that is to say, to the family – and that is to say largely to women – [it] at once: *extends* the role of the family; *diminishes* the state's role in active caring, while further development in the direction of private as opposed to public provision of care, that is, guarding diminishing resources for those who are 'one of us'; *increases* the role of the state in directing that development, that is, it 'arranges' the 'free' market for private care; and in doing all of this, reinforces one rather than another set of definitions and delimitations of 'public' and 'private.'[35]

It also neatly illustrates one of the early themes of the essays in this collection, that of domestic, or intra as well as intergenerational justice. It forces us to ask what are the demands which might properly be put by one upon another, or upon the state.[36] A similar

31 Some of the broader perspectives are canvassed in John Eekelaar and David Pearl, (eds.), *An Aging World – Dilemmas and Challenges for Law and Social Policy*, (Oxford, Clarendon Press and Nihon Kajo Publishing, 1989, esp. chs. 11–31). For the contemporary proposals of the Law Commission of England and Wales to address some of these questions see their three Consultation Papers – *Mentally Incapacitated Adults and Decision-Making: A New Jurisdiction* (No. 128); *Mentally Incapacitated Adults and Decision-Making: Medical Treatment and Research* (No. 129) and *Mentally Incapacitated and Other Vulnerable Adults: Public Law Protection*, (No. 130); (all London, HMSO, 1993). The proposals are the subject of a trenchant critique in David Carson, 'Disabling Progress: The Law Commission's Proposals on Mentally Incapacitated Adults' Decision-making' *Journal of Social Welfare and Family Law*, 1993, 304–20

32 See Gillian Dalley, *Ideologies of Caring: Rethinking Community and Collectivism*, (Basingstoke, Macmillan, 1988)

33 Quoted in *Community Care*, 12 April 1978

34 DHSS, *Growing Older*, Cmnd 8173 (London, HMSO, 1981)

35 Brecher, 'What is Wrong with the Family', Chapter 5, below

36 On the question of intergenerational justice and of children's responsibilities to care for their parents in old age or failing health, see, for example, Norman Daniels, *Am I My Parents Keeper?* (New York, OUP 1988) (it is not possible to define the nature of a filial obligation to support family elders) and compare this with Daniel Callaghan, 'What do children owe elderly parents?' *Hastings Center Report* 15(2), 1985, 32–7, who distinguishes between the obligation to provide affection by maintaining contact and providing emotional support, (which children should provide), physical care in the limited sense of providing help with shopping and transport, (which they should provide if other obligations permit) and financial assistance (which should be provided if no other sources of support and all the needs of the children's own children have been met, since the duty to support those whom we procreate is greater than that to those who have procreated us).

question of inter-generational equity emerges not only in vertical descendant relationships, but ascendant ones too. As Michael King has written:

It is hardly surprising that the law's utterances on children's well-being concentrate upon the parent-child relationship. The law 'knows' children through the parent or parents. Parents have legal rights, duties and responsibilities. These not merely empower the parents to take decisions about their children's lives, but they are the very threads which the law attaches to people who become legal parents, jerking them into response when things go wrong in their child's life.[37]

We can illustrate this movement by looking more closely at the guises of the family.

3. Not Drowning, But Waving: New Uncertainties in the Appearance of Family

Who and what is the family?[38] How does a family come into existence? What are its limits and limitations? Appeals to the enduring value of 'the family' are frequently made by politicians and others who are seeking to divert attention from other intractable problems of social or economic policy. It is assumed without question that we are all for 'the family', and that we all know what we mean by 'the family'; not only that the family has one identity, but that we can identify it. But alongside its proclaimed external nature, developments of new family arrangements, adopted either through choice or necessity, do not fit this identity-kit stereotype, and question the very validity and centrality of the nuclear family.[39] The 'one-parent-family', the household consisting of cohabiting adults only, the grouping of children blended together from different relationships by their parents, the caring for an elderly relative within the home of grown up children. Each of these is an illustration, an affirmation, that we're all family now.

For Michael Freeman what constitutes the family – in the sense that what determines its make up and its functions – is historically and culturally specific; this is something which Plato would have understood well.[40] Bob Brecher puts these concerns concisely in his essay:

... it is precisely the meaning, and our understanding of their scope, of terms such as 'equality', 'power', 'manhood', 'womanhood' and 'citizenship' which are at issue. How exactly we should understand human sympathy and benevolence is what is at issue between supporters and opponents of the family.[41]

Michael Portillo, Chief Secretary to the Treasury, in a speech on Ethics and Public Finance, suggested lately that the British record on teenage pregnancies, better than the United States but seven times worse than Holland and disadvantageous compared with

37 Michael King, 'Child Welfare within Law: The Emergence of a Hybrid Discourse' *Journal of Law and Society*, 18, 1991, 303 at 315

38 Jo van Every, 'Who is "the Family"?' *Critical Social Policy*, 33, 1991–92, 62. O'Donovan's essay in this collection gives some nice examples of relationships that are clearly not tolerated as 'family'. There are good discussions of some of the points canvassed in this section in essays collected in Part III of John Eekelaar and Petar Sarcevic (eds.), *Parenthood in Modern Society: Legal and Social Issues for the Twenty First Century*, (Dordrecht, Martinus Nijhoff, 1993), 279–422

39 See the review snapshot captured by Diana Gittings, *The Family in Question: Changing Households and Familiar Ideologies*, (Basingstoke, Macmillan, 2ed., 1992), passim.

40 *Ibid*

41 Brecher, 'What is Wrong with the Family'

other EC countries, was not a result, 'I think, because the British teenager is more likely to have premarital sex than her Dutch counterpart.'[42]. Rather (this has been interpreted to mean that) teenagers were being attracted to motherhood by over-generous state benefits. Statistics apparently in support of this claim were released only later and then cited as the *moral* justification for the Government's review of the welfare State.

Maybe this is what the Law Commission meant, (although we are sceptical), when it heralded 'increasing public concern about marriage and the family.'[43] The basis of this assumption is not disclosed; increased since when, increased from what, concerned in what way? As Ruth Chadwick observes[44] '... it is not clear how [this] is to be interpreted – whether for example, it is a statement of government policy.' Or whether there is some supposed – but here unsubstantiated – link between the *form* of 'family' and, say, health, employment practices, crime patterns or general social welfare. There is, however, recent evidence which suggests that people, and particularly women, are continuing to assert conscious choices about marriage and family patterning which exhibit a demographic realignment and suggest substantial anthropological disturbance. Two examples will suffice.

First, Marilyn Strathern and her colleagues have shown how the deployment of reproductive technologies are affecting assumptions which we bring to understandings not only of family life but to the very understanding of family itself and cultural practice;[45] '... the way in which the choices that assisted conception affords are formulated, will affect thinking about kinship. And the way people think about kinship will affect other ideas about relatedness between human beings.'[46] And, we would add, the way in which we think about relatedness between human beings will affect the way in which we think about the relationship between individuals, groups and the state.

Secondly, in a study of long term cohabitation in Britain, Susan McRae has reported that for many women the absence of a wedding in their lives is as irrelevant as the proverbial feminist juxtaposition of a fish and a bicycle.[47] For many of the 328 women interviewed marriage does not figure on the agenda; satisfactory cohabiting arrangements or the observed irrelevancies of others' marriage commitments had cancelled marriage from the lifestyle calander. However, financial demands made by a wedding, ebbing religious beliefs and fear of divorce were also cited as reasons for avoiding marital connections. McRae observed that most long-term cohabiting mothers are poor; one in four lived in a household where no one was in paid employment and half had net annual

42 As reported in *The Guardian*, September 17, 1993, p8

43 Law Commission, *Facing the Future*, No. 170, (London, HMSO, 1988) at para. 5.2

44 Ruth Chadwick, 'Moral Reasoning in Family Law - A Response to Katherine O'Donovan'

45 Marilyn Strathern, et. al.,*Reproducing the Future: Anthropology, Kinship and the New Reproductive Technologies*, (Manchester, Manchester University Press, 1993). And see Marilyn Strathern, 'The Meaning of Assisted Kinship' in Meg Stacey, (ed.), *Changing Human Reproduction*, (London, Sage Publications, 1992), 148–69. This essay is a succinct introduction to cultural and linguistic concepts deployed in arguments about the family, demonstrating in her use of examples the way in which what are taken as natural facts are themselves social and cultural constructs. For developments of this sort of argument, applied to various intellectual disciplines, see, inter alia, Michel Foucault, *The Order of Things*, (London, Tavistock, 1970) and Keith Thomas, *Man and the Natural World*, (Harmondsworth, Penguin, 1983)

46 Marilyn Strathern in Meg Stacey, *op. cit.*, at 149

47 See Susan McRae, *Cohabiting Mothers*, (London, Policy Studies Institute, 1993)

household incomes of less that £12.000. She concludes that

Rather than constituting a threat to marriage, long-term cohabiting families more plausibly represent the revival of social marriage, reflecting the diminishment of social norms which sanctioned only particular ways of living.[48]

Changes in 'relatedness' and the economic conditions of modern Britain have also served to expose the assumption that women 'naturally' prefer to care for children, and hence will voluntarily accept responsibility for them. This has been highlighted and challenged in cases such as that involving a woman sentenced to imprisonment for leaving her two year child at home alone all day while she was out at work, because she could not afford to pay for a child-minder. The responsibility of the child's father to take on her care appears not to have been questioned. The only other person who appears to have been contemplated as a carer was the maternal grandmother. Whereas the Child Support Act 1991 appeared to show a recognition of the responsibility of the absent father for his children, the pendulum since its enactment and enforcement has swung back to a concentrated blaming of the mother for both individual difficulties and the general ills. Eekelaar argues that a duty to espouse social parenthood cannot be imposed on a parent, and any statement of such a duty can only be ideological. We cannot force an absent parent to visit his child. But perhaps the 'home alone' cases demonstrate instead that we are prepared to impose such a duty – but only as a 'natural' part of motherhood.

There is a second sense in which the question of being alone at home has appeared on the family agenda in recent years, and that concerns the lack of pension entitlements for women following separation, the only substantial asset which cannot effectively be reallocated at divorce in England and Wales.[49] As Judith Masson has observed, 'Women whose working lives have been shaped by marriage and child care are likely to have pensions which are both inferior to their husbands' and inadequate for a comfortable retirement.'[50] In order to achieve more equitable consideration of women's roles, the pension system, she concludes, '... needs to be redesigned to take more account of the effects of caring responsibilities on employment and thus pensions.'[51] Unlike concern addressed in matrimonial homes legislation, pension loss has not traditionally been perceived as a problem of divorce. It is one manifestation of the concern with justice and equality, to a summary of which we now turn.

48 *Ibid*, and see the National Children's Bureau study, and the commentary in *The Independent*, 11 October 1993, p.3

49 See Heather Joshi and O Davies, *The Pension Consequences of Divorce*, (London, EPR Discussion Paper No.550, 1990)

50 Judith Masson, 'A Poor and Lonely Age – Who Supports Ex-Wives in Retirement?' in Andrew Bainham and David Pearl, (eds.), *Frontiers of Family Law*, (London, Chancery Publishing, 1993), 161–81 at 161. For a comprehensive treatment of the Law of Family Property and proposals for reform of pensions law in a cognate EC country against an international comparative background see Linda Nielsen, *Familie Formueretten; Skilsmisse og Skifte*, (Copenhagen, GEC GAD, 1993). The English summary (at 497-503) gives an introduction to divorce and pension splitting, with the proposal that splitting should be provided for on divorce but not death; 'In the long run the pension system might be reformed in such a way that a pension is tailored specifically for each spouse with the possibility of splitting it on divorce.' For Masson's treatment of this question, see, *op. cit.* 175–81 and, for other proposals, the literature cited at her note 65.

51 *Ibid*

4. Public And Private Philosophy: Liberalism, Principalism and Family

Much of the recent writing in family studies and family policy, especially that influenced by contemporary feminist criticism, has concentrated on the distinction, the disjunction, between the public and the private. Michael Freeman, however, rejects the dichotomy of the public/private dualism. Writing here he dismisses it as

> ... ambiguous and incoherent as well as being illusory. It has been responsible for setting us on false trails, into investigations as to when state intervention in the domestic sphere is justified, whereas, as indicated, non-intervention is itself a form of regulation. The public/private divide distorts. It uses the language of 'privacy' as a justification for non-intervention, ignoring the ways the 'public' constantly shapes, constitutes and restructures the private world of family and sexuality.[52]

Liberal theory continues to project separate worlds of public and private (and largely to ignore the latter) with 'barely a scintilla of recognition of their inter-connectedness or of the patriarchal structure which provides the link ... the form of the welfare state may be public but its content is indubitably private.'

Both Freeman and O'Donovan address the additional formulation of Rawls's 'original position' which Okin advances in her thesis that Rawls has escaped the dilemma of gender order by refusing to recognise that it raises questions antecedent to those of distributive justice of which he treats. Both problematically characterise Okin's attempt to escape the liberal fundamentalism of thinking of persons 'one at a time' (in Lacey's phrase[53]) as an attempt to pre-impose upon the original position a genderless society. O'Donovan witheringly observes that 'It is not clear that Rawls can be adapted to bring justice to the family.'[54] Indeed, Kymlincka has elsewhere shown, tensions in Okin's position which Chadwick reports, is illustrative of the tension between individualism and the marriage-based family. Perhaps the Rawlsian gambit cannot be made to work within the gendered family – the families that *are*, in O'Donovan's world, rather than the families that *ought* to be. The bottom line for O'Donovan is that an obligation of abstraction is possible; 'recognition of a private sphere does not preclude the raising of issues in public, particularly where a violation of the standards of liberty or equality is in question.'[55]

Katherine O'Donovan's thesis is that there has been a move away from the deployment of moral language and judgments in the discourse of family law and its reform. Procedure rather than substance is heralded as what the law can deliver, especially when there appears to be a 'judicial and professional awareness of the law's limitations as a means of social control, particularly where values are unagreed.'[56] The lexicographical legerdemain must, claims O'Donovan be exposed; 'a retreat from overt reference to morality has [not] brought about the end of morals. Rather these live on in

52 'The Private and the Public', Chapter 2, below. His particular subject of critical appraisal is Susan Moller Okin's adaptation of the 'original position' elaborated by Rawls; see the references given at note 10, above.

53 Niki Lacey, 'Theories of Justice and the Welfare State' *Social and Legal Studies* 1, 1992, 323-44 at 335

54 O'Donovan, 'Love's Law', Chapter 3, below

55 *Ibid*

56 O'Donovan, 'Love's Law'

'common sense', 'changed social circumstances' and other phrases employed in justification.'[57]

Changes in family law continue to be based on the moral views of a few and not the shared values of many. Part of this retreat is because shared notions of value are being abandoned, not in favour of pluralistic notions or conceptions of liberty, or justice, but as part of a pragmatic exercise which appears to have much in common with the vaunted Thatcherite conception of rolling back the frontiers of the state.[58] The project of law reform in family law has seen the supposed retreat of the law, rolling back the involvement of principles of justice as substantive rather than procedural and ushering in the consumer values of the IBM decade and 'Texas' homecare. We might see this as one element of the real power of the state – to be able to claim to be rolling itself back while actually extending its control. The Child Support Act 1991 might be seen as an example of this, in that it encourages recognition of private responsibility by establishing a huge state apparatus – much criticised – to enforce that responsibility. The development of the policy of community care mainly as the co-option of women carers into the quasi state we have already briefly mentioned.

The task for Chadwick is how to respond to this tension between individualism and the family; what *values* should inform family law? A core problem is whether general principles – one of O'Donovan's desiderata – can be attached to the family. Chadwick suggests not only that views about the family are culturally and historically specific, but, more fundamentally, that the family can be seen as a distraction from the demands of morality itself, where these are interpreted in terms of impartiality. In thinking about the *values* which should inform family law a central issue will be whether or not the definition of the family employed by the law should be marriage-based or not.

Brecher[59] more precisely than other contributors addresses the question of human nature. His project is located in the communitarian band of the spectrum, and his thesis is that what is wrong with the family, at least 'the present, nuclear, marriage-defined family' is – broadly – everything. The standard arguments in its favour – 'children; the elderly and/or ill; sex; human nature; a bulwark against individualism; and a bulwark against the state' – simply fail.[60] As such, the family is inimical to socialism, and thus to feminism, both projects and philosophies which Brecher seeks to promote. As Susan Mendus has put it; 'The language of domination and subordination is central to individualism and cannot be dispensed with except by abandoning individualism

57 *Ibid*

58 For an examination of government legislation in the 1980s affecting families see Gillian Douglas, 'Family Law under the Thatcher Government' *Journal of Law and Society* 17, 1990, 411. She there suggests (at 421–22) that 'Thatcherism has done nothing concrete and positive to enhance women's rights to equality - indeed, it has made things worse, ... because it prefers to ignore issues of gender entirely. ... What we *do* see is a major shift of interest in looking at the parent/child position. Much of what has been legislated may turn out to be largely symbolic and unlikely to change much in reality. But it is presented as an assertion of the family over the state ...' There, she concludes, however, that the changes in legislation between 1979 and 1990 are responses to changes in family structure and behaviour which were then already in progress, and that this is of more importance than the ideologies of a particular government.

59 'What is Wrong with the Family', Chapter 5, below

60 *Ibid*

itself.'[61] The central difficulty of individualist theories is that they support an atomistic model which cannot readily accommodate social units, such as the family. For Brecher, the hostility which the family presents resides in the sorts of meaning it ascribes to and the understanding it forges of 'notions like sympathy and benevolence.'[62]

5. Who Do You Think You Are?

The most radical challenge to understandings of the family has been presented by assisted conception, or what Singer and Wells have called the 'reproduction revolution.'[63] The legal, biological and social constructs of parenthood have all faced vigorous re-examination, and new definitions and new family forms have become available. Even where families are created without assisted reproduction, parenthood is not a straightforward matter. As John Eekelaar here writes; parenthood can be broken into three distinguishable elements: biological parenthood, legal parenthood and the holding of parental responsibility,[64] in such a way that 'the resulting structure of parenthood in English law is one in which a medieval land lawyer would have taken pride.'[65]

Katherine O'Donovan has elsewhere suggested that this axis, of procreation, is properly understood as the central feature of family law, and not as is usual, the focus on relationships established between adults.[66] The role of the family, and conceptions of personal identity and human nature are underlined in many ways by programmes of assisted conception, especially in the way in which rational women will use and pursue infertility programmes even when they know that the success rates are low.[67]

If the family, by definition, consists of an adult or adults bringing up children, then the new techniques of assisted reproduction raise many issues. Some of them are often phrased in terms of rights; they concern – amongst many other things – which adults should be permitted to make use of assisted conception; what rights and responsibilities should gamete donors or surrogate mothers have in relation to the embryos and children created; what interests might the state or society have in regulating and controlling these techniques, and what should be the rights of children themselves? If the 'wrong' embryos are given to two women patients[68] – ie, they receive non-genetically related gametes –

61 Susan Mendus, 'Kant: "an honest but liberal-minded bourgeois"?' in R Chadwick, (ed.), *Immanuel Kant: Critical Assessments*, Volume III, *Kant's Moral and Political Philosophy*, (London, Routledge, 1992), 377–88 at 385

62 Brecher, 'What's Wrong with the Family'

63 Peter Singer and Deane Wells, *The Reproduction Revolution*, (Oxford, Oxford University Press) 1984. A comprehensive consideration of the issues and questions involved is presented in the two volume final report of the Canadian Royal Commission on the new reproductive technologies, *Proceed with Care*, (Ottawa, Minister of Government Services, Canada, 1993)

64 Eekelaar, 'Parenthood, Social Engineering and Rights', Chapter 6, below, citing the Children Act 1989 for the introduction of the third important element.

65 *Ibid*

66 See *Family Law Matters*, (London, Pluto, 1993)

67 For an excellent analysis of this phenomenon see Lena Koch, 'IVF – A Rational Choice?' *Reproductive and Genetic Engineering: International Journal of Feminist Analysis*, 3, 1990, 235–42

68 As reported, for example, in *The Observer*, August 8, 1993

should this be treated simply as a breach of contract by the clinic, or does it raise more profound questions (can a woman be assaulted by an embryo?) regarding our attachment to the genetic basis of parenthood? Does the easy availability of surrogacy or gamete donation reinforce an increasing tendency to view reproduction as the commodification of human life, or was the alienability of reproductive labour and the commodification of children was more apparent when women were regarded as having no role outside marital motherhood, or when abortion first became legalised? Addressing these questions may lead us to a clearer picture of what it is that we mean by family and what it is in family that we value.

The tensions between genetic and social parenthood, for example, have led Ruth Macklin to suggest that a number of different determinants of what is meant by 'family' can be drawn. In addition to the 'traditional' biological vector, she suggests that law, custom and what she awkwardly calls 'subjective intentions' (more simply what people choose to do despite law or accepted custom) can all be factored to produce an understanding of what family is, or how we understand it or them to be composed. She concludes:

> The effect of artificial means of reproduction on our understanding of the family will vary, depending on which of these three determinants is chosen to have priority. There is no way to assign a priori precedence to any one of the three. ... there is no simple answer to the question of how artificial means of reproduction affect our understanding of family. We need to reflect on the variety of answers, paying special attention to what follows from answering the question one way rather than another. Since there is no single, univocal concept of the family, it is a matter for moral and social decision just which determinants of 'family' should be given priority.[69]

As the generation of women who have chosen to postpone child birth until later in their lives comes of age, the question of a 'natural' span of child birthing is one which is being challenged, both in its logic and its limits. And with an increasing number of second or third relationships seeking to enjoy the pleasures and pains of mutual family life, women and their partners are renegotiating boundaries which previously seemed set as much by convention as constitution. The consequences of this we have hardly begun to hazard at. As Marilyn Strathern has suggested;

> The new reproductive technologies and the legislative and other actions to which they have given rise seek to assist natural process on the one hand and the social definition of kinship on the other. But this double assistance creates new uncertainties. For the present cultural explicitness is revolutionising former combinations of ideas and concepts. The more we give legal certainty to social parenthood, the more we cut from under our feet assumptions about the intrinsic nature of relationships themselves. The more facilitation is given to the biological reproduction of human persons, the harder it is to think of a domain of natural facts independent of social intervention. Whether or not all this is a good thing is uncertain. What is certain is that it will not be without consequence for the way people think about one another.[70]

The discovery of the structure of DNA and the mapping of the human genome has given us a plot of human life, Aldous Huxley has even given us a title to the fabulous world which might be entered, and with which we can advertise the project. What we appear to know about the intimate structure and workings of gametes and embryos,

69 'Artificial Means of Reproduction and our Understanding of the Family' *Hastings Center Report*, 1991, 5 at 6

70 Marilyn Strathern in Meg Stacey, *op. cit.*, at 149. See the discussion of these points in Brenda Almond's essay, 'Parenthood – Social Construct or Fact of Nature', Chapter 7, below

fetuses and babies enables us to speak almost of a quantum theory of reproduction, to be set alongside a theory of general relativity – in which we factor the social, environmental, cultural, and emotional aspects of fertility, parenthood, individuation and society.[71]

There are those who believe that work in present biotechnical research and associated infertility treatment services is like playing alchemy in the crucible of the genetic future. They suspect the danger that the atoms will enter new and unforeseeable trajectories and take on vectors and forces which cannot now be understood. In parallel with this are doubts which have consistently been voiced about the wisdom of investing resources so heavily in the 'reproduction revolution.' The question, 'who do you think you are?' will have new and dramatic significance for the second millenium, but the social problems may not derive from individual choices themselves, but the anthropological consequences of the summation of those individual choices.

6. Conclusion: Plato's Private Problem

Perhaps if he made a fundamental mistake, Plato's particular error was in believing that having 'dealt with the regulations about women' he *had* reduced 'the complexities of family life ... to simple certainties.' Perhaps, indeed, there was a time when such a view might have been fashionable, if of limited accuracy. As the essays here demonstrate, however, (while dwelling more on the role of law and the state than explicitly on theories of human nature) a project which took those as given starting points would be doomed to constitutional chaos, not conversation.

71 See Derek Morgan, 'Undoing What Comes Naturally – Regulating Medically Assisted Families', in Andrew Bainham and David Pearl, (eds.), *Frontiers of Family Law*, (London, Chancery Publishing, 1993), 94–121

Michael Freeman

Austin Lecture:
The Private and the Public

One of the most striking features of moral, political and legal philosophy has been its concentration on the public arena, on the so-called 'big' questions of state and individual. Questions about the state and sovereignty, about political obligation, about the validity of law; questions about the relationship of law to power and law to social change. Questions about justice and about democracy. And now, increasingly, questions about citizenship. These questions have nagged at us for two-and-a-half thousand years. They have been rephrased and reformulated, redesigned in the light of historical specificity and cultural context. And they continue to be asked as the welter of grand theory in the last quarter of a century testifies. So justice is explored,[1] its 'limits' exposed,[2] its 'spheres' tested.[3] Law's 'empire' is justified[4] and the 'morality of freedom'[5] is defended. The state is neutered[6] or at least neutralised.[7] Yet, until the arrival of feminism and sometimes even beyond it, the neglect of domestic relations was deafening. Attention has focused almost exclusively on the 'public' with the 'domestic' assumed to be irrelevant to social, political or legal theory.

How is this neglect to be explained?

To attribute it to the fact that theory has been dominated by male thinkers[8] obviously has some truth, but as an explanation it is little more than trite and question-begging. To observe that cultural systems give authority and value to the roles and activities of men[9] does not explain why thinkers should do likewise or why this should have led to

1 John Rawls, *A Theory of Justice* (Cambridge: Harvard University Press, 1971) His *Political Liberalism* (New York: Columbia University Press, 1993) was published after this lecture was written and presented, and no account is taken of it.

2 Michael J. Sandel, *Liberalism and The Limits of Justice*, (New York: Cambridge University Press, 1982).

3 Michael Walzer, *Spheres of Justice: A Defence of Pluralism and Equality* (New York: Basic Books, 1983).

4 Ronald Dworkin, *Law's Empire* (London: Fontana, 1986).

5 Joseph Raz, *The Morality of Freedom* (Oxford: Clarendon Press, 1986).

6 Robert Nozick, *Anarchy, State and Utopia* (New York: Basic Books, 1974).

7 Bruce Ackerman, *Social Justice In The Liberal State* (New Haven: Yale University Press, 1980). See also John Rawls, 'The Priority of Right and Idea of The Good', *Philosophy and Public Affairs*, 17, 251–276 (1988).

8 Margaret Stacey, 'The Division of Labour Revisited, or Overcoming The Two Adams' in P. Abrams *et al, Development and Diversity : British Sociology 1950–1980* (London: Allen and Unwin, 1981), p. 173 indicts sociology in this way. The men who dominated the development of this in the mid-nineteenth century gave exclusive attention 'to the public domain, to affairs of state and the market-place'.

9 Michelle Rosaldo, 'Women, Culture and Society: A Theoretical Overview' in M.S.Rosaldo and L. Lamphere (eds), *Women, Culture and Society* (Palo Alto: Stanford University Press, 1974), p.19.

ARSP-Beiheft 57. Derek Morgan & Gillian Douglas (eds.)

a concentration on 'the public' – after all, but a minuscule percentage of the male population participates in the public arena.[10] To say that the family is 'beyond justice' as Michael Sandel[11] and Roberto Unger do,[12] is so to idealise domestic relations as to be convinced by the Victorians who told us (and doubtless believed) that the home was 'a shelter for those moral and spiritual values which the commercial spirit and the critical spirit were threatening to destroy'.[13]

The neglect can be explained historically. Although the roots of the dualism of public and private can be traced to Aristotle,[14] its modern rebirth and its centrality to liberalism may be attributed to Locke. In his *Second Treatise* he argued against Filmer[15] that political power is conventional and could justifiably be exercised over free and equal adult individuals only with their consent. But, political power was not to be confused with paternal power over children in the private, family sphere. This, Locke argued, is a natural relationship which ends with maturity, and with it comes the freedom and equality of children, or at least male children. Commentators before Pateman[16] overlooked the fact that Locke's separation of the family and the political is also a sexual division. Locke agreed with Filmer's patriarchal claim that the natural differences between men and women entail the subjection of women to men or, more specifically, wives to husbands. The wife's subordination has a 'Foundation in Nature': the husband's will must prevail in the household since he is naturally 'the abler and the stronger'.[17] But, a natural subordinate cannot at the same time be free and equal with the consequence that women (wives) are excluded from the status of 'individual' and so from participating in the public world of equality and consent.

On one level Locke's separation is of the paternal from the political. But it can be seen also as a separation of the private from the public, for the public sphere embraces

10 See Mary O'Brien's comment that 'the separation of public and private has as little meaning to man on an assembly line, as it did for the medieval serf'.

11 *Op cit*, note 2, p.30–31, 33 ('the values and aims of the participants coincide closely enough that the circumstances of justice prevail to a relatively small degree').

12 *Knowledge and Politics* (New York: Free Press, 1975).

13 *Per* W. Houghton, *The Victorian Frame of Mind 1830-1870* (New Haven: Yale University Press, 1957), p. 343.

14 *Politics*, Book 1. See, further, Susan Moller Okin, *Women In Western Political Thought* (Princeton University Press, 1979), ch.4. In the *oikos*, women could achieve only the limited goodness of the 'naturally ruled' *per* J.B. Elshtain, 'Aristotle, the Public/Private Split, and the Case of the Suffragists' in J.B. Elshtain (ed), *The Family In Political Thought* (Amherst, Mass: University of Massachusetts Press, 1982),p. 52. But there is now a claim that Aristotle was a Feminist. See Linda R. Hirshman, 'The Book of "A" ', *Texas Law Review*, 70, 1992, 971–1012. And see the responses by Richard Posner at p. 1013–1017 and Martha Nussbaum at p. 1019–1028.

15 Sir Robert Filmer, *Patriarcha, Or The Natural Power of Kings* (London: Davis, 1680) See, further, Carole Pateman, *The Sexual Contract* (Oxford: Polity Press, 1988), and T. Brennan and C. Pateman, 'Mere Auxiliaries to the Commonwealth: Women and the Origins of Liberalism', *Political Studies*, XXVII (1979), p.183–200.

16 In addition to *The Sexual Contract* see her 'Feminist Critiques of The Public/ Private Dichotomy' in S.I. Benn and G.F. Gaus, *Public and Private In Social Life* (London: Croom Helm, 1983), p.281, and *The Disorder of Women* (Cambridge: Polity Press, 1989).

17 J. Locke, *Two Treaties of Government*, 2nd ed (ed. Peter Laslett) (Cambridge: Cambridge University Press, 1967), Book I, ch. 47; Book II, ch. 82. See also I. Kant, *Anthropology from a Pragmatic Point of View* (Carbondale: Southern Illinois University Press, 1978), p. 105, 216.

all social life save the domestic. An important result of this conception of private and public is that the public world, or civil society, is categorised and discussed by liberal theory (and not only liberal theory) as separate from the domestic sphere. The principles of association governing the two spheres are quite distinct: the public is governed by liberal criteria (rights, property, equality); the private is based on natural ties of sentiment and blood and marriage relationships – there is no free individualism here, rather natural subordination. By conceptualising civil society as removed from domestic life, the need to examine the latter disappears and only re-emerges when the inequalities of gender are scrutinised by feminist thinkers. The tradition initiated by Locke transforms the public-private dualism into a division within civil society itself (the realm of men). The talk is thenceforth of 'society' and the 'state', of 'social' versus 'political' and of sundry other dichotomous pairs. The legacy of this way of thinking is still apparent in the writing of Rawls[18] and other contemporary philosophers.

To understand why the separation of the two spheres is located within civil society with the consequence that public life is identified with the world of men, it is necessary to delve into history. When Locke wrote, women participated actively in productive activities within a home-based economy.[19] But with the development of industrial capitalism, wives were kept out of economic life or removed to low status ghettoes of employment.[20] They were relegated to dependency, to a status within the private familial sphere, which was all too easily conceptualised as their 'natural' place. The correlativity of dependence and subordination was not questioned: it was taken for granted that civil society could be understood without reference to the inequalities within the domestic sphere. Theory was thus able to marginalise the private, in the sense of the domestic sphere. What this ignores is the centrality of patriarchalism to the theory and practice of liberalism. And yet the image of domestic life as separate from civil society, rather than at its heart, persists. Theory continues to project separate liberal worlds of public and private (and largely to ignore the latter) with barely a scintilla of recognition of their inter-connectedness or of the patriarchal structure which provides the link. The family came to be seen as a private refuge from the exacting demands of public life, a 'haven in a heartless world' in Christopher Lasch's famous expression.[21] It was, and in this image perhaps still is, the 'very antithesis of public life and its discontents'.[22]

But, of course, as is all too readily apparent, the family is no haven and, though its discontents may be different from those within the 'public' world they are nonetheless very real. These have been described elsewhere. The plight of the one-parent family:

18 *Op cit*, note 1, p. 61 and 302 (and see C. Pateman, *op cit*, note 16, p. 301 n. 5).

19 Though there may well have been a division of labour on gender lines. See Alice Clark, *Working Life of Women In The Seventeenth Century* (London: G. Routledge, 1919).

20 But is it motherhood or gender that accounts for this? Heather Joshi concludes that 'the direct consequences of motherhood play a relatively minor part in accounting for mothers' low pay' ('Sex and Motherhood as Handicaps in the Labour Market' in Mavis Maclean and Dulcie Groves (eds), *Women's Issues In Social Policy*, (London: Routledge, 1991, p. 179).

21 *Haven In A Heartless World* (New York: Basic Books, 1977), p. 6. For a critique of Lasch's thesis see Michele Barrett and Mary McIntosh, *The Anti-Social Family* (London: Verso, 1982), p. 110–126.

22 Richard Sennett, *The Fall of Public Man* (Cambridge: Cambridge University Press, 1976), p. 177.

the 'feminisation of poverty'.[23] The failure of divorce equality policies.[24] Marital violence:[25] the pervasiveness of 'domestic hooliganism'.[26] Marital rape,[27] from which the law of England has only just begun to offer protection.[28] To which may be added workplace discrimination[29] and the failure of equal pay legislation,[30] which are integrally related to gender inequalities in the private sphere. Nor is the private sphere a 'haven' for children,[31] though their position is rarely addressed by feminists concerned with the structural inequalities engendered by patriarchalism[32] or for that matter by liberals who often seem more concerned with 'individual freedom and human dignity'.[33]

The public – private dichotomy then needs to be examined though it is the 'private', often ambiguous, frequently mythical and consistently neglected upon which sustained critical attention needs to focus.

It was Carole Pateman who wrote that the 'dichotomy between the private and the public .... is, ultimately, what the feminist movement is about'.[34] Though exaggerated, this reflects an increasing consensus that the battle for sex equality has to go beyond public discrimination to the patterns of domestic labour and the devaluation of women in the private sphere. The battle against public discrimination has anyway on one level

23 In Linda Pearce's expression (see 'The Feminization of Poverty: Women, Work and Welfare', *Urban and Social Change Review* (Winter-Spring 1978), 28–36). See also H. Scott, *Working Your Way To The Bottom* (London: Pandora Press, 1984). But 'throughout the last century women have always been much poorer than men' (see Jane Lewis and David Piachaud, 'Women and Poverty in The Twentieth Century' in Caroline Glendinning and Jane Millar (eds), *Women and Poverty in Britain* (Brighton: Wheatsheaf, 1987), p. 28).

24 See Martha Fineman, *The Illusion of Equality: The Rhetoric and Reality of Divorce Reform* (Chicago: University of Chicago Press, 1991), and John Eekelaar, *Regulating Divorce* (Oxford: Clarendon Press, 1991). For a comparative perspective see Lenore J. Weitzman and Mavis Maclean, *Economic Consequences of Divorce* (Oxford: Clarendon Press, 1992). See also Stephen D. Sugarman and Herma Hill Kay, *Divorce Reform At The Crossroads* (New Haven: Yale University Press, 1990).

25 For the historical context see Linda Gordon, *Heroes of Their Own Lives* (New York: Viking, 1988) and Elizabeth Pleck, *Domestic Tyranny* (New York: Oxford University Press, 1987). For contemporary accounts see R. Emerson Dobash and Russell P. Dobash, *Women, Violence and Social Change* (London: Routledge, 1992), Richard J. Gelles and Murray A. Straus, *Intimate Violence* (New York: Simon and Schuster, 1988) and Jocelynne Scutt, *Even In The Best of Homes* (North Carlton, Victoria: McCulloch, 1990). See also Lorna J.F. Smith, *Domestic Violence* (London: HMSO, 1989).

26 Sir George Baker's description in *Davis v. Johnson* [1979] A. C. 264, 283.

27 Diana E. H. Russell, *Rape in Marriage* (New York: Macmillan, 1982) and David Finkelhor and Kersti Yllo, *License To Rape* (New York: Free Press, 1985).

28 See *R v. R* [1991] 4 All E.R. 481.

29 See David L. Kirp, Mark G. Yudof and Marlene Strong Franks, *Gender Justice* (Chicago: University of Chicago Press, 1986 ch. 7), Sylvia Walby, *Theorizing Patriarchy* (Oxford: Blackwell, 1990 ch. 2).

30 Women earn today, as a percentage of male earnings, no more than they did when the Equal Pay Act 1970 came into force in 1975.

31 Which it clearly is not with physical and sexual abuse rife and children victimised by poverty, unemployment, racial discrimination, bad housing and a multitude of other ills.

32 For critical discussions of which see Michèle Barrett, *Women's Oppression Today* (London: Verso Books, revised edition 1988), Carole Pateman, *The Sexual Contract* (Cambridge: Polity Press, 1988, ch. 2).

33 *Per* Joseph Goldstein, Anna Freud, Albert Solnit, *Before The Best Interests of The Child* (New York: Free Press, 1979).

34 *Op cit*, note 16, p. 281.

been won but the paucity of women in Parliament, amongst the judiciary and in the higher ranks of bureaucracy, the military, the police, the trade unions, and, indeed, in higher education testifies to the impact of inequalities in the private sphere. And decisions taken within a formally equal public arena constantly aggravate the inequalities entrenched in the private world of the family. Thus, the public sphere of welfare provision dictates the content of female tending activities.[35] The effect that seeing women as private non-citizens dependent on men has had in this area has been too little explored.[36] But the projection of welfare as bounty rather than entitlement can surely be traced to a perception of women as residing within the domestic rather than the public world of rights-bearing citizens. The theoretical basis of the welfare state may be egalitarian,[37] but this commitment is not realised either in the rules concerning eligibility or in the patterns of practice.[38] Our welfare system was established on the basis of the concept of the 'family wage',[39] with the presumed contributor and so recipient the 'head of the family'. Indeed, some aspects of it were designed to keep women, more particularly mothers, out of the paid labour market.[40] Most benefits are now formally equally available, but in practice access remains structured along gendered lines.[41] There is considerable irony in the fact that although women are more dependent on welfare benefits than men, the welfare system is constituted by a model of the male as the typical recipient. In similar ways the emptying of 'public' institutions so that 'care' can take place in the 'community',[42] and the embodiment of 'partnership' rather than coercion into the complex of our child care practices[43] are clear demonstrations of how changes in public provision inevitably have repercussions for the lives of women in the domestic sphere. The form of the welfare state may be public but its content is indubitably private.[44]

35 See Clare Ungerson, 'Women and Caring: Skills, Tasks and Taboos', in Eva Gamarnikow *et al,* eds, *The Public and The Private* (London: Heinemann, 1983, p. 62–77).

36 See Linda Gordon, 'The New Feminist Scholarship on the Welfare State' in Linda Gordon (ed), *Women, The State and Welfare* (Madison: University of Wisconsin Press, 1990, p. 9–35, at p. 21).

37 See Carole Pateman, *The Disorder of Women* (Cambridge: Polity Press, 1989, ch. 8); Sylvia Walby, *Theorising Patriarchy* (Oxford: Blackwell, 1990, p. 165–168).

38 See Jane Millar, 'Social Security, Equality and Women In the U.K.', *Policy and Politics*, 17, 311–319 (1989).

39 Hilary Land, 'The Family Wage', *Feminist Review*, 6, 55–78 (1980). So that even where women make a significant contribution to household income there is a tendency to devalue it and treat it as marginal. See Julia Brannen and Peter Moss, *Managing Mothers: Dual Earner Households After Maternity Leave* (London: Unwin Hyman, 1991).

40 See Barbara Nelson, 'Women's Poverty and Women's Citizenship: Some Political Consequences of Economic Marginality', *Signs*, 10, 1984, 221–238.

41 Hilary Land, 'Women, Money and Independence', *Poverty*, 70, 1988, 18–19; Dulcie Groves, 'Women and Financial Provision for Old Age' in Mavis Maclean and Dulcie Groves (eds.), *Women's Issues In Social Policy* (London, Routledge, 1991, p.38).

42 See Michael Bayles's distinction between 'care in' and 'care by' the community (*Mental Handicap and Community Care*, London: Routledge, Kegan Paul, 1973). And see Christine Hallett, 'The Children Act 1989 and Community Care; Comparisons and Contrasts', *Policy and Politics*, 19,1991, 283–291.

43 See Michael D. A. Freeman, *Children, Their Families and The Law* (Basingstoke: Macmillan, 1992, p. 22–25.).

44 See Eli Zaretsky, 'The Place of The Family in the Origins of The Welfare State', in Barrie Thorne (ed), *Rethinking the Family: Some Feminist Questions* (London: Longman, 1982, p. 188–224).

Too often those who point to the public/private dualism do so as if they are two discrete entities which can be described. That there are 'out there' two almost natural realms. That they are value-free. What this ignores is the historical specificity of the conjunction, its relativity to historical period and to culture. Indeed, different concepts of the private are sometimes used in tandem and indistinguishably. Thus it is clear that in talking to-day of the family as private one is referring both to its being (supposedly) outside the authority of the state and outside the scope of market relations, though the latter would not have been understood by Aristotle or Locke.[45]

The constructs of public and private should be seen rather as normative. Every concept of the 'public' presupposes a corresponding delimitation of the 'private'. The language of privacy or intimacy acts as an 'idealising lens'[46] to disguise and legitimate separate and unequal spheres of men and women. Since power is deemed to be situated in the public arena (where the historical struggles for bourgeois religious, economic and democratic freedoms have been fought),[47] power relations in the domestic sphere can be ignored. It is as if they don't exist. This has a number of consequences. It legitimises the status quo. It leaves domestic relations in their pre-liberal world. It ignores the power differentials which are so central to family life. It overlooks the political nature of the family as the place where we learn, or learn in part, our gendered selves.[48] It depoliticises women, marginalising their concerns within the political agenda. The emphasis instead is on 'public' wrongs. Is it thus any surprise that domestic violence should have assumed such a low profile for so long;[49] or that the implications of reproductive technology for women should be sidelined;[50] or that coercive caesareans[51] or involuntary sterilisations[52] should have raised relatively little political interest? Indeed, is it surprising that women were denied the vote for so long? Just as the 'public' in the market sense fails to recognise women's work as work (though there is now a grudging acceptance of this in our divorce legislation),[53] so

45 See Frances Olsen, 'The Family and the Market', *Harvard Law Review*, 96, 1983, 1497–1578.

46 P*er* Seyla Benhabib, *Situating The Self* (Oxford: Polity Press, 1992), p. 109.

47 And see the thesis of Nicholas Abercombie, Stephen Hill and Bryan S. Turner, *Sovereign Individuals of Capitalism* (London: Allen and Unwin, 1986).

48 See Laurie Davidson and Laura Kramer Gordon, *The Sociology of Gender* (Chicago: Rand McNally, 1979), ch. 2. See also the historical insights of D. Gordon, *The Victorian Girl and The Feminine Ideal* (London: Croom Helm, 1982).

49 It re-emerged as a 'social problem' only in the early 1970s. On contemporary concern with the inability of the law to cope justly with battered women who kill, see Holly Maguigan, 'Battered Women and Self-Defence: Myths and Misconceptions in Current Reform Proposals', *University of Pennsylvania Law Review*, 140, 1991, 379–486).

50 Until feminist writing identified some of its implications. Of the many examples of this I single out Gena Corea, *The Mother Machine* (London: Women's Press, 1988). See also Virginia Held, 'Birth and Death', *Ethics*, 99, 1989, 362–88. She makes the point that the devaluing and disregarding of the reproductive act and of reproductive choice both reflect the social subordination of women and distort political thought.

51 See Martha A. Field, 'Controlling The Woman To Protect The Fetus', *Law, Medicine and Health Care*, 17, 1989, 114–129 and *Re S* [1993] 1 F.L.R. 22.

52 See Michael Freeman, 'Sterilising the Mentally Handicapped' in Michael Freeman (ed.), *Medicine, Ethics and The Law* (London: Stevens, 1988), p. 55–84 on *Re B* [1988] A.C. 199.

53 With the contribution to the welfare of the family provision in the Matrimonial Causes Act 1973 (see s. 25 (2) (f)). See for illustrations cases like *Duxbury v. Duxbury* [1990] 2 All E.R. 77.

women's injuries are often not recognised or compensated as injuries by the 'public' as represented by the legal culture.[54] As Robin West has shown[55] such injuries are trivialised[56] or seen as consensual,[57] humorous,[58] sub-consciously wanted,[59] natural,[60] deserved or private,[61] non-existent,[62] incomprehensible,[63] legally pre-determined[64] and, in the case of rape, sporadic or as different from other violence.[65]

There has been considerable debate on the question whether the state should interfere in the family. In the area of parent-child relations much of this was stimulated by the works of Goldstein, Freud and Solnit.[66] But the issue has been raised in other areas as well: domestic violence,[67] non-marital cohabitation,[68] surrogacy,[69] conflict

54 See Adrian Howe, '"Social Injury" Revisited: Towards a Feminist Theory of Social Justice', *International Journal of The Sociology of Law*, 15, 1987, 423–38. See also her 'The Problem of Privatised Injuries: Feminist Strategies for Litigation' in Martha Albertson Fineman and Nancy Sweet Thomadsen, *At The Boundaries of Law* (New York: Routledge, 1991) p. 148–167. Also valuable is Nancy Fraser, 'Talking About Needs: Interpretive Contests as Political Conflicts in Welfare-State Societies', *Ethics*, 99, 1989, 291–313.

55 'The Difference in Women's Hedonic Lives: A Phenomenological Critique of Feminist Legal Theory', *Wisconsin Women's Law Journal*, 3, 1987, 81–145 (a shorter version appears in Fineman and Thomadsen, *op cit*, note 54, at p. 115–134). See also her 'Justice and Gender', *University of Chicago Law Review*, 55, 1988, 1–72. But see the critique of her views in Drucilla Cornell, *Beyond Accommodation* (New York, Routledge, 1991), p. 21–36.

56 For example sexual harassment on the street. 'Sexual harassment' may be seen as an oxymoron with the contradiction expressing the different experiences of the two sexes.

57 For example sexual harassment 'on the job', as West puts it. See also Susan Estrich, 'Sex at Work', *Stanford Law Review*, 43, 1991, 813–862.

58 As in non-violent marital rape (another oxymoron).

59 As in father-daughter incest – a legacy of Freudian thinking.

60 For example, in the case of childbirth. By designating it in this way it can also be seen as inevitable.

61 Domestic violence has for long been so seen. On the invalidation of women's experiences of sexual violence see L. Kelly and J. Radford, '"Nothing Really Happened"', *Critical Social Policy*, 30, 1990–1991, 39–53. See also the excellent article by Martha R. Mahoney, 'Legal Images of Battered Women: Redefining The Issue of Separation', *Michigan Law Review*, 90, 1991, 1–94.

62 Pornography clearly comes into this category. But Emily Jackson, 'Catherine MacKinnon and Feminist Jurisprudence: A Critical Appraisal', *Journal of Law and Society*, 19, 1992, 195–213 offers interesting critical insight into an emergent orthodoxy (see p. 203–207).

63 The example used by West is unpleasant and unwanted consensual sex. And see Jane E. Larson, 'Women Understand So Little, They Call My Good Nature 'Deceit'': A Feminist Rethinking of Seduction', *Columbia Law Review*, 93, 1993, 374–472.

64 As in defence of the marital rape immunity posited by Sir Matthew Hale.

65 But Diana E. H. Russell, *Sexual Exploitation* (Beverly Hills: Sage, 1984) shows it is hardly 'sporadic'. And see Susan Estrich, *Real Rape* (Cambridge: Harvard University Press, 1987) for a sustained challenge to its peripherality to criminal violence.

66 In particular by *Before The Best Interests of the Child* (note 33). But also in their *Beyond The Best Interests of the Child* (New York: Free Press, 1973).

67 There is interesting historical insight into this in Anna Clark, 'Humanity or Justice? Wifebeating and the Law in the Eighteenth and Nineteenth Centuries' in Carol Smart (ed), *Regulating Womanhood* (London: Routledge, 1992, 187–206).

68 See Michael D.A. Freeman and Christina M. Lyon, *Cohabitation Without Marriage* (Aldershot: Gower, 1983).

69 See Peter Singer and Deane Wells, *The Reproduction Revolution* (Oxford: Oxford University Press, 1984).

resolution.[70] The question is, however, totally unreal for non-intervention is a political act: it amounts to intervention to recognise and confirm the status quo and it legitimises existing power relationships. Liberals and libertarians[71] who favour autonomy for the private sphere often rest their case on freedom, but, as Bill Jordan noted in *Freedom And The Welfare State*[72] this is often 'the freedom of more powerful members (usually husbands in relation to wives and parents in relation to children) to exercise their power without restriction'. By contrast, modern history of the 'public' has been an attempt to curb power, to introduce justice and equality. If 'non-intervention' amounts to a failure to apply these values to the sphere then designated 'private', it leaves those whose lives are spent predominantly in the domestic sphere without the benefits acquired by the battles waged in the public arena. So we have in the binary opposition of public and private a discourse of domination which legitimates women's oppression and exploitation, as well as that of children. In the current debates about citizenship,[73] there is little sign that this will change.

And what does modern political and legal philosophy have to say about these injustices? In the modern classics, the authors to whom we all direct our students, Rawls, Nozick, Dworkin, the answer is 'very little'. Before the emergence of feminism the focus in mainstream (or 'malestream')[74] philosophy was very much centred on issues of justice in the public world. Most major theories of justice have had little to say about women or the family.[75] This cannot be satisfactory, for women clearly suffer injustice in the family (most graphically, ironically, when their marriage breaks down).[76] Furthermore, the family is the school of justice for the larger society, the place where children are first exposed to the models of fairness and unfairness that will affect their behaviour in the world outside the family. If children experience injustice within their family, may this not militate against the possibility of establishing a more just society?

This gaping hole has been subjected to an impressive critique in Susan Moller Okin's *Justice, Gender and The Family*.[77] But neither her analysis nor her own prescription for a just family is beyond criticism and improvement.

70 See Michael D. A. Freeman, 'Questioning the Delegalization Movement in Family Law: Do We Really Want a Family Court?' in John Eekelaar and Sanford N. Katz (eds), *The Resolution of Family Conflict*, (Toronto: Butterworths, 1984), p. 7–25.

71 Such as Nozick (see note 6).

72 London: Routledge, Kegan Paul, 1976, p. 60.

73 Major's 'Citizen's Charter' of July 1991 (London: HMSO) being matched by Labour and Liberal Democrat responses the same month. See David Taylor, 'A Big Idea for the Nineties? The Rise of the Citizen's 'Charters'', *Critical Social Policy*, 33, 1991–2, 87–94. See his earlier article 'Citizenship and Social Power', *Critical Social Policy*, 26, 1989, 19–31. On gender and citizenship see Ruth Lister, 'Citizenship Engendered', *Critical Social Policy*, 32, 65–71 (1991).

74 In Mary O'Brien's pithy expression: *The Politics of Reproduction* (London: Routledge, Kegan Paul, 1981).

75 The neglect is discussed in Jean Bethke Elshtain, *Public Man, Private Woman* (Oxford: Martin Robertson, 1981), Susan Moller Okin, *Women In Western Political Thought* (Princeton: Princeton University Press, 1979) and Diana Coole, *Women In Political Theory: From Ancient Misogyny to Contemporary Feminism* (Brighton: Wheatsheaf, 1988).

76 See Lenore J. Weitzman, *The Divorce Revolution* (New York: Free Press, 1985).

77 New York: Basic Books, 1989.

She is especially scathing and pertinent in her critique of communitarian theories of justice. What she has to say about Alasdair MacIntyre's account of justice within traditions is of particular interest since MacIntyre is sensitive to issues of justice for women.[78] But Okin argues convincingly that MacIntyre's appeal to the excellence of traditional arrangements is persuasive only so long as he makes the reader forget to ask what his or her position would be within the traditional society. MacIntyre assumes that if '"we" were members of heroic society, we would be *heroes* ... [and] gives no thought to the far greater probability ... of being ... a slave, an ordinary male member of the underclass, or (more probably still) a woman'.[79] The ethic of the 'heroic society', which MacIntyre claims is 'still inescapably a part of us all'[80] reflects not the 'shared values'[81] he says he finds but 'the dominance of a male warrior elite'.[82]

Her attack on Nozick[83] is less thorough-going if only because it is relatively narrow. She shows that, since only women have the natural capacity to produce people, Nozick's entitlement theory of justice, based on the notion that one owns what one produces, leads to absurd and inconsistent conclusions. 'Instead of a utopian minimal state', Okin states, 'Nozick's individuals are left in a condition of matriarchy, slavery, and dystopia'.[84] As with many other thinkers, Nozick also takes for granted the vast sphere of life in which women take care of others. But Nozick's views are peripheral to the debate about justice in the family – indeed, perhaps they are just peripheral[85].

By contrast, Okin is sympathetic to Rawls and, indeed, wishes to use his theory of justice as a frame for her own account of justice within the family. She is particularly attracted to Rawls's heuristic device of the 'original position', in which hypothetical people in selecting principles of justice are deprived of their own particular place in society, their class, social status, intelligence, strength, even 'special features of [their] psychology',[86] and therefore have to consider the well-being of everyone, from the best-off to the worst-off, on the hypothesis that they could be any one of them. Okin believes that principles chosen in this way would extirpate the gross inequalities between men and women.[87] It will, however, have been noted that Rawls did not stipulate that the persons in the original position are ignorant of whether they will be male or female: in fact in *A Theory of Justice* he says nothing about this question, though in a later article[88] he does make it clear that sex is one of the morally irrelevant contingencies hidden by the veil of ignorance. An additional problem with Rawls, that

78 He certainly tries to show that his Aristotelian – Thomistic account avoids at least some of the discriminatory conclusions of Aristotle's treatment of women. See also Philip Selznick, *The Moral Commonwealth* (Berkeley: University of California Press, 1992), ch. 16.

79 *Op cit*, note 77, p. 51.

80 *After Virtue* (Notre Dame: University of Notre Dame Press, 1981)., p. 122.

81 And see Walzer, op *cit*, note 3.

82 *Op cit*, note 77, p. 52.

83 *Ibid*, p. 76–88. See, further, Samuel Sheffler, 'Natural Rights, Equality and the Minimal State' in Jeffrey Paul (ed), *Reading Nozick* (Oxford: Blackwell, 1981), p. 148.

84 *Op cit*, note 77, p. 80.

85 Okin certainly thinks so, though the influence on Reaganite and Thatcherite politics cannot be underestimated.

86 *Op cit*, note 1, p. 137.

87 *Op cit*, note 77, p. 174.

88 'Fairness to Goodness', *Philosophical Review*, 84, 1975, 537.

Okin acknowledges, is that parties in the original position are 'heads of households', who act on behalf of the interests of their households as a whole, thus not enabling them to determine questions of justice within families.[89] But then Rawls does not seem to have given a lot of thought to the family. He assumes that 'the basic structure of a well-ordered society includes the family in some form' and adds that 'in a broader enquiry the institution of the family might be questioned, and other arrangements might indeed prove to be preferable'.[90] These tentative comments are instructive in the light of challenges to the conventional, nuclear family, but Rawls is clearly reluctant to grasp the nettle. Okin is surely right to respond:[91] 'Why should it require a broader inquiry than the colossal task in which *A Theory of Justice* is engaged, to raise questions about the institution and form of the family?' The answer must be that Rawls did not consider the matter of importance in terms of the construction of principles of justice. This is surprising since he devotes considerable attention[92] to the way in which children learn moral sentiments, and eventually a sense of justice, from their early experiences in the family. But, as Okin rightly asks: how could this happen if the family itself is unjust?

Can then a feminist be sympathetic to Rawls or is his project so essentially flawed as to be beyond reconstruction in the service of those who wish to inject justice into relations based on gender? At the root of the problem is the disembodied individual who occupies the original position. Stephen Guest, writing of Dworkin whose imagined 'auction'[93]is not unlike Rawls' imaginary original position, says that this is 'not at all an odd idea'.[94] But surely it is. The very fact that liberalism has been so blind to gender inequalities suggests that by disembodying the individual, by degendering, you marginalise.[95] And the public-private divide becomes a screen to cloak off the injustices that you accordingly fail to recognise. Do those in the original position know anything relevant to the human condition or are the participants at the same time both everyone and no one? Are they capable of taking the role of the other? Is taking the viewpoint of others compatible with reasoning behind a veil of ignorance? Okin says of Rawls's theory of justice that it 'is itself centrally dependent upon the capacity of moral persons to be concerned about and to demonstrate care for others, especially others who are most different from themselves'.[96] Similarly Jean Hampton says of Rawls's veil that it 'no longer matters to the [person] in the original position who, if anyone, occupies the

89 See S.M. Okin, 'Reason and Feeling In Thinking About Justice', *Ethics*, 99, 1989, 229-249 at p. 235. And see Jane English's comment: 'By making the parties in the original position heads of families rather than individuals, Rawls makes the family opaque to claims of justice' in 'Justice Between Generations' (*Philosophical Studies* 31, 1977, 95). Also useful is Mari Matsuda, 'Liberal Jurisprudence and Abstracted Visions of Human Nature: A Feminist Critique of Rawls 'Theory of Justice'', *New Mexico Law Review*, 16, 1986, 613.

90 *Op cit*, note 1, p. 462-463.

91 *Op cit*, note 77, p. 96.

92 In part III of *A Theory of Justice*.

93 'What is Equality? Part II Equality of Resources', *Philosophy and Public Affairs*, 10, 283-345.

94 *Ronald Dworkin*, (Edinburgh, Edinburgh University Press, 1992), p. 68.

95 This is clearly borne out by history. See Joan Hoff, *Law, Gender and Injustice* (New York: New York University Press, 1991).

96 *Op cit*, note 89, p. 247.

position with him or what its occupants' interests are. What matters to him are the desires and goals of every *actual* member of his society, because the veil forces him to reason *as if he were any one of them*'.[97] Even overlooking the use of the male pronoun here (Hampton was writing in 1980), what Okin and Hampton are failing to grasp is how the hurdle of the empathy they envisage can be surmounted by individuals who know so little about the human condition. What, for example, would they know of anger or envy or pride or desire? Is it to be assumed that we can distil some essence of these 'qualities' which can then be held constant in the original position? Can you individuate moral situations without knowing anything of the character, history or desires of the agents involved?

The problem can be illustrated from within the Rawlsian principles themselves. His second principle posits that social and economic inequalities are to be so arranged that they are both to the 'greatest benefit of the least advantaged' and attached to offices and positions open to all.[98] But how is one to identify the 'least advantaged' and compute the 'greatest benefit' relative to that person? Passing over the utility comparisons, there are real problems here. Rawls purports to find the 'least advantaged' through the prism of 'the expectations of representative men'.[99] But how would they know if they were isolated from the experiences and interactions of the particular society? Who, to take examples drawn from our own society is the least advantaged: the divorced woman in danger of losing her home with young children and no marketable skills or the single mother with children living on income support in a high-rise flat on a 'sink' estate? And would the answer be different if one of these women were black or physically disabled? *We* might be able to answer these questions but would individuals behind the veil of ignorance? *We* can attempt to understand their lives by observing them, by trying to get inside their experiences, by communicating with them. The social-psychological project[100] has its failings (beyond the scope of this lecture) but it offers us insights which disembodied conjecture surely denies us.

And yet Okin for one clearly believes we can build on Rawls. She proposes that we retain the device of the original position but deprive the parties of knowing whether they will be males or females in the resulting society and insist that, since the structure of the family is part of the basic structure of society, the parties would have to consider the basic principles that affect it. From this, she believes, a truly 'humanist justice'[101] would emerge, one that would recognise the privations of the private,[102] the inequalities commonly experienced within the structure of family life and would correct these through legal changes and by transforming the patterns of daily life, in particular activities within the home such as those involved with child-rearing.

97 'Contracts and Choices: Does Rawls Have a Social Contract Theory?', *Journal of Philosophy*, 77, 1980, 315–338 at 335.

98 *Op cit*, note 1, p. 83.

99 *Ibid*, p. 70.

100 See the excellent discussion of its relevance and of some of the issues involved in John Baker, *Arguing For Equality* (London: Verso, 1987), ch. 9.

101. The title of the last chapter of *Justice, Gender and the Family*,.

102 It was Hannah Arendt who, in *The Human Condition* (Chicago: University of Chicago Press, 1958) pointed to the etymological origin of private in privation.

But, like many who have treated the private as an unproblematic given, so Okin seems to regard the conventional, western nuclear family.[103] She acknowledges that it has been peculiarly resistant to justice and yet seems to take it for granted that individuals in the original position, even when deprived of knowledge of their gender, would choose it, although they would have to redesign its internal workings to conform to the basic principles of justice. From Rawls's brief discussion of the family it is clear that he too treats to-day's nuclear family as unproblematic.[104] It is a little odd that Okin should equate her gender-free society with a society of heterosexual couples, even if she believes, as most people do, that children do best when reared by couples of both sexes. This is to take an unduly Euro-centric and modern view of the family: outside Europe and outside modern Europe the extended family, even the village, has often been more central to child-rearing than the couple.[105] It is also to fail to get to grips with modern debates about the family which have come to prominence with the new reproductive technologies but are not unique to them. Questions relating to the propriety of families based on single mothers and lesbian couples. Questions relating to eligibility to adopt[106] (should this be limited to married couples or heterosexual couples or couples?). Questions on eligibility for IVF treatment[107] which came to the fore with the debate over 'virgin births'[108] and the passing of s.13(5) of the Human Fertilisation and Embryology Act in 1990.[109] And debates which have surfaced with the implementation of the Child Support Act 1991 such as over the liability of a sperm donor to maintain a child engendered by him in this way.

The Child Support Act indeed is a useful test-bed for some of Okin's ideas. She favours 'the added weight of responsibility given to fatherhood in a gender-free society'.[110] This would 'surely give young men more incentive than they now have not to incur the results of careless sexual behaviour until they were ready to take on the responsibilities of being parents'.[111] She likes a proposal of David Ellwood[112] that the paternity of all children of single mothers (but why just single mothers?) should be

103 See, for agreement, Will Kymlicka, 'Rethinking The Family', *Philosophy and Public Affairs*, 20, 1991, 77–97. See also Jo Van Every, 'Who is "the Family"? The Assumptions of British Social Policy',*Critical Social Policy*, 33, 1991–2, 62–75.

104 Rawls begins his account of moral development by saying: 'Given that family institutions are just' (*Op cit*, note 1, p. 490). See also D. Kearns, 'A Theory of Justice – and Love: Rawls on the Family', *Politics*, 18(2), 1983, 36–42.

105 See Michael Mitterauer and Reinhard Sieder, *The European Family* (Oxford: Blackwell, 1982) for extensive historical evidence.

106 As to which see Department of Health/Welsh Office, *Review of Adoption Law* (London: Department of Health, 1992).

107 See Andrea L. Bonnicksen, *In Vitro Fertilization: Building Policy From Laboratories to Legislatures* (New York: Columbia University Press, 1989) p. 104-105, referring to the Texas and Massachusetts laws. See also *R v. St. Mary's Hospital, Manchester Ethics Committee ex parte Harriot* [1988] 1 F.L.R. 512.

108 See Hilary Rose, 'Victorian Values in The Test-Tube: The Politics of Reproductive Science and Technology' in Michelle Stanworth (ed), *Reproductive Technologies* (Cambridge: Polity Press, 1987), p. 151.

109 On which see Gillian Douglas, 'Assisted Reproduction and the Welfare of the Child', *Current Legal Problems*, 46(2), 1993, 110. *Op cit*, note 77, p. 178.

111 *Idem.*

112 *Poor Support: Poverty In The American Family* (New York: Basic Books, 1988), p. 163–174.

established at the time of birth and support payments (admittedly of a rather low amount) levied thereafter. On one level this may look just: it seems to restore, partially at least, an inequitable balance of responsibility between mothers and fathers. And, it is true, it may also save some public money (which is, of course, the real aim of our new legislation).[113] But, in terms of justice within the family, it overlooks the impact of increasing a man's responsibility. It may serve to increase his control over her.[114] Robert Goodin warned some years ago that 'depending on their families for assistance subjects beneficiaries to the arbitrary will of another'[115]

He may demand rights, both over her and the child; rights over such questions as a child's upbringing, education, religion, medical treatment; he may claim access rights,[116] just at a time when we have begun to recognise that these inhere in the child rather than the parent. He may also try to stop her having an abortion: although the courts have resisted such attempts in the past,[117] there is no guarantee that this line will hold. Indeed, the argument that the foetus is part of her body[118] may backfire because it is part of his also. And if he is the commissioning father in a surrogacy arrangement, he may demand the child be handed over to him.[119] Would individuals in Okin's reconstructed Rawlsian original position, not knowing whether they might become mothers or fathers (or neither) advocate a system of responsibility with the potentiality for use (abuse) in these ways? At the very least I suspect they would deliberate at length and make changes very warily.

But go back to Okin's premise: a just society being a gender-free society in which the difference between being male and female would be no more significant than 'one's eye colour or the length of one's toes'.[120] I think the analogy untenable, as I shall argue presently. But at this juncture it is worth pointing to the inconsistency of, on the one hand, emphasising paternity and, on the other, treating a gender-free society as the ultimate goal. It is difficult to see how they can be compatible. By imputing responsibility to those who father children Okin, whether she wishes to do so or not, is attaching social significance to gender. But, if gender is really as socially irrelevant as eye colour, it is difficult to prioritise the married heterosexual couple over other combinations

113 This is admitted, to all intents and purposes, in the government report which heralded the Child Support Act, *Children Come First* (London: HMSO 1990).

114 There is research evidence suggesting that some divorced and separated women prefer the poverty of lone parenthood to their economic position within marriage (will the Child Support Act impose a quasi marital relationship?). See H. Graham, 'Being Poor: Perceptions of Coping Strategies of Lone Mothers' in Julia Brannen and G. Wilson (eds), *Give and Take In Families* (London: Allen and Unwin, 1987). Also Jonathan Bradshaw and Jane Millar, *Lone Parent Families in the U.K.* (London: DSS/HMSO, 1991).

115 'Self Reliance v. the Welfare State', *Journal of Social Policy*, 14, 25–47 at p. 37.

116 But see Alison Kitch, 'Conditioning Child Support Payments on Visitation Access', *International Journal of Law and The Family*, 5, 1991, 318–50.

117 *Paton v. British Pregnancy Advisory Service Trustees* [1979] Q.B. 276 and *C. v. S* [1988] Q.B. 135.

118 See Judith Jarvis Thomson, 'A Defence of Abortion', *Philosophy and Public Affairs*, 1, 1971, 47–66. In the United States it is privacy doctrine which has laid the basis for the legal right to abortion. See Catherine Mackinnon, '*Roe v. Wade*: A Study in Male Ideology' in Jay Garfield and Patricia Hennesey (eds), *Abortion: Moral and Legal Perspectives*, (Amherst: University of Massachusetts Press, 1984, p. 45–54).

119 As in the notorious *Baby M* litigation in New Jersey: 337 A. 2d 1227 (1988).

120 *Op cit*, note 77, p. 171.

– though Okin seems to wish to do so. The social reality is that there is a world of difference between gender and eye colour and, if those behind the veil of ignorance cannot make the distinction, it is yet another indication of the incoherence of the concept of the individual in the original position: the experience of being male or female and the experience of sexual attraction cannot be seen as like the feelings about oneself or others associated with eye colour.

Writing of Okin's position, Nicola Lacey suggests that it leads ultimately to an original position inhabited by the 'super-imaginative'.[121] A world, perhaps, where Ronald Dworkin's Judge Hercules might well feel at home. Dworkin's liberalism and his theory of adjudication are not targets of Okin. His *Taking Rights Seriously*[122] is cursorily dismissed as a book which pays 'even less attention'[123] to issues of family justice than does Rawls. But no critical attention is focused on *Law's Empire*[124] or on his series of articles on equality.[125] This is somewhat surprising when Dworkin's claim to find the answer to the puzzle of legitimacy lies in so obvious a target, namely 'fraternity'.[126] The political connotations of this concept have been explored by Carole Pateman in *The Sexual Contract*.[127] I will accordingly address a different issue here: the moral position of the judge when his (or her) view conflicts with that of the community, though it will inevitably become necessary to return to the association of community and fraternity.

In the last chapter of *Law's Empire* Dworkin writes of Hercules's dilemma when he thinks 'the best interpretation of the equal protection clause[128] outlaws distinctions between the rights of adults and those of children that have never been questioned in the community, and yet he .... think[s] that it would be politically unfair .... for the law to impose that view on a community whose family and social practices accept such distinctions as proper and fundamental'.[129] The paradox of a 'right answer' which is at the same time a 'wrong' answer has been little noticed. The implications of what Dworkin says, however, are significant in the context of justice for women (and children, though this is outside the scope of this lecture).

Dworkin's sentence may have passed relatively unnoticed because most of his readers and critics would not question discrimination against children any more than the communities of which they are a part. But travel the time machine backwards less

121 'Theories of Justice and The Welfare State', *Social and Legal Studies*, 1, 1992, 323–344, at p.
122 London: Duckworth, 1977.
123 *Op cit*, note 77, p. 9.
124 See note 4.
125 See 'What is Equality? Part I: Equality of Welfare,' *Philosophy and Public Affairs*, 10, 1981, 185–246; 'What is Equality? Part II: Equality of Resources', *Iowa Law Review*, 73, 1987, 1-54; 'What is Equality? Part IV: Political Equality, *University of San Francisco Law Review* 22, 1987, 1–30. I do not consider them either in this lecture.
126 See *op cit*, note 4, p. 200–201, 206–208. See also Rawls, *op cit*, note 1 at p. 105 where fraternity is 'the idea of not wanting to have greater advantages unless this is to the benefit of others who are less well off'.
127 See *op cit*, note 15, p. 78–82. See also 'The Fraternal Social Contract' in *The Disorder of Women* (Cambridge: Polity Press, 1989, ch. 2).
128 Amendment 14 prohibiting the denial to 'any person within its jurisdiction [of] the equal protection of the laws'.
129 *Op cit*, note 4, p. 402.

than one hundred years (and that is being generous) and substitute for 'children' 'women' and then interpret Dworkin.[130] Would Hercules in an earlier time have had to allow his convictions that discrimination against women was wrong to be 'trumped'[131] by those of a community which did not question it?

We must examine the concept of 'community', a concept to which Dworkin devotes considerable space.[132] As Guest explains, 'a proper community, one in which it is fraternal association that provides the justification for political obligation, places weight on concern for well-being and equality. Dworkin calls such a community a "community of principle". Such a community fulfils the four conditions of having special obligations to the group, being personal, showing concern for the well-being of others and showing an equal concern for all'.[133] 'A community of principle ... can claim moral legitimacy – that its collective decisions are matters of obligation and not bare power – in the name of fraternity'.[134]

What is the status of children to-day in relation to this 'community'? Or women yesteryear or to-day? Practices in relation to both have been and are justified by paternalism and Dworkin stresses that the conception of equal concern, which is a constitutive feature of the community of principle is not incompatible with paternalistic practices.[135] It is rather unfortunate that 'equal concern and respect' in his earlier writings[136] has now become 'equal concern', making it much easier to reconcile paternalism.[137] It may also be an unhappy coincidence that the example Dworkin uses is that of a culture which 'accepts' equality of the sexes but 'in good faith thinks that equality of concern requires paternalistic protection for women in all aspects of family life'.[138] Nor is this assisted by some opaque reasoning and ambiguous language, for Dworkin acknowledges that if this 'institution' of the family is 'otherwise seriously unjust', then it 'cannot be justified in any way that recommends continuing it'. But serious injustice is exemplified by Dworkin as forcing family members to commit crimes in the interest of the family – a strange example and one which compounds errors already perpetrated. What is the 'interest' of the family? How does a 'culture' think? And, most pertinently for this discussion, how is membership of a community tested? Dworkin does not question why certain persons who he takes for granted are members of the group need protection. Perhaps they would not see themselves as members of the group. Perhaps they need protection because of cultural practices of the past.[139] And, even if they identify with the group and accept its practices, even those which hold them down, could this not be false consciousness rather than preference, the result of inculcation of a dominant ideology over generations or centuries?[140]

130 In the 'best possible light', of course. See, further, *op cit*, note 94, ch. 2.

131 To use Dworkin's own metaphor in *Taking Rights Seriously*, *op cit*, note 122, p. XV.

132 *Op cit*, note 4, p. 206–215.

133 *Op cit*, note 94, p.88.

134 *Op cit*, note 4, p. 214.

135 *Ibid*, p. 200.

136 *Op cit*, note 122, p. 198–199.

137 *Op cit*, note 4, p. 200–201.

138 *Ibid*, p. 204–205.

139 See Robin West, 'Taking Preferences Seriously', *Tulane Law Review*, 64, 1990, 659–703, which is particularly valuable in this context. There is, of course, a huge literature on dominant ideology.

140 And see Alison M. Jaggar, *Feminist Politics and Human Nature* (Totowa, N. J.:Rowman and

I think it is clear from Dworkin's discussion of the paternalistic family that he regards its female members as included within that community. But would they? Or is this a community defined by those who also define the practices? And if the same applies to the wider community, as by definitional fiat it must, then, as we return to the moral dilemma posed in the conflict between the 'right answer' and the answer deemed by the 'community' to be fair, we reach the conclusion that the 'community' can fictively prescribe membership to those it denies participatory rights and then in *their* name justify that exclusion. And rely on the judiciary to legitimate their actions for, as Dworkin conceives the judicial role,[141] questioning the unquestioned[142] clearly exceeds its appropriate bounds.

Some of these strands must now be drawn together and some conclusions offered. It would be trite to say that liberalism has failed women for so too have libertarianism,[143] communitarianism[144] and Marxism.[145] The focus in this lecture was on liberalism and its vision of justice in part because of its historical importance and contemporary significance, but also because a leading feminist account of gender and justice is in large part a reconstruction of a leading liberal exposition (and Okin's is an increasingly influential book). And, of course, it is within liberalism that the public/private dualism is most clearly articulated. But, as has been shown, the dichotomy is both ambiguous and incoherent as well as being illusory. It has been responsible for setting us on false trails, into investigations as to when state intervention into the domestic sphere is justified, whereas, as indicated, non-intervention is itself a form of regulation. The public/private divide distorts. It uses the language of 'privacy' as a justification for non-intervention, ignoring the ways the 'public' constantly shapes, constitutes and restructures the private world of family and sexuality. By dividing the world into two spheres, it purports to create a private space where the rules of the public do not intrude. So that in the 'private' world we are private beings, not social ones. So that the ideals and principles of democracy can be left at every front door. And the emphasis on the rights-culture of the public realm deflects from the importance of some of the qualities like benevolence, altruism and care[146] which are associated primarily with the private sphere.

Allanheld, 1983) and Sandra Lipsitz Bem, *The Lenses of Gender* (New Haven: Yale University Press, 1993).

141 See text at note 128.

142 Cf Martha Minow, *Making All the Difference: Inclusion, Exclusion and American Law* (Ithaca, New York: Cornell University Press, 1990). See also Katharine Bartlett's comment: 'Feminists consider the concept of community problematic, because they have demonstrated that law has tended to reflect existing structures of power' ('Feminist Legal Methods', *Harvard Law Review*, 103, 1990, 829 at p. 841.

143 The 'private' is worshipped, but is rarely problematised. It is hardly surprising, then, that the situation of women is given so very little attention by its most prominent exponents.

144 See Marilyn Friedman, 'Feminism and Modern Friendship: Dislocating The Community', *Ethics*, 99, 1989, 275–290.

145 It is remarkable that the recent plethora of literature on Marx and justice has ignored (or at least skirted) this question. A good summary of the debate is Norman Geras, 'The Controversy About Marx and Justice', *New Left Review*, 150, 1985, 47–85.

146 See Carol Gilligan, *In A Different Voice* (Cambridge, Mass: Harvard University Press, 1982); Nel Noddings, *Caring: A Feminist Approach To Ethics and Moral Education* (Berkeley, California: University of California Press, 1984). See also O. Flanagan and K. Jackson, 'Justice, Care and Gender', *Ethics*, 97, 1987, 622–637.

A theory of justice which embraces issues associated with the domestic must be the goal. There is a need to politicise, to renegotiate and to redress. The status quo has to be challenged, not justified. Part of the value of Okin's project is to confront abstract theories of justice with the problems of real lives, with issues which have for so long resided in, what was thought of as, a 'haven': child care,[147] domestic violence,[148] the problems of divorced women.[149] Failure to make this conjunction has led to policies like the trend away from awarding alimony which could only have been initiated and sustained because the realities of women's lives were not addressed. Such a policy is the result of translating from the public sphere a principle of equality on to a realm where custom, the conventional division of labour and discrimination in employment have worked to the detriment of women.[150] But this should teach us to be wary about the dangers of piecemeal transplants. Justice in the home requires more than the extension to the domestic situation of principles and concepts used to constrain power elsewhere. Too many feminists have assumed the answer lies in contract.[151] This may have value in some areas (in regulating cohabitation[152] and as an alternative to the status of coverture created by marriage[153]) but could be an unmitigated disaster in others (surrogacy[154] and the adoption of children[155] being two examples).

A detailed account of this theory of justice must await a further lecture – though it would need a book. It must seek to create equality whilst recognising difference. It must demand changes in both the 'private' sphere and in all of the 'public' spheres. It must build on an understanding of the interests of others, an understanding which cannot be acquired by the disembodied individuals who inhabit the original position or attend auctions, and upon an empathy with their lives and problems. It must examine real lives of real people and the social and political culture and the institutions (employment, education, the welfare state, transport as well as marriage and parenthood) which structure and sustain these lives. It will reject the public/private dualism, but recognise its legacy and seek radically to change it. A beginning has been made – but there is a long way to go before justice in home can become a reality.

147 See Carol Smart, 'The Legal and Moral Ordering of Child Custody', *Journal of Law and Society*, 1991, 18, 485–500.

148 See, amongst an extensive literature, Betsy Stanko, *Intimate Intrusions* (London: Routledge, Kegan Paul, 1985).

149 Mavis Maclean, *Surviving Divorce* (Basingstoke: Macmillan, 1991) is a useful source.

150 Barbara R. Bergman, *The Economic Emergence of Women* (New York: Basic Books, 1986); Sylvia Walby, *Patriarchy At Work* (Minneapolis: University of Minnesota Press, 1986); Linda M. Blum, *Between Feminism and Labor* (Berkeley: University of California Press, 1991).

151 See, for example, Carmel Shalev, *Birth Power: The Case for Surrogacy* (New Haven: Yale University Press, 1989) and Marjorie Schultz, 'Contractual Ordering of Marriage: A New Model for State Policy', *California Law Review*, 70, 1982, 207–334.

152 See Michael Freeman and Christina M. Lyon, *Cohabitation Without Marriage* (Aldershot: Gower Press, 1983).

153 See Lenore J. Weitzman, *The Marriage Contract* (New York: Free Press, 1975).

154 See Martha A. Field, 'Surrogacy Contracts – Gestational and Traditional: The Argument for Non-Enforcement', *Washburn Law Journal*, 31, 1991, 1–17. See also Zillah Eisenstein, *The Female Body and The Law* (Berkeley, California: University of California Press, 1988, ch. 6).

155 See Richard A. Posner, 'The Regulation of The Market in Adoptions', *Boston University Law Review*, 67, 1987, 59–72.

If the 1990s are truly to be the decade of the 'citizen'[156], we must construct a new concept of 'citizenship', one which serves the goals and needs of all people. And it will have to address not just abstract rights in the public sphere, but how that sphere has been created and by whom, as well as the power relationships that are involved both in this and the private sphere and in creating and sustaining the dualism. In doing so it will question and reconstruct the very concept of citizenship. If this could come out of the current debates about citizenship, if 'charters' could penetrate the iron curtain surrounding the home, if women could attain full citizenship status, the decade of the 'citizen' might be truly memorable. But these are big 'ifs'.

156 But the critique of universality in Iris Marion Young's writings needs to be taken very seriously. See her 'Polity and Group Difference: A Critique of the Ideal of Universal Citizenship' in *Ethics*, 99, 1989, 250–274 and her *Justice and the Politics of Difference* (Princeton: Princeton University Press, 1990). See also now David T. Evans, *Sexual Citizenship* (London: Routledge, 1993).

Katherine O'Donovan

Love's Law: Moral Reasoning in Family Law

This paper proposes that changes in family law, emanating from law reformers, legislators, or the judiciary, are based on the moral views of a few but not on the shared values of many. This proposition is often denied by those with power to change law, who claim to speak on behalf of others or who deny that morality is involved. The paper supports the proposition with evidence from recent changes and current reform proposals; examines the reasons for the denial of morality; and suggests that morality being an inevitable part of family law reform, this must be acknowledged, the values debated openly, and theories of the family subjected to the scrutiny of those who share their lives with others.

Popular Opinion and Common Sense

Legal philosophers such as Raz[1] or Dworkin[2] acknowledge the place of morality or principles as a safety net onto which the judiciary may fall when a gap opens up in the law. The question is: whose views and whose morality? The role of the 'ordinary person', the 'ordinary man', the 'silent majority', as a reference point for the judiciary in family law cases has not been acknowledged and explored in the literature. Reference is not confined to 'common sense', but is sometimes extended to 'changed social conditions', particularly to justify a proposed change in the law not sanctioned by past practice. Perceptions of popular opinion also play a part when legislative changes to family law are proposed by the Law Commission or in parliamentary argument. But do such references relate to personal preferences and values of the justifiers and arguers? Or are they based on the legislator's knowledge of beliefs and desires of the majority of people?

Popular Opinion as Judicial Gap Filler

What is a family? Faced with this question the English judiciary calls on the 'ordinary person'. It is said that:

> in no case has the court found it possible to identify the necessary ingredient or quality that distinguishes a familial nexus from a nexus less than familial. The approach of the courts has been to look at the circumstances and then seek to answer the question: What would an ordinary person characterize the relationship as?[3]

Reference to an 'abuse of the English language'[4] has been used to deny the title of family member (and therefore of rights of succession to a tenancy) to the survivor of a

1 J. Raz, *The Morality of Freedom* (Oxford, Clarendon Press, 1986).
2 R. Dworkin, *Taking Rights Seriously* (London, Duckworth, 1977).
3 *Sefton v. Cairns* [1988] 2 *Family Law Reports* 108.
4 *Gammans v. Elkins* [1950] 2 *All England Law Reports* 140.

ARSP-Beiheft 57. Derek Morgan & Gillian Douglas (eds.)
Constituting Families. © 1994 by Franz Steiner Verlag Stuttgart

twenty-year long heterosexual cohabiting relationship. However a later case has stated that the word family is 'not restricted to blood relationships and those created by the marriage ceremony', but must be considered according to the 'popular meaning of the word'.[5] Yet if the cohabiting couple do not conceal their lack of mutual marriage the court may deny the status of 'member of a family' to them, for it has been said that without a pretence of marriage they cannot satisfy pre-conceived notions. The test is 'what the ordinary man would say'.[6] But there is some doubt as to who precisely this man is: 'Do you listen to the vociferous minority or do you imagine what the silent majority might have said at a particular time?'[7] A functional approach which looks inside the relationship has been advocated by some lawyers, but has been rejected by the courts. The notion of family goes beyond function, but to what exactly?

As can be deduced from the above references to the ordinary man create a flexibility, which might be thought to encompass new patterns of living. But this reference to popular views is neither functionally nor empirically based. There is no empirical research to support the judge's surmise. Nor even is a jury polled for its opinion. Not only does the habit of reference assume that the judiciary is in touch with public opinion, but it leaves open to the discretion of the individual judge the definition of popular morality, which may be confused with personal preference. A normative approach follows from this reference. In other words the reasonable man stands for popular opinion which stands for ought statements about how we should live.

There are a variety of arrangements for living together. Yet the status of family member has been judicially denied to the survivor of a relationship between two women who lived together as sisters for forty-five years. They were denoted 'strangers' by the court, which claimed the authority of the ordinary man.[8] Since their relationship was not legitimated as a family relationship benefits derived from membership could not be received.

What emerges from the references in these cases is a model of family form which does not depart very far from the heterosexual, marital tradition. For example, where two women lived together in a 'committed, monogamous, homosexual relationship', the status of family member was refused to the survivor who argued that the relationship was similar to marriage. The judge's view was that 'the ordinary man and woman...would in my opinion, not even remotely think of there being a true resemblance between these two very different states of affairs'.[9] The judges in these cases attribute to the ordinary person limited, normative views of what a family is. At present this includes heterosexual cohabiting relationships, particularly those with children. Gender, parental roles based on tradition, seem to be regarded as significant.

It might be objected that a normative view of what a 'family' is must necessarily result from the discretion conferred on the interpreter. But an empirical or a functional definition might also be applied. This could refer to the kind of relationship involved, love, help, support, what the members give to one another.

5 *Dyson Holdings v. Fox* [1975] 3 *All England Law Reports* 1030.
6 *Helby v. Rafferty* [1978] 3 *All England Law Reports* 1016.
7 *Ibid* at p.1018.
8 *Sefton Holdings v. Cairns*, see above note 3.
9 *Harrogate Borough Council v. Simpson* [1986] *Family Law Reports* 91.

Popular Opinion Affected by Changed Social Circumstances

The courts have recently decided that rape of a woman by a man, with the status of husband, is a crime. In so doing the House of Lords overturned an exemption from the criminal law of rape, believed by the judiciary to date back two hundred and fifty years, and which had hitherto been upheld as a principle throughout the twentieth century.[10] Although this may be welcomed as a departure from the content of tradition, examination of the judgments in the House of Lords and in the Court of Appeal reveals that 'changed social circumstances' are the key words in justifying the alteration of what was held a significant legal principle. That is, the concept of 'changed social circumstances' is used to undo an immunity from prosecution for rape based on marriage. But what does the concept of 'changed social circumstances' stand for? I suggest it stands for changed perceptions, attitudes, understandings, in other words popular morality. On one level marriage has changed very little. Its magic, rites, status, familiarity continue. On another level, everything about marriage has changed, only its shell remains. The point here is not to debate change or its acknowledgement by the judiciary, but to highlight not only the lack of definition of a concept such as 'changed social circumstances' in the overthrow of an established principle, but also to highlight in legal discourse the use of such vague phrases in justifying new departures. In establishing that circumstances have changed socially the judiciary does not call on the Central Statistics Office, or the Office of Population and Census, or on market analysts, but on common sense. This may appear as a criticism from within the realist, jurisprudential school. But it is intended to go further and to illustrate the use of 'common sense' as a point of closure which cannot be questioned.

Family law does not draw on a privileged, technical discourse, or on empirical research, to establish 'common sense'. Rather common sensical opinions are said to be those of the reasonable man. In this family law depends on a way of knowing, of defining the 'normal', of stigmatising the 'unusual', of silencing what is not approved. Is there slippage between what is denoted common sense by a judge and the personal preferences of that judge for how others should behave? In other words, if common sense exists how is it to be recognised and differentiated from personal opinion? Does not the common part of common sense imply shared views, agreement? Or is 'common sense' an attribute of a legal subject constructed by legislation and courts? This is an important question particularly where we legislate for others.

It might be objected that reference to 'changed social circumstances' is preferable to the maintenance of precedent, especially where precedent is anomalous or offensive. Perhaps so, but it may involve the creation of a new norm without full justification. There remain inarticulate major premises about popular opinion, or what Alastair McIntyre calls shared values in *After Virtue*. These are presumed to exist without investigation, yet there is evidence of uneasiness.

10 *R v. R* [1991] 4 *All England Law Reports* 481.

The Denial that Popular Opinion is Morality

References to the common sense of the reasonable man as a justification for legal provision or decision are made not only in the course of judgment by the judiciary, but also by law reformers in and out of Parliament. An example is available from divorce debates. Divorce law was last reformed in 1969.[11] In late 1980s the Law Commission undertook a major review and new divorce legislation has been proposed.[12]

A comparison of the 1966 paper which preceded the 1969 reform with the current reform papers produced in 1988 and 1990 reveals a lack of overt reference to 'shared values' in the community in the latter papers. Whereas the language of the earlier document was concerned with the promotion of the 'stability of marriage, reconciliation, maximum fairness, protection of children and the economically weaker spouse',[13] the 1988 document states that,

> law and practice can no longer be founded on the assumption that people affected by divorce are a small and deviant proportion of the population. Secondly, the 'consumer interest' in both the substantive and procedural aspects of the divorce law is proportionately that much greater and must be taken into account in any evaluation of the present law or proposals for reform.[14]

Thus the language has shifted from confident morality albeit often based on 'common sense', to consumer led opinions as the standard of justice. But are these any less 'moral'? We are seeing the emergence of a new construction of legal subjects allegedly concerned with efficiency rather than justice.

The language of 1966 contained humanitarian values. There was talk of 'maximum fairness, and minimum bitterness, distress and humiliation', of decency and dignity.[15] The language of 1988 is of efficiency, pragmatism and resignation. For example it is said that the reforms of 1969 led to procedures which 'were often unnerving and humiliating for the petitioner'; that there was 'a rapid escalation of legal aid expenditure and divorce'; that 'registrars act as little more than "rubber stamps"'; that there is no adequate system for checking whether the petitioner has proved the contents of the petition.[16] The sub-text is that the seemingly just system of divorce devised in the 1960s is open to abuse and perjury, is costly to the taxpayer, and is unsatisfactory to those divorcing.

Of particular interest is the discussion of 'fault'. One of the jewels in the crown of the common law is its procedures for ascertaining truth, allocating fault, responsibility and blame. A trial, whether civil or criminal, is designed to establish the facts, apply the law, draw conclusions, and produce a result; a fine, a not-guilty verdict, compensation for a wrong. A trial is a recreation of 'what happened' with blame for those at fault. This was the method applied to family law in its ecclesiastical origins, and in its judicial phase from 1857. Doubts about the suitability of this method of inquiry for marital termination are now instated. In 1966 there was some discussion of the limits of judicial inquiry into the breakdown of marriage. Whereas the Archbishop of Canterbury's Group, which had

11 The Divorce Reform Act 1969 now consolidated in the Matrimonial Causes Act 1973.

12 Law Commission, *Facing the Future*, no.170 (London, HMSO, 1988); Law Commission, *The Grounds for Divorce*, No. 192 (London, HMSO, 1990).

13 Law Commission, *The Field of Choice*, No. 6, Cmnd. 3123 (London, HMSO, 1966), para.15.

14 *Facing the Future*, see above note 12, para.2.22.

15 *The Field of Choice*, see above note 13, para.2.3.

16 *Facing the Future*, see above note 12, paras.2.6; 2.8.

published a report entitled *Putting Asunder*[17], favoured court adjudication of marriage breakdown, this was officially rejected on the grounds that breakdown was not a justiciable issue. But the notion of fault, which had previously dominated divorce law, was retained in relation to 'adultery' and 'behaviour', two 'facts' which could be elicited as evidence of breakdown. In other words, fault was retained, and with it law's claims to establish truth and blame. Fault gave the prospect of a quick divorce, as other non-fault based 'facts' required a minimum wait of two-years. The point of this discussion is that the 1988 text admits that law's ability 'to conduct a proper inquiry'[18] into irretrievable breakdown of marriage is strictly limited; and the 1990 document says that the courts are only capable of assessing marital fault 'in the crudest possible way'.[19] Thus, law's claim to establish 'truth' in divorce cases has been abandoned. Although this is justified in terms of encouraging 'the parties to look to the future rather than to dwell in the past'[20] the significance of the abandonment of this site should not be overlooked. It is part of the retreat of family law from an overt moral discourse, because the notion of shared, or imposed, values is being abandoned. However, it seems that policy-makers are reluctant completely to abandon their claim to make 'a coherent and consistent moral law'[21] and such perspectives remain embedded in family law in the wider sense, and in the legal subjects constructed within the law.

The 1988 document, whilst criticising the 1966 text, is an indictment of the present divorce law. It may also be read as placing the limits to law's powers in human relationships. The Divorce Reform Act 1969 is held up as having failed to perform the humanitarian tasks of ensuring the stability of marriages whilst destroying the 'empty shell' of those which are dead, promoting 'maximum fairness' with 'minimum bitterness, distress and humiliation'.[22] This indictment, which is supported by considerable empirical research, enables the Law Commission to move to its own preferred solution, presented in terms of consumer choice, efficiency, and pragmatism. Justice is now defined in terms of procedure rather than substance. Underlying the 1988 text is resignation, a retreat from the earlier confidences of 1966 in the essential goodness or even perfectibility of man.

The retreat identified may be welcomed as making way for pluralism. But it takes place in the name of pragmatism and not liberty. Thus 'virtually any spouse can assemble a list of events, which taken out of context, can be presented as unreasonable behaviour sufficient to found a divorce petition'.[23] An adultery petition is an 'easy option' for 'determined parties', who may perjure themselves.[24] Not only are consumers manipulating the law but it is not possible to allocate blame as in 'most divorces the spouses will both be "at fault" in varying degrees'.[25] And the legal process may itself be 'such as to provoke or exacerbate unnecessary antagonism between parties'.[26]

17 The Archbishop of Canterbury's Group, *Putting Asunder*
18 *Facing the Future*, see above note 12, para.2.8.
19 *The Ground for Divorce*, see above note 12, para.3.6.
20 *Ibid.*, para.3.3.
21 *Ibid.*, para.3.40.
22 This was the language used in *Putting Asunder,* see above note 17 and in *The Field of Choice*, see above note 13.
23 *Facing the Future*, see above note 12, para.3.8.
24 *Ibid.*, paras. 3.45 and 5.16.
25 *Ibid.*, para.3.16.
26 *Ibid.*, para.3.22.

One of the values of a good divorce law, according to the Law Commission, is fairness. The present law is seen as unfair and as exacerbating bitterness and hostility; so it is the legal divorce 'system' which engenders conflict.[27] The elimination of fault and of consensual divorce, where the spouse who least wishes to divorce is given an 'unfair advantage in negotiations about children, finances and property',[28] will lead to the avoidance of the unfair stigmatisation of one party. Fairness, then, is to be realised by leaving divorce to be worked out as 'a process over time'.[29] Law's aspirations in divorce are to be limited. Enter then the figure of the respondent to a 'behaviour' petition who has 'been guilty of violence or other forms of serious misconduct'. Whilst 'undeserving of sympathy',[30] the bringing out of such behaviour in public, the paper says, will not reduce conflict. It may further upset the children. Thus ideas about justice, in the sense of a public hearing and condemnation of conduct which falls below a certain standard, are no longer considered appropriate to family law. What we are seeing is judicial and professional awareness of law's limitations as a means of social control, particularly where values are unagreed. The research evidence of courts' reluctance to become involved in tricky or sticky family disputes already exists.

The quotations from the Law Commission documents above are designed to illustrate the extent to which legal policy makers are abandoning law's claims to knowledge and judgment of human domestic behaviour. For example, although children are traumatised by divorce, there are said to be cases in which this is still the best course for them, but 'others in which it is impossible to tell which course will be best'.[31]

The epistemological consequences of the abandonment of the claim to know are significant. A lack of confidence about the values that the law should uphold is also evident. It might be argued that, whatever the reasons for a retreat from judgment, liberty will be increased by law's retreat. This is a consequentialist argument, possibly susceptible to empirical confirmation, but only after the fact. However the reasons for law's proposed abandonment of the epistemological high ground are not couched in terms of liberty. This value has not been discussed by the Law Commission; rather the concern is pragmatic. Procedural issues, costs, efficiency, rationing of legal services: these are important concerns of the administration of justice. But this must not obscure from us the retreat from proud confidence. Nor must we conclude that a retreat from overt reference to morality has brought about the end of morals. Rather these live on in 'common sense', 'changed social circumstances' and other phrases employed in justification.

Reasons for Denial that Popular Opinion is Morality

'The complexities of family life are no longer capable of being reduced to simple certainties'; thus spoke the Law Commission in 1990.[32] Accordingly the current pretence of inquiry into truth on divorce is false. It is better therefore, according to the

27 *Ibid.*, para.3.41.
28 *Ibid.*, para.5.18.
29 *Ibid.*, para.5.22.
30 *Ibid.*, para.3.27.
31 *Ibid.*, para.3.37.
32 *The Grounds for Divorce*, see above note 12, para.3.6.

reformers, to look to efficiency and consumer satisfaction. Judgment about behaviour has become unfashionable. But is it so easy to abandon the highground? And if family law does so on divorce, can we still find a language to justify the traditional legal structures for regulating marriage, or for dealing with disputes over parenthood and child custody? This is not to suggest that English family law based on judeo-christian tradition is justifiable. On the contrary it can be criticised as failing to meet standards of liberty and equality. But these are ethical standards, against which it can be openly measured. At present morality assumes a disguise in the language of efficiency, consumerism and common sense.

In this section of the paper the language used to discuss parenting by lesbian and homosexual persons will provide the illustrations. There is evidence of search for a neutral language to deal with cases of applications by homosexual parents for custody of or visitation rights to their children. As David Bradley points out in his extensive review of cases 'descriptions of a homosexual way of life as "odd", "unusual and irregular" or "rather extraordinary" were not unusual'.[33] Pragmatic considerations do play a part and much depends on the circumstances: a home with an 'unusual' parent is better than none.[34] But a home with 'usual' parents is better than either, according to case-law.

Summing up the cases is difficult. As already established there has been a judicial change away from explicit moral language. *Re D* (1977) provides an example of judicial outspokenness where a homosexual father wished to visit his child and therefore opposed adoption by the mother and stepfather. The judgment in the House of Lords refers to

> 'the risk of children, at critical ages being exposed or introduced to ways of life which, as this case illustrates, may lead to severance from normal society, to psychological stresses and unhappiness and possibly even to physical experiences which may scar them for life'.[35]

Putative common sense was used to suggest that 'a reasonable man would say "I must protect my boy, even if it means parting with him forever, so that he can be free from this danger"'.[36]

By comparison, more recent cases have introduced notions of 'corruption', which is usually rejected as a justification for denial of visitation rights, and 'reputation', which is usually upheld. 'Corruption' relates to good and bad example by a parent and is based on assumptions about morality. 'Reputation' relates to 'expressions of ridicule and scorn' by some sections of the community leading to teasing and embarrassment of the child.[37] In this way judicial language avoids moral condemnation of an 'unusual' parent and places the decision onto external factors, such as the attitudes of the community, the difficulties for the child at school and with friends, what the neighbours say.

33 D. Bradley, 'Homosexuality and Child Custody in English Law' *International Journal of Law and the Family*, 1 (1987) p.155 at p.189.

34 See also the language of 'unusual background' for child rearing in *C v C* [1991] 1 *Family Law Reports* 223 at p.225.

35 *Re D* [1977] *AC* 617 at p. 634.

36 *Ibid*. at p. 630.

37 *Re P* [1983] at p.404.

This was a more overt opinion than is usual today. It is these moral standards which judge the 'abnormal', and they are not easily escaped in family law, despite a language of usual/unusual. The legislature is not sympathetic. Lesbian partners cannot register their relationship and legitimate it, as can be done in Denmark. Nor can homosexual partners.[38] Thus tradition is upheld despite the Law Commission's views of a lack of 'simple certainties.'

If it is not a Moral Question, what Kind of a Question is it?

Thus far I have noted a tendency for the judiciary and the Law Commission to move away from the expression of preferences in moral terms, to expression in terms of external preferences, views of the community, consumer opinion, efficiency. I have further noted that such an escape may be illusory. It might be objected that no example has been given of 'moral talk' by government and legislators. The government White Paper, *Children Come First*, which preceded Child Support Act 1991 provides such an example.[39] Although the discussion is of 'the benefit of a child', the focus is on ensuring 'that parents honour their legal and moral responsibility to maintain their children whenever they can afford to do so'.[40] The needs of children are stated to be primarily defined by parents and to depend on their financial means. The language of 'rights' is avoided, being replaced by language that 'it is nevertheless right that a child should look first to his own natural parents for his maintenance'; 'personal responsibility towards children is too important a principle to be ignored'; 'it is not right that the absent parent should choose to transfer his obligation to pay maintenance to the state if he can afford to meet that obligation himself'.[41] This is the language of clear state preference that parents should financially support their children, which has been couched in a legal principle. But in other areas of family law, such as divorce, moral principles are less easily articulated.

Whether the reformer, the legislator, and the judge acknowledge that the reference to common sense and consumer desires is a reference to external preferences; or whether the reference is to 'principle' or to what 'is not right', the ultimate arbiter seems to be the constructed figure of the reasonable man. By this I mean that there is a purported understanding of the preferences, the tastes, and the views about the 'good', of the populace at large, even if not reducible to simple certainties. There is a further assumption about the external preferences of this populace as to the imposition on others of the morality attributed to the majority. This 'popular morality' I define as a blend of religious ideas, tradition, and ideas about the 'natural'.

Particular examples in family law may be taken from rules about who can marry whom, when, where and how, and the reinforcement of marriage not only by other laws but by state practices and policies. What we find is that preferences are expressed by the state, through legislation, for marriage as a heterosexual union of two consenting adults,

38 L. Nielsen, 'Family Rights and the "Registered Partnership" in Denmark' *International Journal of Law and the Family*, 4 (1990) p.297.

39 Department of Health and Social Security, White Paper, *Children Come First*, Cm 1264 (London, HMSO, 1990).

40 *Ibid.*, para.2.1.

41 *Ibid.*, paras.3.30; 5.33.

classified as man and woman. Thus marriage is confirmed by a ceremony and a particular type of heterosexual act, referred to as consummation. It is not denied that such state preferences derive from tradition, history and religion. As the Danish example shows, however, legislators are free to express other preferences, or to recognise the desire for legitimacy of partners in other forms of unions.

Members of the judiciary in interpretation, psycho-social workers in administration, also express their preferences for the behaviour of others. The denial of the right to marry to the post-operative transsexual illustrates the imposition of preferences by the judiciary for the behaviour of others (external preferences). Adoption practices, constituting informal law, provide an illustration in relation to other government agents of a sub-text of approved and rewarded behaviour and disapproved and disbenefitted behaviour. The thesis advanced here is that these external preferences, whether expressed in legislation, interpretation, discretionary decisions, informal rules, are expressions of morality.

It has been argued that family law is a procedural area; that it has moved from a system of remedies; that it has forgotten to look for what is right in principle. Brenda Hoggett, a member of the Law Commission, says "the present (family) law produces inconsistent and unpredictable results because it fails to express the underlying principles, and values to a sufficient extent, thus allowing the courts to invent their own."[42] This statement assumes that there are principles and values underlying family law. If so, who is articulating them and where are they to be found? Whose view on morality is expressed in these underlying principles? Whose sense is called 'common sense'?

My position, as argued thus far, is that, despite its procedural mask, and despite reformers' attempts to so deny, family law is based on moral views. It is particularly based on a few people's expressed views, not necessarily consistent, about how others should behave. Depending on the power one has as legislator, Law Commissioner, judge, or adoption social worker, one can lay down rules for others in reports, rules, law, legal decisions or discretionary decisions. In other words, if it is not morality what is it?

If it is not a Moral Question there is no Need for Justification

If the reader accepts the thesis advanced so far, she may ask 'so what?' After all, I have proposed, from the outset, that morality is an inevitable part of family law. Does it matter whether the morality is disguised as procedure, or as efficiency? Does it matter whether judges present their personal views as the basic values and principles of family law? I think it does. The aspect which bothers me is that of justification. If it is inevitable that family law is in the morality business: that the choice of Family A rather than Family X as adopters is moral; that the choice of Parent B rather than Parent Y to bring up a child is moral; that the legitimation of heterosexual but not homosexual relationships is a moral choice; then these choices and their underlying principles and values have to be acknowledged, debated and justified. Personal views of the powerful imposed on others as an expression of external preferences are not sufficient and neither are phrases about common sense, changed social circumstances, consumer efficiency.

42 B. Hoggett, 'Family Law Reform: Where Will It End?', *The King's College Law Journal*, 3 (1992) pp.64–78 at p.72.

It is justification for family law rules and decisions in terms of Kantian universalizability that I am seeking. But the universal principle can be formulated in terms of acceptance of difference, pluralism and beneficence. Sex and gender are constructed in family law and its discourse. Indeed the legal discourse of family cannot conceive of a person in whom gender is not a fundamentally determining attribute. This affects all of us who deviate from the dominant paradigms of the feminine and masculine as constructed in law. Even those accultured to their appropriate role may be involved in a denial of self. This accounts in part for law's inability to accept lesbian, homosexual and transsexual relations as family relationships, or as marriage. 'How you should be' as woman or man also affects your abilities as a parent, in the eyes of the law. There are a number of ways in which this can be discussed, of which observations about moral underpinnings is one. Law expects persons to conform to traditional roles, living out in their bodies normative modes of femininity and masculinity. Yet the justification for this is circular, calling only on tradition. This is not confined to law: the judges of gender normality are to be found in doctor's surgery and in hospital; in adoption committees of social services departments; in educational and corrective institutions; in factory, plant and office.

Despite efforts to use gender neutral language, removing specific references to women, men, husbands, wives, mothers and fathers, and instating spouses, parents, and partners in their places, legal discourse has not escaped its transmission of gender normality. So long as legal marriage as heterosexual union remains a central concept in family law, giving rise to a privileged status, the gender message will continue to be transmitted. It may be objected that this is a matter of culture rather than law. It is true that the heterosexual dyad is a union of opposites, a bi-polar model of attributes, bodies, gestures, conduct, aptitudes and expectations of what a gendered person is and what a gendered person does. It is true that the social and cultural notion of parenthood is not gender neutral. However the distinction between law and culture is that the former requires justification.

A further objection may be made that marriage calls on the past, on the sacred, on romance, for its justification; that it is not to be justified in rationalistic terms. But do we want to say the same for law? Some have indeed done so, looking to the religious origins of law, authority, hierarchy.[43] But such callings up from the dead seem more akin to explanation than to justification.

Justification

Why I am insistent that family law has to be justified? And if the reader accepts that this is so,. may she not proffer tradition and the personal choices of the powerful for the behaviour of others as sufficient justification for current law? What brings Kant to public institutions for the regulation of families? Is justification in terms of universal principles not discredited in late modernity? These are questions this paper must attempt to answer.

43 P. Goodrich and Y. Hachamovitch, "Time out of Mind", in P. Fitzpatrick (ed.) *Dangerous Supplements* (London, Pluto Press, 1991).

Questions about the justification of law in terms of tradition and the views of the powerful have been implicitly answered in earlier sections of the paper. The consent of legal subjects (however constructed) is assumed as axiomatic in a democracy. Liberty and equality are standards against which law can be measured, and family law, particularly where it governs personal relations, continues to fail miserably. Perhaps this restatement is philosophically naive. It does not broach those problems, so pressing to moral philosophers, of law's limits, of appropriate state intervention. Further the paper's focus on the IS of family law, the critique of family law's gendered nature, tends to displace the OUGHT. The trouble is that we do not start from nowhere, and efforts so to do run into troubles of their own, as we shall see with Susan Moller Okin's prescription of a genderless family. Furthermore the retreat into arguments about what is desirable in principle can be a form of evasion.

Okin, in a strong effort to break the family free of its gendered past, uses John Rawls's mind experiment as her solution.[44] Tradition, and what IS, are dead; instead we return with open minds to agree terms of a social contract not knowing our sex or gender. According to Okin we will choose a genderless family. This assertion is backed with illustrations about the injustice of contemporary gendered families, of the bad example this gives our children, and by calling on fairness as the standard. It is a tough case to oppose. Three counterpoints can be raised about understandings of fairness, about self-interest and empathy, about the special place of the family in political philosophy.

Okin's case would be stronger if she could show that understandings of fairness encompass gender, and that gender issues are not silenced by general theory. As she graphically illustrates political philosophers seem unwilling to tackle this. Rawls does not shine, seeming to assume that all is well with the gender order and that distributive justice is where ink must be spilled. With a few exceptions[45] the Rawls industry agrees. Books on justice rarely concern gender. We can dismiss this, if we wish, as the dead white male myopia, but I suggest there is something, worrying, an acceptance of exclusion, which must be challenged. *Theory of Justice* made such an impact on philosophers because it got away from utility and yet enshrined an element of self-interest: 'is it not just to ensure equality and the fairest possible system of distribution, within the principles, in case I end up poor?' From self-interest the leap is made to justice. Empathy is not required. Yet Okin is caught in a contradiction. She does not like the self projected by Rawls so tries to rescue that self with the idea of empathy.

To explain further: critics have said that the person choosing the principles of justice from behind Rawls's veil of ignorance is egotistical and individualistic. It may be that the idea that liberalism assumes an atomistic and disembodied individual, abstracted from his or her social context, has been exaggerated. But as Lacey[46] points out, 'liberalism's primary focus on the individual, on persons *one at a time*, abstracted from their social context, as moral units, is inimical to giving issues of gender the central place in political theory ...' In order to escape from such a person Okin endows him (and Lacey emphasises that the chooser is male) with empathy, thinking 'from the perspective of

44 Susan Moller Okin, *Justice, Gender and the Family* (New York, Basic Books, 1989).

45 J.S. Fishkin, *Justice, Equal Opportunity and the Family* (New Haven, Yale University Press, 1983).

46 N. Lacey, 'Theories of Justice and the Welfare State', *Social and Legal Studies*, 1 (1992) pp.323–344 at p.335.

everybody, in the sense of *each in turn*' with 'a preparedness to listen carefully to the very different points of view of others.'[47]

Although Rawls uses the language of forcing the individual to take others into account it is in terms of a rational choice because one does not know what kind of self one will turn out to be. This is not empathy, nor does Rawls require it; rather he deliberately creates a hypothetical original position in which it is unnecessary.

Okin's rational choosing persons 'must be persons whose psychological and moral development is in all essentials identical'[48] (i.e. genderless). The only way to produce such persons is through genderless institutions and customs. Only when men nurture and women take part 'in what have been principally men's realms' will 'members of both sexes be able to develop a more complete *human* personality than has hitherto been possible.'[49] It seems therefore that a genderless society must precede the original position, for presently constituted human beings are inadequate to choose principles of justice. But transcending the handicaps of one's upbringing may not be possible.

It is not clear that Rawls can be adapted to bring justice to the family. But Okin does reveal the hidden agender of family law. Furthermore she makes the original point that the raising of children in unjust gendered families may affect and limit their conceptions of justice. She does not tackle the injustices to children themselves in such families; this is a further item for the agender of justification.

It is a puzzle to know why political theorists have so avoided theorising the family. My own answer relates partly to the hidden agender. But placing the family in the realm of the sacred or the natural not only enables non-justification but also non-confrontation with the issue of what shared values, if any, underpin the institution.

In a review of Okin, Kymlicka[50] points to issues which remain undiscussed in her book. These relate to the issues I raise in the early part of my paper. Who has the right to form a family, to bear children, to parent? Before we talk of equal parenting by adults of both sexes, as Okin does, we need to determine a theory of family justice which might look radically different from Okin's version. Otherwise we are accepting the old ideology of the natural family and merely redistributing its tasks. Kymlicka's point is that liberal theories of justice if applied to the family based on freedom of contract, might lead to 'a universal market in bodies and services'.[51] Perhaps the reason why liberal theorists avoid theorising the family is that they would be confronted with the commodification of babies, intimacy, personal relations and persons.

I am not advocating commodification of babies and bodies, the commercialisation of sex nor the sexualisation of commerce. Whilst the failure to theorise the family has been, in my view, dishonest and unjust, I do not propose to replace tradition with trauma. Rather I am advocating a reconstruction, a theory which takes account of identities and universals.

47 Okin, see above note 44, p.101.
48 *Ibid.*, at p.107.
49 *Ibid.*
50 W. Kymlicka, 'Rethinking the Family', *Philosophy and Public Affairs*, 20 (1991) pp.77-97.
51 *Ibid.*, at p.94.

Conclusion: Love's Law Applies

This paper argues that current family law is unjust, excluding those who want to create family relationships but are denied the legal capacity to do so; perpetuating an unfair sex/gender system; educating children in injustice. This is done in the name of morality, which turns out to be "common sense", the views of the constructed reasonable man, which further deconstructed turns out to be tradition. The legal practice is to create an artifact embodying common sense; thus silencing and closing debate.

In reconstructing what is now called 'family law' I would bring together in conversation: citizenship where persons voice their concerns and beliefs, and family membership (in the broad sense) where most of us live. It is sometimes proposed that citizenship should include an obligation of abstraction: a stepping outside one's individual concerns and seeing one's point of view as one among many; a juxtaposing of other points of view. This is not so-called common sense, but it is what happens in conversation. The difficulty is that each person in this model is assumed to be capable of empathy and the judgement of Portia. Putting self-interest aside becomes the mark of the citizen, a rather different person from the rational chooser. Those who have been traditionally urged to altruism in the family may be suspicious. And who is to identify universal principles and values as agreed?

An additional step of universality is to a collective sphere of justification in which actions can be challenged when an infringement of liberty is in question. It makes no difference whether it is a child or an adult who is affected, or whether the infringement takes place in private or stems from the personal belief of the actor. In other words, no claim to infringe or to have been infringed, is beyond discussion. The traditional separation of public and private must be brought into conversation, despite ideas about privacy. This might ensure a standard within the family which can be justified in the public realm, particularly where actions of one family member are queried by another. Surely this is what we want: a standard which respects liberty and equality, which is acceptable to the community and to the family, and which recognises a necessary zone of privacy.

Getting to such a standard will not be easy. Extensive conversation will be required. The boundary between public and private has been the subject of discussion throughout western philosophy's history. This paper restates the point that the lines must be publicly agreed, but goes further. It agrees with the view that we should also be entitled to discuss openly and publicly all issues, if we so wish, and 'none should be excluded from public discussion as inappropriate or trivial or better suited to the private domain.'[52] In other words recognition of a private sphere does not preclude the raising of issues in public, particularly where a violation of the standards of liberty or equality is in question.

The idea of family law as conversation is directed against current distributions of power to define families and their contents, and to define justice. Justice may not be common sense but it does belong to all of us.

52 A. Phillips, 'Citizenship and Feminist Theory' in G. Andrews (ed.) *Citizenship* (London, Lawrence and Wishart, 1991) pp.76–89.

Ruth Chadwick

Moral Reasoning in Family Law – A Response to Katherine O'Donovan

Katherine O'Donovan argues that despite overt protestations to the contrary, family law is informed by moral views, but in the wrong way. It reflects the personal preferences of judges or of legislators. Sometimes these are dressed up as appeals to common sense or to changing social circumstances; at other times, in more recent documents emanating from the Law Commission, the law is said to be responding to consumer demand.

One of the things that worries O'Donovan is that the covering up of the way morality in fact enters family law sidesteps the question of justification. What is required is that the premises be revealed and measured up against the demands of morality. Despite a present-day questioning of the possibility of universal morality, O'Donovan asks whether something akin to the universalism of Kant would be appropriate.

In my response I want to do two things: the first is to say to what extent I agree with O'Donovan's analysis. The second is to explore the kind of resources available to us for thinking about the family in moral and political philosophy.

The Analysis

O'Donovan argues that in the Law Commission's reports on divorce law reform, justice is defined in terms of procedure rather than substance. To a large extent this seems to me to be correct. In addition I want to suggest, however, that in *Facing the Future*, in particular, we find the inevitable result of an attempt to apply the language of late Thatcherism to a context to which it is scarcely appropriate.[1] This creates a site of struggle between competing value systems.

The Ground for Divorce states that:

"'Justice' in this context has traditionally been taken to mean the accurate allocation of blameworthiness for the breakdown of marriage".[2] This is a backward looking, 'desert' model of justice[3], which has been held to be relevant in two ways – in regulating the ground for divorce, and in allocation of goods. The backward looking approach is rejected in favour of a forward looking one. This might be thought to pave the way for a 'need' model of justice[3], and we do find one or two references to the needs of the affected parties, particularly children. This is not the main contender however, for replacement of the desert model, as is clear from a study of paragraph 2.22 of *Facing the Future* where it is stated that:

1 Law Commission, *Facing the Future,* no. 170 (London, HMSO, 1988)
2 Law Commission, *The Ground for Divorce,* no. 192 (London, HMSO, 1990) para. 2.13
3 For an exposition of the desert and need models of justice see D.Miller, *Social Justice* (Oxford, Clarendon Press, 1976)

ARSP-Beiheft 57. Derek Morgan & Gillian Douglas (eds.)
Constituting Families.

... law and practice can no longer be founded on the assumption that the people affected by divorce are a small and deviant proportion of the population. Secondly, the "consumer interest" in both the substantive and procedural aspects of divorce law is proportionately that much greater and must be taken into account in any evaluation of the present law or proposals for reform.

The use of the word 'deviant' is significant. This is a word, after all, which is used to indicate behaviour that is considered not only unusual but also appropriate for disapproval. The implication of the paragraph is that once the number of people becomes large enough, they can no longer be regarded as deviants but have to be regarded in a different way. They are reconstructed as consumers. The use of scare quotes around the term 'consumer', however, perhaps suggests that it is recognised that it is not entirely appropriate.

Consumer interest is appealed to again in paragraph 5.2 of *Facing the Future*, again with quotation marks: "Although many of the "consumers" interviewed by Davis and Murch thought in general it was too easy to obtain a divorce, few petitioners thought that it had been too easy for them personally". The oddness of the language of consumerism here becomes evident if you substitute for the word 'divorce' the name of any commodity, such as a loaf of bread.

The tensions in the language of Thatcherism become apparent too if the sentence is looked at in its fuller context. It is preceded by one which says that there is "increased public concern about marriage and the family".[4] Unlike some of the claims made in *Facing the Future*, which are based on empirical research, it is not clear how it is to be interpreted – whether, for example, it is a statement of government policy.

In the light of the fact that the Thatcher Government did have a pro-family policy the following statement is significant:

... income and wealth today depend upon trade and employment rather than inherited property ... Combined with increased prosperity it has enabled couples to marry, or set up home together, as soon as they please, and even (it has been suggested) to apply consumer society's "throwaway attitude" to marriage.[5]

Such quotations show the difficulty of maintaining a pro-family policy while also supporting consumerism.

It is true to a large extent that other considerations in *Facing the Future* give way before pragmatic ones – despite concern about the family, it is said not to be feasible to prop it up, for example, by toughening divorce law.[6] The language of *Facing the Future* shows that while it is hard to avoid the language of desert – it recognises that some respondents are "undeserving of sympathy" – and that some petitioners may be both needy and deserving[7], the problem is that it is impossible in practice to allocate blameworthiness: "The complexities of family life are no longer capable of being reduced to simple certainties".[8] And yet it is said that a public opinion survey has found that fault as a ground for divorce, alongside other grounds, is regarded as acceptable by 84% of the population.[9] What does this say about consumer choice?

4 *Facing the Future*, see above note 1, para. 5.2.
5 *Facing the Future*, see above note 1, para. 2.19
6 *Facing the Future*, see above note 1, paras. 2.16–2.17, 3.6–3.8
7 *The Ground for Divorce,* see above note 2. para. 3.24
8 *The Ground for Divorce*, see above note 2, para. 3.6.
9 *The Ground for Divorce*, see above note 2, para. 3.8.

The paramount consideration, however, seems to lie in cost: " ... the expense (both public and private) ... of any proposed divorce law is a crucial factor. ... Present Government consideration of procedural reform and conciliation services is very much dependent on the cost-effectiveness of the proposals"[10].

As O'Donovan states, a consequentialist might argue that the proposals are for the best, as they promote a forward-looking approach which might increase liberty[11], even though they are not done in the name of liberty (despite the link with Thatcherism) but ultimately in the name of cost-effectiveness and pragmatism. What needs to be considered, however, is whether it is sufficient to say that a system that maximises liberty is to be welcomed without considering whether there are other competing values to be taken into account.

Arguably, the tensions to be find here are to be expected, in that they are indicative of the tensions within Thatcherism – on the one hand a moralistic tendency and promotion of the family policy, while on the other hand promoting the ideology of consumer choice, freedom of the individual and cost-effectiveness. The financial considerations, however, are paramount and hence morality has to play second fiddle to these considerations (although the primacy of cost-effectiveness may itself be seen as another moral view).

These tensions are at the heart of individualism itself. As Susan Mendus has pointed out: "All individualist theories share this difficulty: in construing persons as essentially independent, free and equal, they support an atomistic model which cannot readily accommodate those social units, such as the family, which transcend mere atomism. The choice is then between abandoning individualism and construing the family as itself as a single unit...." [12] There is of course another option, and that is to decline to accommodate this social unit. Charles Taylor has argued that since the prime target of individualism is political obligation, rather than living in relationship with other human beings, it has no reason to reject the family.[13] Mendus' point shows, however, that there is a problem about attempting to define family law in terms of satisfying individual consumer interests, while on the other hand if the family itself is regarded as a single unit, it appears impossible to escape the 'head of the family' problem. Kant on this subject is instructive: "If a union is to be harmonious and indissoluble, it is not enough for two people to associate as they please; one party must be *subject* to the other."[14]

The fact that Kant talks about indissolubility here is not crucial to the point about subjection, for Mendus, commenting on this, says: " ..... it is never in doubt that *someone* must be the head and decision-maker. The language of domination and

10 *Facing the Future*, see above note 1, para. 5.4

11 K. O'Donovan, "Love's law: moral reasoning in family law", in this volume, p. 40.

12 S.Mendus, 'Kant : "an honest but liberal-minded bourgeois"?' in R.Chadwick (ed.) *Immanuel Kant: Critical Assessments*, Volume III, *Kant's Moral and Political Philosophy* (London, Routledge, 1992) pp. 370-388 at p. 385

13 C.Taylor, 'Atomism', in S.Avineri and A. de-Shalit (eds.) *Communitarianism and Individualism* (Oxford, , O.U.P., 1992) pp. 29–50

14 I. Kant, quoted in S. Mendus, see above note 12, at p. 386

subordination is central to individualism and cannot be dispensed with except by abandoning individualism itself'. [15,16]

In thinking, then, about the values that we might want to inform family law, we have to think about how to respond to this tension between individualism and the family. Should we abandon individualism, or the family, or try to mediate between them?

What Values Should Inform Family Law?

In political philosophy the family has always posed a problem, partly because viewed as a distraction from public responsibilities,[17] and partly because of its privileged position within a private sphere. Michael Walzer, however, says that it is a mistake to see kinship and sexual relations as lying in a realm beyond the realm of distributive justice:

> There are a hundred ways in which the basic distributive question – Who...whom?- is asked and answered. Who can sleep with whom? Who can marry whom? Who lives with whom? ... The answers to these questions constitute an elaborate system of rules, and it is a feature of the earliest understanding of political power that chiefs or princes who violate these rules are tyrants. The deepest understanding of tyranny probably lies here: it is the dominance of power over kinship.[18]

While the family is arguably a suitable case for treatment by theorists of social justice, it might be objected that the search for values to guide family law is a non-starter. Although the possibility of universal principles of morality is regarded as generally problematic, their applicability to the family is even more so. This is not simply because of the fact that views about the family vary between cultures, which have very different ideas about what the constitution and role of the family should be. The family can also be seen as a distraction from the demands of morality itself, where these are interpreted in terms of impartiality. On the other hand, once we give up complete impartiality, as Walzer argues, "no arrangement of family ties seems to be theoretically required or even generally preferable. There is not a single set of passional connections that is more just than all of the alternatives".[19] While within moral philosophy there is an increasing number of challenges to the view that morality demands impartiality[20], and thus the law would not be at variance, on such views, with morality in encouraging people to be partial to family, it is not clear that these approaches can give guidance on which particular set of partialities, if any, should be promoted by law. For much depends here on how one's family is to be defined.

15 S.Mendus, see above note 12, at p.386

16 It is significant in this connection that in the course of the implementation of the community charge, households were asked to designate someone as the responsible person for a given household.

17 The history of this view stretches back at least as far as Plato's *Republic*

18 M.Walzer, *Spheres of Justice* (Oxford, Blackwell, 1983) at p.228

19 *Ibid.* at p.231

20 see, e.g., L.Blum, *Friendship, Altruism and Morality* (London, Routledge & Kegan Paul, 1980); A.Oldenquist, 'Loyalties', *Journal of Philosophy*, 74 (1982) pp. 173–193; N.Noddings, *Caring: A Femininist Approach to Ethics and Moral Education* (Berkeley, University of California Press, 1984)

Definition of the family

It might be thought that the definition of the family must be the first priority in thinking about the moral issues surrounding it.[21] This is precisely the problem, however, as illustrated by O'Donovan in her analysis of judicial definitions. Attempts to found a definition on some idea of the 'natural' are doomed to failure, because of the social variation noted above.[22] Further, in our own time, as has been pointed out in another context, the roles of 'mother' and 'father' are in a state of flux because of the increasing use of assisted reproduction techniques.[23]

It is far from clear that it is possible to give a value-free account of the family. Raymond Williams has pointed out the usefulness of remembering the "major historical variations....and the sense, through these, of radically changing definitions of primary relationships".[24] Not only is there the distinction between nuclear and extended family to consider, but a crucial point turns on whether or not marriage is taken to be part of the definition. The wording of Article 8 of the European Convention on Human Rights, for example, which reads "Men and women of marriageable age have the right to marry and to found a family", is ambiguous as to whether the first item is a necessary condition of the second. Different world-views will obviously have different implications for this.

For present purposes what can be said is that family can be understood either in a narrow (monogamous) marriage-based sense or in a wider one that allows more fluidity of family relationships. So in thinking about the values which should inform family law a central issue will be whether or not the definition of the family employed by the law should be marriage-based or not. Having made the point that the answer will depend on prior value commitments it is time to examine the implications of different political philosophies.

Individualism and contracts

The tension between individualism and the family has already been noted. Will Kymlicka[25] has pointed out, in reviewing Susan Moller Okin[26], that the logical conclusion of individualism is to reject the family as an institution in favour of freedom of contract. Individuals should be free to contract with other individuals for reproductive and domestic services. In this sense the marriage-based family is certainly incompatible with individualism, because marriage has traditionally been more than a contract. Further, 'family' obligations on this model would not include those simply based on the fact of a blood tie, but would be the result of freely entered relationships.

21 See. e.g., W.Kymlicka, 'Rethinking the family', *Philosophy and Public Affairs*, 20 (1991) pp. 77-97
22 The idea that certain arrangements are natural has, however, recently made a come-back in debates about single-parent families. See e.g., 'Absent fathers', *Independent on Sunday* (11 July, 1993)
23 E. Kingdom, 'Birthrights: equal or special?' in R.Lee and D.Morgan (eds.) *Birthrights* (London, Routledge, 1989) pp. 17–36
24 R.Williams, *Keywords: A Vocabulary of Culture and Society* (London, Fontana, 1983) at p.134
25 W.Kymlicka, see above note 21
26 S.M.Okin, *Justice, Gender and the Family* (New Haven, Yale University Press, 1983)

One immediate objection to this, noted by Okin, is that it would not secure stability for the welfare of children. Wesley Cragg, similarly, points out that on a contractarian system it would be irrational for parents to make the kind of sacrifices for children with which we are familiar.[27] It is not clear, a priori, that the contract system would *necessarily* be unable to find a way to protect children's interests as well as the institution of the marriage-based family currently under threat. The law would presumably have an interest in regulating the contracts, however.

It might be argued that from the point of view of individualism which advocates autonomy and choice, individuals could, if they wanted to, still subscribe to the life-long commitment type of marriage. Cragg, however, rejects this possibility:

> On an instrumental view of social relationships, a marriage commitment will be considered binding only while it serves the purposes of each of the individuals taken separately, This means that marriage as traditionally understood is impossible unless backed by a "Hobbist sovereign" who is prepared to enforce the promises of those involved beyond the point where the resulting arrangement has instrumental value for one or both of the two people who have contracted into it. But modern society and liberal theory cannot justify a "Hobbist sovereign"[28].

In other words, liberal individualism removes the possibility of marriage as a rational option and thus may actually decrease options for some. Thus it cannot actually carry through its avowed aim of being neutral between different versions of the good life.

A further objection to the freedom of contract system is that individuals do not have equality of bargaining power. This worry has already been expressed with regard to surrogacy contracts.[29] In particular, it may be felt to be disadvantageous to women as a group, as their earning power is on average considerably less than that of men (something that may itself be changed by alterations in family relationships).

Gender

To overcome the problems of inequality between the sexes, some feminists have argued for a revamped form of liberalism to try to avoid this. Mendus argues, however, that simply modifying it to take into account the fact that some families have women as their head will do nothing to overcome the problem essential to individualism, that it requires subordination within the family.[30] Similarly, Okin notes that revising Rawls' Original Position to make the contractors sexless does not really make sense in a gender-structured society.[31]

27 W.Cragg, 'Two concepts of community in moral theory and Canadian culture', *Dialogue*, XXV (1986), 31–52

28 Cragg, see note 27, at p. 37

29 See. e.g., J.Merrick, 'The case of Baby M', in D.M.Bartels, R.Priester, D.E.Vawter and A.L.Caplan, *Beyond Baby M: Ethical Issues in New Reproductive Techniques* (Clifton, N.J., Humana Press, 1989) pp.183–200

30 S.Mendus, see above note 12

31 S.M.Okin, 'Justice and gender', *Philosophy and Public Affairs*, 16 (1987) pp.42–72

Okin has argued, as O'Donovan points out, for a genderless family. Kymlicka argues, however, that there are tensions in her position because she apparently wants to hang on to genetic parenthood and mother and father roles, suggesting that each child should have the care of both a mother and a father. In the absence of a genderless society the ideal of non-discrimination aimed at by liberal feminists remains important and will clearly have implications for the law's regulation of relationships between men and women, whether marital or contractual.

The consideration of the tension between individualism and the marriage-based family has pointed to an internal contradiction within individualist thought. An anxiety about protecting the needs of children, and the importance of non-discrimination, have also been noted. It remains to be seen, however, whether an alternative political philosophy has any insights to offer about the family which should inform the law.

Communitarianism

A standard objection from the communitarians to individualism is that the latter rests on a false view of people. Within a communitarian philosophy, individuals do not come as atomistic units; they are essentially related. Some of their moral obligations are discovered rather than chosen and these will be, among others, family ones. Thus Alasdair MacIntyre writes: "I am someone's son or daughter, someone else's cousin or uncle; ... I inherit from the past of my family, my city, my tribe, my nation, a variety of debts, inheritances, rightful expectations and obligations."[32]

As regards the family, MacIntyre's point highlights genetic relatedness, itself under increasing threat in the light of changes in reproductive techniques. What of marriage? An aspect of communitarian thought is that relationships do not have value purely insofar as they facilitate the achievement of the objectives of individuals. A community such as the marriage-based family, rather than being the irrational choice of individuals, might be a necessary condition of social behaviour.

The communitarian insight about the essential relatedness of persons does not commit us, however, to accepting the moral claims of any particular relation. Socialist feminism for example has long recognised the family as a source of women's oppression, and so-called universal biological 'facts' about women's mothering urges as social constructs. As Marilyn Friedman has pointed out, the communitarians sometimes make the mistake of turning a point about moral psychology into a moral requirement, whereas in fact the communities to which they appeal are "exploitative and oppressive towards many of their own members .... the communitarian emphasis on communities unfortunately dovetails too well with the current popular emphasis on 'the family' and seems to hark back to the oppressive world of what some sociologists call communities of 'place', the world of family, neighbourhood, school and church, which so intimately enclosed women in oppressive gender politics".[33]

32 A.MacIntyre, *After Virtue* (London, Duckworth, 1981) 204–5.

33 M.Friedman, 'Feminism and modern friendship' in S.Avineri and A. de-Shalit A. , see above note 13, pp.101–119, at p.107.

Friedman therefore asks why, if we need communities, the family is privileged rather than, say, Alcoholics Anonymous. Others, such as Roy Weatherford optimistically suggest that the family of the future will avoid the sort of criticism that Friedman advances:

While there have certainly been, and continue to be, many patriarchal and authoritarian families, they belong to the past, not the future, of the human race. The family of the future, both locally and globally, will consist of people who *choose* to belong, who *want* to contribute, who *value* the family and its members...true obedience is only possible when one is truly free, and neither loyalty nor affection can be commanded. [34]

Neither individualism nor communitarianism is satisfactory on its own. It is possible that at the theoretical level some accommodation can be found between individualism and communitarianism, and then the tension between them mediated within the context of the family, as Weatherford suggests. This would then represent a possible model for family law. But the question of the role of law adds a further dimension to the dispute between individualism and communitarianism concerning the family.

What is the role of Family Law?

It has been suggested that family law has the following functions: the protective function, when the family environment threatens any of its members; the adjustment function, when the family disintegrates; the supportive function (propping up the institutions of the family) and the preventive function (education of the population in the problems of family living).[35] Of these I shall discuss only the protective and supportive.

A preliminary point I want to make is that while the possible functions above clearly have moral dimensions, the enforcement of morality is not itself to be found on the list. Given the doubt about the appropriateness of the law's enforcement of morality at all, as evidenced in the Hart-Devlin debate, we should surely not expect to find it in family law more than in other areas. In other words, in so far as it is appropriate for family law to make moral judgments, it will be to the extent that this is necessary for it to carry out one of these functions.

There is clearly a general minimum requirement that the law act to protect individuals from harm that they may suffer at the hands of other individuals, and it seems uncontentious that family law should not be at odds with this. Despite some claims that the family is itself a protective agent for individuals against the state,[36] it has also increasingly come to be recognised that the very fact of the existence of the family as an institution has made it less likely that the law will carry out this task – that the claims of privacy can serve as a cover for violence. Latterly, steps have been taken to overcome this, but as experience with child abuse has shown, this is a very difficult area. What is clear is that the family cannot serve as a substitute for society.

34 R. Weatherford, *World Peace and the Human Family* (London, Routledge, 1993) at p.88
35 J. Eekelaar, *Family Law and Social Policy* (London, Weidenfeld and Nicholson, 1978)
36 P. Johnson, 'Family reunion', *Observer* (10 October, 1982)

The claim that the law should support some particular form of family would require further argument. If marriage is thought to be a prerequisite for the formation of a family such a proposal would suggest measures to bolster that institution. This might be thought to require explicit disapproval of certain types of behaviour, such as adultery.

The Law Commission in *The Ground for Divorce* makes it clear that it does see one of its functions as to support marriage:

> The aim of supporting those marriages which can be saved can be distinguished from the aim of upholding the institution of marriage itself. For some of our respondents, as for our predecessors, it was important that divorce law should send the right messages, to the married and the marrying, about the seriousness and permanence of the commitment involved. We agree. Despite a rapid recent growth in cohabitation outside marriage, marriage remains an extremely popular institution. Couples see it as offering, not only an "important signifier" of their commitment to one another, but also a home of their own, financial and emotional security, and an "accepted context" for having children. Marriage involves mutual legal obligations of support and sharing which other relationships do not. The law should certainly do its utmost to recognise and enforce these.[37]

It is possible to disentangle different strands of argument in this passage. The first concerns the quality of relationship between adults. It was noted above that from the point of view of individualism, marriage is an irrational institution, and yet it remains something that apparently individuals want. There is thus an argument for the law to enable this type of commitment, from the individualist perspective, in so far as the latter supports use of the law to reflect pluralism.

Further argument is commonly provided (though not in the above passage) by citing the [marriage-based] family as a moral educator, a place where values are instilled. This begs the question, however, as to what values it is desirable to instil, and where relationships are concerned this takes us back to the individualist versus communitarian debate. If on the other hand it is respect for the values of law and order that is the issue, as is sometimes claimed,[38] then it is far from obvious what the connection between these and marriage is.

A crucial point seems to be the Law Commission's remark concerning an accepted context for the upbringing of children. It is significant that marriage is said to be *an* accepted context, but the above quotation does not claim that it is the only one. While it is clearly desirable to set some boundaries of acceptability (as in the Human Fertilisation and Embryology Act), it has not been shown to be necessary for the law to support the marriage-based family rather than a variety of freely chosen patterns of living. These arguments are therefore insufficient to ground the desirability of a supportive function as regards marriage.

37 *The Ground for Divorce*, see above note 2, para. 3.4.

38 P. Johnson, see above note 36, cited the family as one of the institutions (the others being organised religion and the State) that counter the lawless and destructive instincts of human beings.

Conclusions

Analysis of Law Commission materials has exposed a tension, which is partly to be understood in terms of problems within individualism itself. The family provides a focus for dispute between the rival political philosophies of individualism and communitarianism. Given the lack of resolution to this debate, it is not surprising that the question of what values should inform family law is problematic. Law has to be sensitive to changing social conditions (opinions about which should be empirically based). Rather than maintaining an idealised picture of marital relationships, the important consideration is what set of problems the law is required to solve, at a time when people are choosing to regulate their relationships in a variety of ways, including the increasing use of techniques to assist reproduction with their weakening of the importance of genetic relatedness. There is, nevertheless, room for appeal to moral principles, not about individual 'behaviour' but about fairness to different parties. To maximise individual choice in choosing patterns of relationship is compatible with the constraint of the protective function of law with regard to weaker parties, particularly as concerns the needs of children. (It is significant in this context that children are increasingly being recognised as the bearers of rights of their own). Considerations of justice also suggest that one constraint on family law is that it should avoid discrimination on irrelevant grounds such as gender, and have regard not only to changing roles of men and women, but also to the different patterns of relationship between the worlds of work and of family life.[39] Thus in so far as it supports a kind of institution that we might want to call 'family', law should avoid reinforcing gender-based stereotypes. In the light of the fact that the arguments for the supportive function of the law as regards marriage are unconvincing, these very general precepts seem to be the closest we can come, if we want universal morality by which to judge family law.

39 C. Veile, *Marriage : Trends and Implications,* St. Catherine's Conference Report no. 30 (Windsor, St. Catherine's Foundation, 1992) at p. 9

Bob Brecher

What is Wrong with the Family

Abstract

The nuclear family has in recent years enjoyed something of a rehabilitation, with the left arguing that as 'a haven in a heartless world' (Lasch) it demands defence and sustenance. But this is a delusion. The standard arguments in its favour (concerning dependents, sex, "human nature" and its constituting a defence against either or both individualism and the State) fail; and questions of what, if anything, the contemporary family embodies that might be worth retaining await eludication. Meanwhile, its current constitution is hardly an advance on Mill's description of its actuality – while its ideological role in helping maintain the liberal status quo renders it both incapable of reform and a central bulwark of capitalism.

This article is no more than a prolegomenon for a possible critique of the family, directed at questioning certain assumptions: and it is perhaps indicative of the depth at which some of these run that a question-mark should have crept its way to the end of the title I had originally submitted for the conference at which it was originally given.[1] Such an intrusion sums up rather well what I think is wrong with the family: namely the **ideological** role which both 'the family' and its contemporary nuclear instantiation currently play in our society. What I have to say in what follows, then, is not directed at anything like – *per impossible* – 'the family' in itself; nor at all and any possible forms of the family: but rather at its currently central ideological manifestation, namely the contemporary nuclear couple and its offspring. Furthermore, I shall be almost entirely negative, since critical dissatisfaction seems to me a necessary condition of any constructive change, change which I think cannot consist in reform or improvement of the internal workings of the nuclear family – just because of the depth and extent of its ideological role. What different ways, if any, there might be of retaining those aspects – again, if any – of the nuclear family which today offer some means, however attenuated, of articulating and realising values whose worth transcends the circumstances of their present instantiation is a question I do not tackle. For not only would that require, practically, a further article, or perhaps a book; but, more importantly, and at a theoretical level, I am not at all certain that any such values there might be are capable of being clearly and unambiguously identified outside their actual context. Companionship, intimacy and friendship, to mention just three possible candidates, would not under some different dispensation take exactly the same form as they do either within or – but nevertheless under its tutelage – without the contemporary nuclear family. We just do not know exactly how things might be in some quite different socio-political structure: merely that the present structure is at the very least

1 I should like to thank in particular Carol Jones and Sandra Marshall for helping me maker clearer a number of points which would otherwise have obfuscated matters: whether they are sufficiently clear is of course something readers will decide.

ARSP-Beiheft 57. Derek Morgan & Gillian Douglas (eds.)
Constituting Families. © 1994 by Franz Steiner Verlag Stuttgart

less than entirely satisfactory. The temptation to succumb to the demand for blueprints is to be resisted.

I

First, a few reminders of youth, or even, I dare say, of childhood. In 1967, Edmund Leach say during the course of one of his Reith Lectures – and gained considerable notoriety as a result – that

(F)ar from being the basis of the good society, the family, with its narrow privacy and tawdry secrets, is the source of all our discontents.[2]

In 1964, R. D. Laing and Aaron Esterson had put forward the view in *Sanity, Madness and the Family*[3] – albeit while not understanding, disingenuously or otherwise, the logic of what they were arguing – that it was family relationships and contexts which caused schizophrenia, a view further elaborated at the end of the decade in Laing's *The Politics of the Family*,[4] where he refers to the

families, schools, [and] churches [which] are the slaughterhouses of our children (p. 91).

By 1970, Shulamith Firestone had published *The Dialectic of Sex*,[5] in which, among other things, she argued that the biologically-based oppression of women required for its elimination that they take control of reproduction, just as economic class-oppression required that the working-class seize control of the means of production. Giving birth being 'barbaric ... [like] shitting a pumpkin .. [and] (P)regnancy (is) the temporary deformation of the body of the individual for the sake of the species' (pp. 188-9), motherhood itself had to be abolished. The family could hardly be expected to survive the 'freeing of women from the tyranny of reproduction by every means possible ...' (p. 183). And by 1971 David Cooper had offered in The *Death of the Family*[6] a critique which

applies to the first-world working class, second-world societies and third-world countries in so far as these have been indoctrinated into a spurious consciousness that ... is definitive of the secret suicide pact conducted by the bourgeois family unit, the unit that labels itself the 'happy family'; the family that prays together and stays together through sickness and health till death us do part or releases us into the terse joylessness of the epitaphs on our Christian tomb-stones erected, for want of any other sort of erection, by those who mourn for us in the curious mode of remembering very hard to forget us very hard ... [: a critique of] (T)he bourgeois nuclear family unit ... [which] has become, in this century, the ultimately perfected form of non-meeting and therefore the ultimate denial of mourning, death, birth and the experiential realm that precedes birth and conception (pp. 5-6).

Since then, things have changed. Leach seems the archetypal bored academic in search of a wider and younger audience; Laing was shortly to change his mind and

2 As quoted in Lynne Segal, '"The most important thing of all" – rethinking the family – an overview', in Lynne Segal (ed), *What is to be Done about the Family?* (London: Penguin, 1983), p. 35.

3 London: Tavistock Press, 1964.

4 Harmondsworth: Penguin, 1976.

5 London: The Women's Press, n.e., 1979.

6 Harmondsworth: Penguin, 1971.

deny the substance of what he had asserted; Firestone is condemned even, or especially, by feminists for 'proposing such an extreme solution ... which becomes ... a way of not examining or analysing motherhood in relation to modern women',[7] and Cooper is rightly seen as part of a self-indulgent vanguard whose radical, and sexist, libertarianism paved the way not for liberation, but for the New Right. By the beginning of the 1980s, let alone by now, and for feminists as well as men nostalgic for the good old days of unquestioned patriarchy, for socialists as well as conservatives, for the young as well as those too old for the sixties, '... the family ha[d] come to represent nurturing, enduring, and noncontingent relations governed by feelings of morality ... (I)n contrast [to] market relations [which] are characterized as impersonal, competitive, contractual, and temporary'.[8] Even the attempts of the mid-1980s by those (then?) identifying themselves as socialist feminists to resurrect questions asked of the family in the 60s in a more coherent, non-patriarchal and less anti-realistic manner were exceptions; rearguard actions conducted against the increasing espousal by socialists of the view that the family was, in Christopher Lasch's classically eponymous words, a *Haven in a Heartless World*.[9]

How much credence **should** we then place in the claim enshrined in the constitution of Eire that the family is a moral institution which possesses inalienable rights, rights which are antecedent to all positive law? Is 'the nineteenth-century conceptualization of heaven as an eternal family reunion' commented upon by Phillipe Ariès in T*he Hour of Our Death*[10] just a ghastly nightmare? Or was Christ, '... come to set a man at variance against his father, and the daughter against her mother, and the daughter-in-law against her mother-in-law' perhaps right to insist that '... a man's foes shall be (they) of his own household'?[11] I am not, of course, going to attempt to settle such questions. For I am not going to offer any sort of historical analysis of the family; nor do other than simply take it for granted both that gender roles are in our society largely transmitted by families and that this is a matter for regret; nor attempt yet another evaluation of the adequacy or otherwise of Engels' or Lenin's – or any of their followers' – understanding and critique of, or attitude to, the family or 'the family'; nor offer any sort of empirical evaluation of the role, or indeed the nature, of families in our society or our culture.[12] Rather, my concerns ar two-fold. First, I shall try to clear some ground for **this** question. Is the present, nuclear, marriage-defined family, even if as a matter of fact the form adopted by only some 30% of households in the UK today, inevitably inimical to socialism, and thus to feminism; and **to that extent** unsatisfactory? (An explicit defence of particular varieties of socialism and of feminism is another

7 Ann Dally, *Inventing Motherhood* (London: Burnett Books Ltd., 1982), p. 171.

8 Barrie Thorne, 'Feminist rethinking of the family: an overview', in Barrie Thorne and Marilyn Yalom (eds), *Rethinking the Family: Some Feminist Questions* (New York: Longman, 1982), p.18.

9 New York: Basic Books, 1977.

10 Trans. H Weaver (New York: Knopf, 1981), p. 611: cited by Charles Taylor, *Sources of the Self* (Cambridge: CUP 1989), p. 562, n.22.

11 Quoted by Ferdinand Mount, *The Subversive Family* (London: Cape, 1982), p. 15: he cites Firestone, *op. cit.*, p. 75, as the source, but the quotation does not in fact appear there.

12 The best **brief** survey of the Laslett/Mount – Ariès/Shorter debate about the history of the nuclear family, and of the notorious "Lasch thesis" is still, I think, in Michèle Barrett and Mary McIntosh, *The Anti-Social Family* (London: Verso, 1982), pp. 86ff. and 110ff. respectively.

matter, and not something I can attempt here.) Second, I shall attempt to suggest – and no more than that – some reasons why it is indeed inimical to both of these: and that that is what is wrong with the family.

II

What, then, are the answers which one might reasonably expect in response to the rhetorical question, 'What's wrong with the family?'? Leaving aside religious considerations (since if we are indeed God's children, for instance, then I would rather leave theologians to sort out the ensuing problems) I think that there are, broadly speaking, six such – partly overlapping – answers. They concern: children; the elderly and/or ill; sex; 'human nature'; a bulwark against individualism; and a bulwark against the state.

Children

Even critics of the family appear to accept, and without argument, that children constitute a good reason – although not necessarily a decisive one – for familial arrangements. I do not mean that there are no debates about alternative forms of childcare (kibbutzim; nurseries): but rather that it is simply **assumed** that producing and looking after children is both necessary and a good – and that because of an unarticulated assumption about the moral desirability of the survival of the species. The issues this raises are of course too large to pursue in detail here: nevertheless, since some would argue that the question, 'Why should the human species continue?' is a nonsense, a question which it just makes no sense to ask, I have to say something about its probity. Certainly, it may be psychologically the case that the question cannot seriously be asked: but that does not show that it is logically out of order, any more than does Dr. Johnson's kicking a stone dispose of Bishop Berkeley's analysis of 'the material world', or psychological incredulity tell against Descartes' questioning of whether or not he is awake. The point is that the question, like Descartes', is a thought-experiment, a way of asking about the grounds we have for what we seem clearly to know is the case. And just as attending to Descartes' question clarifies what it is to know that something or other is the case, so attention to the question of the worth, or point, of our continuing serves to bring out the context of what is, at least, one important basis of moral value. It will not do, simply to assume the overriding value of human survival *tout court* without saying anything at all about what sorts of things about it are valuable: for that would rule out the very possibility that certain means of ensuring survival, or certain of the contingent conditions of any particular manner of survival, might be such as to require being set against sheer survival. But surely whatever might be required to ensure the greatest possible chance of survival is not thereby simply right: another course of action, even at the price of **some** risk to survival, might be morally preferable, even if one supposes – and many do not – that in extreme cases human survival justifies just anything. To know one's way around specific examples requires precisely having some notion of the different things about human survival which are worthwhile.

The authors of *The Anti-Social Family*, for instance, simply accept that children constitute evidence in its favour; and Mica Nava's critique of Firestone as unrealistic is similarly based on unargued assumptions about bringing up children.[13] But even if one were to allow, however temporarily and albeit only for the sake of argument, that the nuclear family is indeed the best structure for turning children into adults, this is wholly inadequate. For even if the argument for a particular form of social arrangements is that it constitutes the best available means of ensuring the survival of human beings, it nevertheless remains to be shown that such-and-such a means and manner of survival is indeed the greatest possible good in the circumstances. Sheer survival must be set against what is likely to arise from the prosecution of the most efficient means of ensuring such survival; and the question asked of whether or not they outweigh the different harms or disadvantages arising from different social arrangements to ensure human survival, which, although less efficient, did not entail such harms or disadvantages. Unless a particular form of social arrangement – in this case the nuclear family – is a **necessary** condition of survival *tout court*, such a question always arises (and even then, some would think it arises nevertheless). But clearly the nuclear family is not a necessary condition of our survival. Do the disadvantages of the nuclear family, then, outweigh the advantages of the species' surviving in the forms and with that degree of efficiency which the family allows and/or entails?

Such a question requires debate of a peculiarly difficult kind, difficult because the criteria according to which it might be settled are themselves part of what is at issue. This article is intended as a small contribution to that debate: but for the moment it is perhaps worth noting that the main argument against various forms of social provision of childcare – the family as the largest, and least readily detectable, site of all sorts of abuse of children notwithstanding – is circular, consisting simply in the allegedly anti-familial nature and/or consequences of such provision. What, then, is it about the survival of human beings as a species which is a good? Even allowing that the question is not one which simply invites an answer, but is rather a sort of thought-experiment, does it just follow, for instance, that we have moral obligations to as yet unborn (and thus merely possible) future generations, and that current arrangements to ensure this have at least that function in their favour?[14] I do not seek to deny that many people feel such obligations; or that they feel fulfilled by playing a part in the process: but such feelings are no argument. Until and unless some adequate account is offered of what is valuable about the survival of the human species, however, discussions of possible forms of child-care are irrelevant for an assessment of the family: for we have nothing concrete about the benefits of the – comparatively distant – consequences of such forms against which to weigh their – more immediate – content.

13 'From utopian to scientific feminisim? Early feminist critiques of the family', in Lynne Segal (ed), *op. cit.*, pp. 65–105.

14 Even such perceptive discussions of inter-generational obligations and responsibilities as John O'Neill's 'Future generations: present harms', *Philosophy*, 68, 1993, pp. 35–51, tend to assume rather than to offer grounds for the supreme importance of survival, and of survival *tout court*; and this goes for anti-anthropocentrists as much as for the unabashed speciesists.

The aged and ill

The same considerations apply here as in the case just adumbrated. The fact that properly resourced social arrangements would be disruptive both of the economy of the family and of its moral rationale is, while true, no argument *per se* in favour of the family. It is simply one important element in the debate about its role and meaning, an element that needs to be set against others.

Sex

Incest and marital rape notwithstanding, (comparative) familial monogamy is said to help maintain a balance between individuals' autonomously seeking gratification and some sort of social stability; the alternative is Hobbes's 'state of nature'. To the extent that this is an empirical claim, and even allowing that it is in any way supported by evidence, something which seems to me extremely dubious, it nevertheless assumes what its seeks to show, namely that some particular states of affairs regarding sexual activities are morally preferable to certain others. To the extent that it is an explicitly moral argument, addressing directly the issue of the family, it is either quite unsupported; or turns merely on protagonists' preferences; or depends on claims, views and assumptions about human nature.

Human nature

This is of course the central argument, whether in its (quasi-)biological form or in the form of some sort of non-biological claim about human potential. Thus Ferdinand Mount's objection in *The Subversive Family* (op. cit.) to marxist criticism of the family is based on his accurate observation that it

> is essential for the view of human development proposed by Marx and Engels that man [*sic*] should be freed from the legacy of any biological imperative ... For the charm of marxism is that it liberates you from nature – and from the duties and restrictions of the family (p. 45).

This is indeed the crux of the issue, as the course of his argument illustrates. The family is claimed to be a 'natural' arrangement: hence the central role of historical and anthropological debate. But such debate, about the incidence of monogamy, maternal love and so on in human cultures – let alone among non-human animals[15] – is entirely irrelevant to the issue. Mount writes that the

> Marxist trick is to shift the definition of nature along the range until it means virtually the same as instinct. At that point, the Marxist can say 'nature is an illusion' – because people can and do behave unnaturally, often violently so and in great numbers. Because some mothers are cruel or indifferent to their children, the idea of a maternal instinct as being natural to women must be rejected. Because in most societies a percentage of men and women are homosexual, we must reject the idea that heterosexual behaviour is natural ...
>
> But the commonsense idea of nature is no way damaged by the argument that so-called natural human behaviour needs, at least in part, to be learnt by example or precept. So does much natural animal behaviour. It is easier to be an affectionate mother if you knew affection as a child; happy marriages breed happy marriages. To say this is to do no more than observe that water prefers to run downhill (p. 46).

15 e.g. O'Neill, *op. cit.*, p.47 ff.

Apart from their entertainment value, the confusions of these two paragraphs serve nicely to illustrate the shortcomings of the position. There can be no question of water preferring to 'run downhill', or, of course, preferring anything at all. But this is no mere slip. Mount, like so many others, thinks of nature anthropomorphically, imbuing it with purposes and intentions: his whole concern with history arises from this absurdity, as must that of all the protagonists in such debate, since only on such an assumption can it be thought to be relevant. As Mill clearly pointed out more than a hundred years ago,[16] to observe of some piece of behaviour that it is natural is either just to say that it is statistically normal; or that it is neither the outcome of, nor dependent upon, human intervention. **Human** behaviour – or, better, action – is of course not susceptible, by definition, of the latter description: indeed, human beings may in part be characterised as, uniquely, able in principle to intervene in the world, and thus, in their own character. Mount's 'commonsense idea of nature' is commonsensical only insofar as it admits of the possibility of alteration in respect above all of human activity: thus no one need, and self-respecting marxists do not, suppose that nature 'means virtually the same as instinct'; that it is 'an illusion'; or that it is not the case that 'natural behaviour', whether human or otherwise, 'needs, at least in part, to be learnt by example or precept'. Observations (whether accurate or not – do 'happy marriages breed happy marriages'?) of the incidence of maternal affection, homosexuality or anything else show precisely nothing at all about any biological imperative or anything like it. Mount's biologism on the one hand, and the willingness of his opponents to take seriously arguments of the sort he puts forward on the other, are equally mistaken. Indeed, his willingness to devote the whole of the second part of his book to the '*moral* objection' that the family is 'selfish and materialistic, inward-looking, indifferent to the sufferings and struggles of the outside world' (p. 153) runs contrary to such biologism: for moral objections and evaluations are intelligible only insofar as things **could** be otherwise. If biology really were wholly and completely determinative of human possibility, as in some sociobiological fantasies, rather than something which simply sets material limits – and those contingently – then neither moral disapproval nor approval would make any sense. Finally, Mount might well be right to suppose that '(U)topian feminism needs Marxism.' But he is quite wrong to suppose that this is so, if it is, because '(W)ithout the underlying theory that economic conditions ultimately and basically determine social existence, feminism runs up against biology' (244): for he is confused about what it means to say that feminism 'runs up against biology'. Feminism certainly does run up against biology and is of course not alone in so doing; and the extent of biological determination is an empirical issue which requires to be reasonably accurately decided before one can evaluate the appropriateness or otherwise of Shulamith Firestone's prescriptions. But biology does not necessitate. Interestingly, Mount seems to be at least to some small extent aware of problems in his understanding of 'natural', for he immediately goes on to say that for utopian feminists and marxists, the

> family has to be entirely created and thoroughly penetrated by the economic process; otherwise we shall have to concede that it has a life of its own, that in some sense the family is *natural* (ibid.).

16 *'On Nature', 'The Utility of Religion', and 'Theism'* (London: Longmans, Green, Reader and Dyer, 1874).

Both the italics and the qualification give away the notion's shakiness. And while the nuclear family was, here and recently, but is no longer, here and now, statistically normal, neither fact is to the point.

A bulwark against rampant individualism

A traditional strain of praise for the family arises from its allegedly constituting a curb against excessive individualism. Thus de Tocqueville refers to an individualism

> which disposes each member of the community to sever himself from the mass of his fellows and to draw apart with his family and his friends, so that after he has thus formed a little circle of his own, he willingly leaves society at large to itself.[17]

The family has a morally educative role, nurturing on a small scale that sympathy, benevolence and concern which on a larger scale is required by society for its very possibility. In short, the family not only teaches morality, but affords a space for its practice. Thus Mill argues in *The Subjection of Women* that while '(T)he family is a school of despotism, in which the virtues of despotism, but also its vices, are largely nourished ... justly constituted, [it] would be the real school of the virtues of freedom ... a school of sympathy in equality, of living together in love, without power on one side or obedience on the other',[18] while Bosanquet went on to say that the 'family may be the nursery of manhood (including womanhood) and citizenship, or their grave').[19] The empirical evidence, however, is hardly conclusive, as any child social worker, battered women support worker, or even perhaps many a prison warder can clearly testify. But such evidence as there is on the other side from alternative structures is both too scarce to be conclusive and too conceptually dominated by the 'norm' to be terribly helpful.[20] The first problem might in the forseeable future be overcome, as the nuclear family comes as a matter of fact to constitute a decreasing and distinctly minority form of arrangement. But the second problem, rather as in the case of debates about the alleged causal relation of the availability of pornography to crimes of sexual violence, is far less tractable. For it is precisely the meaning, and our understanding of their scope, of terms such as 'equality', 'power', 'manhood', 'womanhood' and 'citizenship' which are at issue. How exactly we should understand human sympathy and benevolence is what is at issue between supporters and opponents of the family; and its role in forging certain understandings of these terms and notions is just one of the accusations which its critics make. I shall return to this central ideological issue in section IV.

17 *Democracy in America* (New York: Knopf, 1983) II, p. 98: cited by Charles Taylor, *op. cit.*, p. 561, n. 13.

18 In John Stuart Mill, *Three Essays* (Oxford: OUP, 1975), p. 479. Cf. p. 469: 'if the family, in its best forms is, as it is often said to be, a school of sympathy, tenderness, and loving forgetfulness, unbounded self-indulgence, and a double-dyed and idealized selfishness, of which sacrifice itself is only a particular form ...'.

19 *Social and International Ideals* (London: Macmillan, 1917), p.5.

20 Bruno Bettelheim's *Children of the Dream* (London: Paladin, 1971) is an influential example.

A bulwark against the incursions of the state

Apparently ironically, the moral-political claim which these days is made with even greater vehemence on behalf of the family is just the opposite of those about socialization. Lasch's *Haven in a Heartless World* (op. cit.) is usually taken as the standard example, but it is important to realize that its view echoes that of those, like Mary Whitehouse or Ferdinand Mount, whose political convictions are otherwise quite different, and whose only point of contact with a disillusioned left is a shared distrust of the Welfare State.[21] Charles Taylor's comments in the course of his historical location of a 'new sense of the significance of ordinary life' in the eighteenth century sum up this sense of the family as 'haven':

> This whole development leads to a progressive withdrawal of the family from the control of the wider society. People today are appalled to learn, for instance, how much the pre-eighteenth-century village presumed to control its members' lives, even what we would consider today their intimate family lives. Take, for instance, the 'charivari' that henpecked husbands had to undergo, not to speak of fornicators ... This couldn't be seen just as a matter between himself and his wife; it was everybody's business, because the order was a shared one within which all individuals lived (op. cit., pp. 290-291).

One's identity is not fully determined by the wider order of the society in which one lives, but rather, to at least a considerable extent, by the smaller-scale, more intimate, less alienating domestic order. The family is literally the haven in which one can be oneself and take shelter from the world's unreasonable and unpleasant demands; and in providing such shelter and such scope for building identities, it constitutes a political and not just an individual bulwark against the state. Thus Mount speaks of

> the family's permanent revolution against the State, and of the working-class family as the only true revolutionary class. For the working-class family provides, every day, its own living refutation of the accusation of passivity and manipulation (op. cit., p. 162).

This sort of view is ubiquitous, and goes a long way to explain such phenomena as the increasing popularity of marriage,[22] the extent to which the gay and lesbian movements are (although not without internal controversy and objection) fighting for marital recognition, and the disarray which the notion of 'community care' causes on the left. Betty Friedan, for example, 'reminds us that most women are very committed to the family' and that 'the identification of feminism with an anti-family position'[23] has lost it much support:

> for women, as for men, it is the symbol of that last area where one has any hope of individual control over one's destiny, of meeting one's most basic human needs, of nourishing that core of personhood threatened now by vast impersonal institutions and uncontrollable corporate and government bureaucracies

21 For particularly telling examples of the genre and of responses to it, see Anthony Skillen, 'Welfare state versus welfare society', *Journal of Applied Philosophy*' 2, 1985, pp. 3–17; *idem*, 'Active citizenship as political obligation', *Radical Philosophy*, 58, 1991, pp. 10–13; Gregory Elliott and Peter Osborne's reply to the latter, 'Community as compulsion?', *ibid.*, pp. 14–15; and Skillen's riposte, 'Compulsive communism', *ibid.*, 59, 1991, p.33.

22 In discussion of her paper at the ALSP Conference ('Love's Law: Moral Reasoning in Family Law', pp. 40–52) Katherine O'Donovan wondered aloud why marriage continued to be such a popular institution, despite so much work by feminists over the last twenty years or so; that a similar concern lies behind this article, and that it is the institution of marriage which – in defining the nuclear family (and much else besides) – is my ultimate target, is I hope obvious to the reader.

23 Barrett and McIntosh, *op. cit.*, pp. 16–17.

and the bewildering, accelerating pace of change. Against these menaces, the family may be as crucial for survival as it used to be against the untamed wilderness and the raging elements, and the old, simple kinds of despotism. For the family, all psychological science tells us, is the nutrient of our humanness, of all our individuality: our personhood.[24]

By contrast, Lasch's thesis, although equally pro-family, is far more pessimistic. While Friedan at least urges, however inconsistently, that the family needs to be reconstructed rather than abandoned, Lasch is convinced that although 'the family is the last stronghold of the realm of the private, [it is] now invaded by public policy and increasing state control'[25] to such an extent that the protective shield it once afforded agains the capitalist state has disappeared – with feminists in the vanguard, doing capitalism's work for it. These are both substantial viewpoints; and certainly form a large part of today's "commonsense" response in defence of the family.

But however sincere, both are inadequate: Friedan's in its acceptance of liberal parameters and the "facts" it claims, and Lasch's in its romantic nostalgia. Let me go back, first to what I omitted from the passage I quoted earlier from Taylor, and then to the continuation of Mount's peroration on behalf of the working-class family. Having mentioned 'henpecked husbands' and 'fornicators', Taylor gives us more details:

Charivaris were noisy manifestations of public collective ridicule. In France, for instance, a husband who had beaten his wife, or who did women's work, or who was cuckolded, could be the target of one of these. Presumably this was because he was allowing an inversion of the proper, patriarchal order (op. cit., pp. 290–1).

This is what could not be left 'as a matter between himself and his wife': quite so. For of course the family is not some sort of 'haven' with no particular form or content, other than as a cosy playground for platonic forms of sympathy, benevolence or whatever. The haven that the family affords men against the demands of society is at the expense of the control it enables them to exert over it, and in particular over the women in it. For every male social nonentity to whom it gives an at least domestic and agreeable identity there is another male to whom it gives a similarly domestic, but entirely disagreeable, identity, and whose alienation in the public world is made more bearable by his control, all too often literally violent, of his domestic world. The public world of the European village of the past may well be intrusive and oppressive: but it was no less than a haven for those on the receiving end of family life than is the family today for those on the receiving end in the public world.

The gender-blindness of our "common sense" which enables the "family as haven" argument to be taken as conclusive rather than as pointing to one factor to be taken into account in any overall assessment receives a particularly extraordinary airing in the evidence which Mount adduces for his view of the family, and especially the working-class family, as an agent of permanent revolt against the state. This is how he seeks to show that it is a 'living refutation' of perhaps more guarded assessments:

24 *The Second Stage* (London: Abacus 1983), pp 229–230. Friedan's simple acceptance of 'all psychological science' and of 'equality' helps to make hers a particularly illuminating statement of "second wave" liberal feminism '... new research shows that virtually all women today share a basic core of commitment to the family and to their own equality within and beyond it, as long as family and equality are not seen to be in conflict' (p. 219, italics in original). The book is nevertheless an important and eloquent statement of the position I am attacking: see especially pp. 39–40, 53, 84, 92–3, 99 and 102.

The simplest way to demonstrate this is to refer to talk in public houses – the working class equivalent of parliamentary debate or the talk of Left Bank cafés – and regarded by its practitioners with just the same sentimentality ... First, pub talk is critical and sceptical ... Second, pub talk is habitually discontented... Third, pub talk is prosy ... (pp. 162–163).

It is not the sub-Orwellian romantic nonsense which this represents, nor even its curious cultural specificty, that I want to point out: but rather its extraordinary exclusion of women. Despite the social changes creeping up upon even pub life – at least in Britain – I have yet to hear of locals where women, working-class or not, regularly and habitually engage in this sort of subversion, and on an equal footing with men, again whether or not working-class, similarly engaged. Mount's implicit inversion – an understanding of it he unhappily has in common with an increasing number of feminists of a postmodern persuasion – of the feminist slogan that 'the personal is political' would be merely funny if it were not also serious. Certainly the personal is **political**: family life has political meanings and repercussions; but that is quite different from maintaining that the **personal** is political, that one's personal life is what is in the end all that is politically important.

III

Conservatives at least tend to be quite clear where they stand on all this: '(T)here is no such thing as society, only individuals and the family', Thatcher once told us.[26] Liberals are somewhat less clear. On the whole, they tend either to take for granted or explicitly to accept the "common sense" views I have outlined: thus, for instance, not only Mill and Bosanquet, but the whole of today's liberal left, from Rawls and his 'original position' to the Labour Party. Interestingly it is perhaps the more consistently libertarian wing of liberalism which, in the name of the individual, begs to differ:

The human essence, then, is the true individuality of every person. The bourgeois individual is the first occurrence in human history when men and women are not first of all members of a tribe or a clan or even a family, but are recognised for what is most essentially human, namely self-responsibility. Bourgeois men and women belong by nature to no one; they are sovereigns ...[27]

The Left is, I have already indicated, largely muddled, and this is partly, I suspect, because the classic texts are somewhat ambivalent. While, for example, T*he Communist Manifesto* is clear in its denunciation of the bourgeois family,[28] it is not at all clear whether this is intended as a diatribe against only that bourgeois family – as contrasted

26 Quoted in an interview in *Woman's Own*, 31 October 1987.

27 Tibor Machan, *Capitalism and Individualism* (Brighton: Harvester Wheatsheaf, 1990), p 106.

28 'On what foundation is the present family, the bourgeois family based? On capital, on private gain. In its completely developed form this family exists only among the bourgeoisie. But this state of findings finds its complement in the practical absence of the family among the proletarians, and in public prostitution. The bourgeois family will vanish as a matter of course when its complement vanishes, and both will vanish with the vanishing of capital ... The bourgeois clap-trap about the family and education, about the hallowed co-relation of parent and child, becomes all the more disgusting, the more, by the action of modern industry, all family ties among the proletarians are torn asunder...': Karl Marx and Friedrich Engels, *The Communist Manifesto* (London: Pelican, 1967), pp. 100–1.

with some (idealized?) non-bourgeois form – or whether it is intended *tout court*: for Marx was as clearly 'worried that the dynamic of capitalism was destroying the sphere of family life'[29] as Engels was clear that 'the patriarchal family ... [originally involving] the organisation of a number of persons, bond and free, into a family under paternal power ...'[30] would disappear.

IV

What is to be made of all this? Having cast at least some doubt on immediate and "common sense" defences of the family, I shall indicate in outline what I think is wrong with it: its actual ideological role. For whatever the precise balance of the considerations earlier adumbrated, and quite regardless of its historical provenance and/or the extent of the dependencies and interdependencies between its particular forms and those of political and social structures such as capitalism, it is its present and actual ideological role that constitutes what is positively wrong with the family. What follows, then, is a brief gesture towards the arguments which await the full and detailed treatment I think they demand: it neither is, nor is intended to be, any more than that.

The family is inimical to socialism, and thus to feminisim; and this because of the sorts of meaning it ascribes to, and understanding it forges of, for example, notions like sympathy and benevolence. Despite the sociological statistics, it is ideologically as powerful as ever, and, arguably, becoming more so as sections of the left and of other opponents of elements of the status quo adopt, and adapt to, it: for example, marriage as a statement against the state; the family as a haven which should be as open to gays and lesbians as to heterosexuals; the institutionalization of surrogacy agreements in the name of 'a woman's right to choose'; and calls for more 'equal' adoption rules, to extend the term 'family' rather than to deny its necessity. What, then, is that ideological function?

'Unlike the modern family', writes Ross Poole in *Morality and Modernity* (op. cit.), 'friendship does not buy its place in the modern world through exclusion and oppression; nor does it attempt to provide guarantees of the reassurance it provides by barring one of the participants from the values of the wider public world' (pp. 144–145). Such a contrast between family and friendship gives a clue. What is it about the family, as against at least some conceptions of friendship, that make it as much a cornerstone of Stalinism as of western conservatism and liberalism? In the immediate aftermath of 1918, 'the [Soviet Communist] party did not and could not accord specific attention to questions of the everyday life of the working masses'.[31] By 1936, however – homosexuality having become a criminal offence in the Soviet Union in 1934 – *Pravda* was telling its readers that 'Marriage is the most serious affair in life'[32]: and, according to Stalin, the 'enemies of the people, the vile fascist hirelings ... covered the family in the USSR with filth, spreading the counter-revolutionary "theory" of the

29 Ross Poole, *Morality and Modernity* (London: Routledge, 1991), p. 46.

30 *The Origin of the Family, Private Property and the State* (London: Pelican, 1972), pp. 120–1.

31 H Kent Geiger, *The Family in Soviet Russia* (Cambridge, Mass., Harvard UP, 1968), p. 77.

32 *ibid.*, p. 94. (In the circumstances, I rather think that 'matter' might have been a better translation than 'affair').

dying out of the family, of **disorderly** sexual cohabitation in the USSR, in order to discredit the Soviet land.[33] Thus, and unsurprisingly – and despite some of the convolutions through which his defence of the family as a bulwark against the State and the Church has to rotate in order to escape the doubts raised by Stalin's support of the family – Mount is quite right when he says that 'the main reason [for Stalin's turn] was surely that the regime had simply allowed too large an area of Soviet life to escape its control'.[34] Stalin's allusion to 'disorderly sexual cohabitation' would suggest, however, that it is Reich's rather than Mount's assessment of the role and function of the family which is accurate: its 'cardinal function, that for which it is mostly supported and defended by conservative science and law, is that of serving as a factory for authoritarian ideologies and conservative structures ...'.[35] This is as important for the state capitalism of Stalin's USSR as it is for the more orthodox capitalism of today's Britain. The apparent paradox noted earlier, in the "commonsense" insistence on the family's being a bulwark both against rampant individualism and the long arm of the state, is here dissolved. For '(T)he construction of "the family" as a privatized zone with rigid barriers to prevent the intrusion of the social ...'[36] is at one and the same time a construction which permits 'the social' to have control over that zone. In short, the thesis that the family is a bulwark against the state is not at all inimical to the thesis that it helps socialise individuals: and this on two, complementary, levels.

First, on a more practical level, there are two sides to every bulwark: the drawing of a line around the family might protect elements of its members' lives against the everyday world and its demands (the rules concerning giving evidence against one's spouse, for example); but at the same time it delimits that domestic interior (marital rape has only recently been recognised). In short, just as the family may be to some – small – extent a no-go area for the state, so the state, the public world, is – very largely – a no-go area for familialized everyday life. Consider contemporary Britain: the family sanctions 'forms of life' which are publicly inadmissible and at the same time ensures that they remain out of the public sphere and thus not in need of attention by the state, other than in terms of punishment to discourage overspill. For were the state to be required to intervene directly in people's 'private' lives to any greater extent, its role would be seen to be bigger than it seems; and so one element of its real power – its claiming to be 'rolling itself back' while actually extending its control – would be threatened. Community care, for instance, would be clearly seen for what it is. 'Returning' people to 'the community', that is to say, to the family – and that is to say largely to women – at once: **extends** the role of the family; **diminishes** the state's active role in caring, while furthering development in the direction of private as opposed to public provision of care, that is, guarding diminishing resources for those who are 'one of us'; **increases** the role of the state in directing that development, that is, it 'arranges' the 'free' market for private care; and in doing all of this, **reinforces** one rather than another set of definitions and delimitations of 'public' and 'private'.

33 Quoted in *ibid.*, p. 104: my emphasis. I owe the last three citations to Mount, *op. cit.*, pp. 36–37.
34 Mount, *op. cit.*, p. 37.
35 Wilhelm Reich, *The Sexual Revolution* (New York: Noonday Press, 1962), p. 72.
36 Barrett and McIntosh, *op. cit.*, p. 89–90.

Second, and more importantly because more insidiously, the ideology that is in part constituted by the family actually **requires** the appearance of paradox in order to assist in its own maintenance. The values of capitalism – the 'impersonal, competitive, contractual, and temporary'[37] relations of the market – need a home, a place from and in light of which such relations can appear tolerable; and a home, the furtherance of which is claimed as their ultimate goal. Why make the effort, why go through the pain, if not to support the family, the home which is at one and the same time a haven from those values? 'If it didn't hurt', as the current British prime minister once remarked, 'it wouldn't be working': the values and requirements of the market, of the public world of arms sales, unemployment, lies and the rest of it are justified by their being said to offer the best possible support for the private, family world of 'nurturing, enduring, and noncontingent relations governed by a feeling of morality'.[38] Hence, of course, the threat that feminism presents to capitalism: for it challenges the governing assumptions of its ideological needs. In disturbing the '"public-private" settlement' on which the market in part depends, feminisim suggests at least the possibility not simply of a (more) equal distribution of its goods between women and men, thereby threatening the comparative privileges of the latter; but, in the longer run far more seriously, also the possibility of a re-evaluation of such goods and the means for their attainment. Thus it is in part Stalin's reversal of the Bolshevik Revolution's earlier rejection of the traditional family that constitutes evidence in favour of the thesis that what he instituted in the Soviet Union was a form of state capitalism: as in the early phases of the Industrial Revolution in western Europe, so the rapid industrialization of the USSR required the discipline, order and 'public-private' distinction for its own version of capitalist accumulation to operate.

But is it just that capitalism, Stalin's included, makes use of whatever is to hand – in this case the nuclear family? Or does it in some way require the family? I am agnostic about this question, and am not attempting to argue that the family is a necessary condition of capitalism. Rather, what I am suggesting is that, now that capitalism has made the use of the family that I have briefly outlined, the family has come to be one of its central ideological carriers. Something else, some other social formation, might perhaps have done: but as it is, it is the family which performs a central role – and its so doing thus cannot but be an aspect of what the family is.

Thus 'sympathy' and 'benevolence' mean one thing in the 'public' sphere, another in the 'private': and this is a distinction which capitalism requires in order to justify its playing by the rules of a Hobbesian 'state of nature' for the sake of the non-Hobbesian 'private' sphere of the family; and to help ensure that 'the private' forms the locus of 'real life' so that those concerned with the real real world of the market are not too easily disturbed in it. Now, unless one takes a wholly economistic view of the development and life of capitalism, one is driven inexorably towards the view that the false consciousness thus engendered, and this not necessarily in any conspiratorial manner, is something that capitalism reqires: in short, towards the conclusion that capitalism needs people to suppose that it is the **personal** which is political. The double ironies this creates is well illustrated by Mount's objection in T*he Subversive Family*

37 Barrie Thorne: see n.8.
38 *ibid.*

that 'if you start from that end ["feminist history" or the economic approach] you are likely to suffocate the evidence of the inner life of the family':

If, for example, you start from the evidence of property arrangements, you may conclude that women in traditional society were usually considered primarily as pieces of property. From the legal point of view, this may well be true of certain societies – although we shall need to modify the conventional view on this too – but the economic preparations for marriage need not and cannot wholly determine what happens after marriage. The fact of living together in the same household inescapably creates emotional connections. We know this to be true even in cases where the relationship is one of officially sanctioned, legal oppression. How much greater is the possibility in relations within a family consisting of two and only two adults of the same class living together for twenty or thirty years, until one of them dies (op. cit., p. 220).

It may at first appear that some women in some societies are sometimes regarded – although not entirely – as 'pieces of property'. But as one is not a vulgar Marxist, one has to remember that the economics of marriage do not at all determine its nature or its course: emotional factors can make all the difference, as presumably battered wives in particular know only too well. But if only one sticks at it for long enough, all will be well, and, with the owner dead, the previously owned will no longer be a piece of property.

Contrary, I think, to the claim occasionally made the '(T)he benefits of family life depend upon the suffering of those who are excluded',[39] it seems to me that they depend even more on the suffering of those included. And that is why an analysis of the family in terms of its inability to deliver what it claims for itself is inadequate: for in seeking to understand the content of such claims outside the context in which they are made, and in which they therefore carry specific meaning, such a critique cannot but appear incredible. It is this self-reaffirming and self-perpetuating aspect of the family, and the particular meanings it gives to apparently universal terms, that constituts a critical objection to it. Take, for example, this critique of the family:

The needs and satisfactions to which we refer – affection, security, intimacy, sexual love, parenthood and so on – are not artificial. We see these as human needs, not pathological constructs. The form in which they are currently met, however, we regard as both unsatisfying and anti-social.[40]

But why suppose that if they are artificial – that is to say, if they are constructed within a particular set of social formations, by particular groups of specific people – 'affection, security, intimacy, sexual love, parenthood' must be 'pathological constructs' rather than being 'human needs'? It is just this implicit appeal to the natural, or to 'human nature', as something not 'constructed', which, as I have suggested, vitiates quasi-biological defences of the status quo; mistaken there, it is no more acceptable as part of an attempt to counter such a view. However, to advocate affection, sexual love, etc., without approving of 'the form in which they are currently met' is to invite the immediate question, 'In which form would you approve of them?' And that is of course why the critiques of so many feminists and socialists cannot but appear incredible: why Firestone is not taken seriously; why the intellectual probity of the feminist and socialist refusal to prescribe the future is so often held against it. What exactly is

39 Barrett and McIntosh, *op. cit.*, pp. 132–3.
40 *ibid.*, p. 133.

'affection', let alone 'intimacy', outside the family? Barrett's and McIntosh's mistake is to imply that they do know; and to use that purported knowledge as the basis of their critique of what it actually is within the family. Our notions of what these are and/or might be, like the more general notions of sympathy and benevolence, determine critique.

What I mean is this. Some concepts, and this is most readily recognizable in the case of newer ones, like, for instance, 'racism', are what I term **'morality-affecting'**.[41] Actions, practices and events issue not only in direct consequences for specific individuals or groups, but may also affect the moral and related attitudes of people: the moral climate within which such consequences are recognised. An example might be the Race Relations Act, which has had among its consequences the fact that some people have come to regard racism as a real harm who had not previously done so. Or consider slavery as an example. What is wrong with it? The classical liberal's objection to a person's voluntarily selling themselves into slavery (other things being equal of course, and the wants of no party involved being adversely affected – a not at all unimaginable scenario) is basically that, to quote Mill, 'By selling himself for a slave [a man] abdicates his liberty; he forgoes any future use of it beyond that single act. He therefore defeats, in his own case, the very purpose which is the justification of allowing him to dispose of himself ...'.[42] But there are at least *prima facie* grounds against even the "well-regulated", one-off deal which Mill's argument fails to address. Regardless of the specific conditions of sale, and regardless of the intensity of the parties' wants, it is wrong. Why? Well, in very rough outline, the mere possibility of one person's owning another might well encourage the prevalence of certain sets of relations; certain sorts of use to be made by people of each other; certain further harms to come into being (the full use, according to the owner's wishes, of the slave, for example); and so on. As a practice comes to be accepted, so it becomes acceptable: and where this is a morally wrong state of affairs, the harm done in engaging in the practice is one which is morality-affecting, since its having become acceptable constitutes a moral change. The harm done in owning a slave is not just that which accrues to the slave; but rather the practice of slave-owning itself has further consequences which affect what is taken to be morally right and wrong.

The family's ideological power, and its ideological role in late capitalism, is to construct and conduct debate in its own terms and its own image; and to determine the nature and content of the very moral terms in which a *prima facie* critique of capitalism – and/or of the family itself – might be offered. In respect of the family, such a critique would centre on its inwardness, its limiting both such notions as sympathy and benevolence and their application to specified groups, thereby putting the onus of justification, and even of intelligibility, on those who seek to base their thinking on, say, humanity at large. It would stress the way it limits the extent to which the Hobbesian 'state of nature' is tamed by seeking both to contain and to maintain antagonistic competition between families (in order the better to ensure the demand

41 Cf. Ted Honderich's 'morality dependent harms': '"On Liberty and morality-dependent harms', *Political Studies*, 30, 1982, pp. 504–514. I am indebted to Honderich for thus suggesting to me the idea of 'morality-affecting' harms.

42 *On Liberty*, in (Mary Warnock, ed), J S Mill *Utilitarianism* (London: Fontana, 1962), p 236.

that capitalism requires while avoiding the danger of disorder and indiscipline) – competition which all too easily spills over into nationalism.[43] The 'public collective ridicule' of the charivaris referred to by Taylor has been replaced by a private, familial version, all the more difficult to challenge because it is not public: again, the observation that the self-discipline required by capitalism is more efficiently policed from within than from without is hardly a new thought. Most importantly of all, I think, such a critique would focus on the family as a system of ownership, a living denial of Kant's claim that the central injunction of morality is that we treat each other as ends and not as means. For even while elements of the ownership of children appear to be coming under challenge – I have in mind recent cases of children 'divorcing' their parents – the challenge seems primarily to concern the conditions of particular ownerships rather than the fact of possession; and certainly does not extend to marriage. For whatever the extent of small changes in income tax arrangements; the wording of contracts; or the misguidedly sincere protestations to the contrary of some of the parties to them: such contracts – marriages – constitute the ownership of one person by another. Kant's view of marriage simply as an agreement between two people for the 'reciprocal use of each other's sexual organs'[44] was as optimistic and patriarchally partial in its assessment as was gender-blind and, understandably, exaggerated that of Thomas Webbe, rector of Langley Burhill, when he reportedly opined, while on trial for adultery, that 'there's no heaven but women, nor no hell save marriage'.[45]

43 See ch 5 of Ross Poole's *Morality and Modernity*, *op. cit.*, for an excellent analysis of the way in which the logic of liberal morality leads inexorably towards nationalistic expression.

44 Quoted in Roger Scruton, *Kant* (Oxford: OUP, 1982), p 9.

45 Cited (no reference) in Ferdinand Mount, *op. cit.*, p. 155.

John Eekelaar

Parenthood, Social Engineering and Rights

Introduction

In two recent cases dealing with the placement of children, a judge in the Court of Appeal warned against "social engineering". In one,[1] the parents (who were married to each other) had handed their six week-old baby to an older, childless, couple because they were in financial difficulty and the mother was receiving treatment for heroin addiction. A few months later, the mother asked for its return. But the trial judge refused the application, observing that the child had now settled into a loving family and that the removal would cause it "upheaval and upset". Reversing this decision, Butler-Sloss L.J. said: "The mother must be shown to be entirely unsuitable before another family can be considered, otherwise we are in grave danger of slipping into social engineering. The question is not: would the child be better off with the parents? but: is the natural family so unsuitable that, as Fox L.J. said, 'the welfare of the child positively demanded the displacement of the parental right'".

In a later case, *re O.*[2] unmarried parents had lived together for three months, but separated when the child was born, the mother returning to her former husband. She strongly objected to the father being involved with the child, which she placed with an adoption society. The society, in turn, placed the child with foster-parents. The father, however, wanted the child, and the trial judge ordered it to be returned to him. This time the Court of Appeal upheld the decision. Butler-Sloss L.J. said: "If it were a choice between the known defects of every parent with some added problems that the father has, against idealised perfect adopters, in a very large number of cases children would immediately move out of the family circle and towards adopters. That would be social engineering and it is important to bear that in mind in looking at the problems which arise in this case." She went on to approve an observation made by Lord Templeman[3] that "public authorities cannot improve on nature".

I do not wish to take issue with the solutions the Court of Appeal found to those cases. Yet the words used by Butler-Sloss L.J. are very revealing of what that judge *thought* to be the basis upon which the decisions rested. A contrast seems to be drawn between "social engineering" (which would be a wrong basis) and a basis which is somehow "natural". This is particularly strong in the second case, because the father was not married to the mother, and, as the law stood both before and after the passing of the Children Act 1989, he had no parental "rights" or "responsibility".[4] His claim lay solely in the fact that he was the "natural" father.

1 *re K. (a minor) (wardship: adoption)* [1991] 1 F.L.R. 57.
2 [1992] 1 F.L.R. 77.
3 In *re KD* [1988] 2 W.L.R. 398.
4 These concepts will be explained below.

This is not an isolated example of framing the issues which arise in the placement and care of children in this way. Indeed, as I have argued elsewhere,[5] it lies at the very heart of the Children Act 1989. This is premised on the assumptions that "parenthood" is a phenomenon of the "natural" world, that biological parents will "naturally" act responsibly towards their children, that interferences in this relationship, though sometimes justified, are suspect as intrusions into natural behaviour and that it therefore falls to parents, rather than the state, to exercise "responsibility" with respect to their children.

The argument I wish to make in the first part of this paper is that, to a very large extent, parenthood is a social and not a "natural" concept, and that therefore this opposition between the social and the natural is false. Apart from the brute facts of conception, gestation and birth, and sometimes even these, attributions of parenthood are social, so the choice is not between "social engineering" and "following nature", but between different kinds of "social engineering". In the second part, I wish to show how concepts of parenthood thus created relate to a complex of rights and obligations which are themselves intellectual constructs.

Parenthood and Social Engineering

(a) Social Engineering

The expression "social engineering" is clearly used by Butler-Sloss L.J. in a perjorative sense. Yet its origins are impeccable. In 1923, Roscoe Pound sought for a new model according to which to interpret legal history.[6] Pound believed that Kohler's 1908 work[7] advanced on the nineteenth century comparative method, which sought merely to reconcile abstract legal propositions, divorced from their social context, but thought its Hegelian thesis that law should be interpreted as an emanation of civilization, reflecting the progress of societies towards their highest unfolding, incorrectly presented law as being *caused by* some historical force. Pound preferred an instrumentalist view which saw the legal order and its institutions as means by which society was consciously moulded. He found a metaphor in engineering:

> "We require an analogy which will not postulate formal and logical determinism nor positivist determinism, and yet will remind us that what we do in law is conditioned by many things. It must give us an interpretation in terms of activity, leading us to think of legal institutions not merely as things that have come to us, but as things that were made at some time and are made by those who believe in them and will them. Yet it must give us an interpretation in terms of conditioned activity, conditioned by the capacities, the characters and prejudices of those who plan and make, by the materials with which they must work, by the circumstances in which they must work, and by the specific purposes for which they work. Such an analogy seems to be one to be afforded by engineering. Let us think of jurisprudence for a moment as a science of social engineering".[8]

5 J. Eekelaar, "Parental Responsibility – State of Nature or Nature of the State?" *Journal of Social Welfare and Family Law* [1991] 37.

6 Roscoe Pound, *Interpretations of Legal History* (Cambridge, Cambridge University Press, 1923).

7 *Lehrbuch der Rechtsphilosophie,* 1908.

8 Pound, n.6 above, pp. 151–152.

Within jurisprudence, this has been seen as a call to extend legal study beyond "law in the books" and to include in it the social sciences, psychology and even the physical sciences.[9] In 1945 Karl Popper appropriated Pound's usage to contrast a political theory which saw humans as agents, capable of adapting social institutions in accordance with chosen ends, with historicism, which saw such ends as being dictated by historical circumstance.[10] But Pound wrote contemporaneously with the "Progressive" movement in the social sciences in the United States, associated with John Dewey and William James, which sought the application of social science to the organisation of society.[11] It has been argued[12] that "democratic social engineering" in the United States replaced the more authoritarian efforts of social control of the nineteenth century with methods designed to manipulate people's wishes so they would more readily consent to the capitalist democratic social order. The movement operated through small groups, such as Sunday Schools, the YMCA, Boy Scouts and recreational clubs. It reached into the family through books such as Spock's *The Common Sense Book of Baby and Child Care* (which maintained that confrontation with children should be avoided so they would learn to *want* to conform) and in consumer relations through works like Dale Carnegie's *How to Win Friends and Influence People* (which promoted sales techniques directed at making people *want* to buy).[13]

In Britain, however, the expression "social engineering" seems to have been associated with the politics of pragmatic socialism, and in 1919 was used to describe the goals and methods of the Fabian Society.[14] Its contemporary perjorative flavour seems to have a more immediate and local origin in Conservative Party disapproval of left-wing interventionism, particularly in education and social policy.[15] Right-wing interventionism, designed to promote a market economy, or to shore up individual or family responsibility,[16] and which seems closer to the "utopian" social engineering of which Popper disapproved,[17] seems not currently to attract this epithet.

9 See Sidney Post Simpson and Ruth Field, "Social Engineering through Law" *New York University Law Review* 22 (1947) 145–193. This is the dominant endeavour of socio-legal studies.

10 Karl Popper, *The Open Society and its Enemies*, (London, Routledge, 1945) vol. 1, pp. 22–23.

11 The influence of this movement on Gunnar Myrdal had important consequences for post-war social policy in Sweden: see Walter A. Jackson, *Gunnar Myrdal and America's Conscience: Social Engineering and Radical Liberalism 1938–1987* (Chapel Hill, University of North Carolina Press, 1990).

12 See William Gruebner, *The Engineering of Consent: Democracy and Authority in Twentieth Century America* (Madison, University of Wisconsin Press, 1987).

13 There is a parallel with the process of "normalization" as a means of social control described by Jacques Donzelot, *The Policing of Families* (London, Hutchinson, 1980).

14 M. Beer, *The History of British Socialism* (London, Allen & Unwin, 1919) vol. 2, p. 287.

15 See, for example, the cartoon in *The Independent*, 29 July 1992, p. 1, depicting a Conservative government White Paper on education as replacing a document on which is written "Educashun: social engineering, truancy, low standards, sink schools".

16 See Gillian Douglas, "Family Law under the Thatcher Government" *Journal of Law & Society* 17, 1990, 411.

17 Popper, n.10 above, pp. 157–158, distinguished "utopian" social engineering, when the "engineer" sought social change to achieve an *a priori* idealised blueprint for society, with "piecemeal" social engineering (of which he approved), where the engineer primarily sought to identify and remove the main ills of society.

(b) Parenthood as a Social Construct

Nevertheless, parenthood might be thought to be at least one feature of life which is rooted in nature. Begetting and bearing children are, of course, fixed natural events. But those events do not constitute "parenthood" in any full sense. In her definitive study of fostering and occupational roles in west African societies, Esther Goody analyses parenthood in terms of its roles in achieving social replacement. These roles are: (i) bearing and begetting; (ii) endowment with civil and kinship status; (iii) nurturance; and (iv) training and sponsorship into adulthood.[18] The following passage is important in view of the subsequent argument of this paper:

> "If parenthood is best considered as a set of roles which may be allocated to different people, how are we to define the 'real' parents? It is significant that such a question should even arise. Why should one feel the need to be able to say of a child – 'these are his "real" parents'? The question is partly anchored in our cultural experience. For us it means 'who are his biological parents?' While this aspect of parenthood carries very different weight in different societies, I doubt that there is any society in which it is impossible to ask the question in a meaningful way. But 'real' parenthood may be linked to different combinations of parental roles in different societies. Very often it is defined in physiological terms. But in many societies the 'real' parents are seen as those through whom civil/kinship status is transmitted. And there are a few societies ..... in which 'real' parents are defined by the rearing relationship itself....We are left in a position of having to recognize that there are 'kinds' of parenthood – physiological, jural, educational – which are differently weighted in different societies. The weighting is not arbitrary, but is a response to a balance of cultural and institutional features in a given social system".[19]

The analysis of contemporary parenthood which follows is thus consistent with the anthropological evidence of the social construction of parenthood. Such an analysis does not ignore, nor reflect an evaluative attempt to downgrade, the significance which may be attached to biological parenthood, nor to deny (which would hardly be possible) the naturalness of conception, pregnancy and childbirth. But it places those fixed elements within a social matrix which relates them and their perceived significance to other aspects of parenthood in varying ways, just as societies through the ages have sought to control the circumstances in which they should occur. In this sense it is true to say that parenthood is socially determined.[20]

(c) Legal Parenthood, Biological Parenthood and Social Parenthood

The example given by Goody of wet-nursing in Italy, France and England from the fourteenth to sixteenth centuries is one illustration of a detachment between child-bearing and nurturance which might seem "unnatural" in many modern eyes.[21] But,

18 Esther N. Goody, *Parenthood and Social Reproduction* (Cambridge, Cambridge University Press 1982) p. 8.

19 Goody, n18 above, pp. 17–18.

20 This is not the place to grapple with the claims of socio-biology that social behaviour is biologically (genetically) determined. Such arguments are partly definitional, but also raise deeper questions of the origins of all human behaviour. For a discussion, within the context of family behaviour, see Janet Finch, *Family Obligations and Social Change* (Cambridge, Polity Press, 1989) pp. 218-220.

21 The children would often be taken from the natural mother to the wet-nurse's home for almost two years. Goody points out that the re-integration of the child was not *seen* at the time as being a problem: Goody, n.19 above, p. 25.

even to-day, particularly in the case of men, procreation does not necessarily raise a right, or even expectation, of rearing the child. Suppose a child is conceived by a married woman as a result of an adulterous liaison. In such circumstances, continental European legal systems have developed complex rules controlling not only whether the father may have any part in the upbringing of the child, but whether his fatherhood can be recognised at all. The law will start with the presumption that a child born to a married couple who are living together is the child of the husband (*pater est quem nuptiae demonstrant*). Although this rule was partly designed to confirm the paternity of the person most likely to be the biological father, it is more than that. In the Napoleonic Code, the rule applied even if the spouses were legally separated. However, the husband (but not the wife) could disavow his paternity. In that context, the rule was a manifestation of patriarchal concerns and the protection of the legitimate status. Since the early 1970s, the Netherlands and France have allowed the *mother* to disavow the husband's paternity, but only if another man accepted the child as his, showing a movement from the original motivations to a concern to protect a child's social parentage. And even this may be barred (in systems based on French law) if the child has *possession d'état*: i.e. if she has been treated by the husband as if she were his child. Nor is it likely that the mother will be permitted to challenge her husband's paternity once she has accepted it. In any case, the disavowal must be made within a specific period from the child's birth.[22] Unless these conditions are met, the child remains legally and socially the child of the married couple, even though scientific tests, if carried out, might prove she was not "theirs".

Although English law is remarkably free of such rules, the results are probably the same. In *re F. (a minor) (blood tests)*,[23] a man's claim to be awarded "parental responsibility" with respect to a child he had allegedly fathered by a woman who was married to another man was rejected. The court refused to order tests to determine the paternity of the child.

The reasons for these restrictions are clear enough. Where a child is born into a functioning marriage, the social parentage exercised over the child would be threatened if it were proved that she was conceived adulterously. So strongly does the law view the social institution of marriage that it assumes nature conforms to social appearance. Parenthood is "socially engineered". As the judge remarked in *re F.*, he would not make an order which might "disturb the presumption of legitimacy": not, presumably, because of the legal advantages of legitimacy over illegitimacy, for these nowadays are miniscule, but to protect her social parentage. "This court will not order (DNA "finger-printing") against the wishes of the parents who have responsibility for the child, at the behest of a stranger to the marriage to satisfy his own desire to know whether he is the father".[24]

22 See P. Senaeve, "The Reform of Affiliation Law in France and the Benelux Countries" and Ioannis Deliyannis, "Establishing and Contesting Parentage: the Approach of Greek Law in Comparative Perspective", chs. 6 & 7 in J. Eekelaar and P. Sarcevic (eds), *Parenthood in Modern Society: Social and Legal Issues for the Twenty-First Century* (Dordrecht, Martinus Nijhoff, 1993).

23 [1992] 2 F.C.R. 725. The appeal by the man claiming to be the father failed: *The Independent*, 6 February 1993.

24 This is not to deny that the people concerned may not be aware of the biological facts. The point is that, despite these facts (and possible awareness of them) one powerful social force (the law) and perhaps others does not recognise the biological father's parenthood.

This is only one example. Much stronger instances appear in the context of artificial reproduction and surrogacy. It is, for example, provided that where a married woman, or an unmarried woman who receives treatment with a man, conceives a child as a result of artificial insemination with the semen of someone other than her husband or that man, her husband or that man will be treated in law as the father of the child unless he did not consent to the insemination.[25] Of course in these cases, unlike the father in *re O.*,[26] the sperm donor will not wish to act as social father. But it was not the man's wishes which constituted the belief that it was "natural" to award the child to the father in *re O.*, but his biological link with the child. In the artificial insemination case, on the other hand, it is the mother's partner's consent and his potential as the social father which displaces the preference for the biological link. But if the partner does not consent, and proves the child is not his, he will not be the legal father; nor will the donor, but only if licensed facilities were used to perform the insemination.[27] If he did not use them, the donor will be treated as being the legal father. Here, therefore, the legal definition of fatherhood is made to serve social ends: encouraging the use of licensed facilities. Although none of these provisions apply if an infertile couple elect to overcome the infertility by agreeing that the woman should conceive through natural intercourse with another man, the result will be much the same if the couple are married and claim the child as their own because the the presumption of legitimacy might prevent that man establishing his paternity. But if the couple are unmarried, it is unlikely that the true father will be prevented from asserting his fatherhood, should he choose to do so.

One of the most remarkable recognitions of social parenthood is found in section 30 of the Human Fertilisation and Embryology Act 1990. The Act settles[28] that, if a woman is implanted with an embryo or sperm and eggs which do not contain her genetic material, she will nevertheless be treated as the legal mother of the child she consequentially bears. But section 30 provides that if a woman hands over a child she has conceived by artificial means (whether it originated in her own fertilized ovum or that of another woman) to a married couple in consequence of a surrogacy agreement the court may, if certain conditions are met, make an order the result of which is to convert the married couple into the child's legal parents. The section does not make surrogacy arrangements enforceable. On the contrary, section 36 of the Act proclaims that they are not enforceable. But a court will find it difficult to resist giving *ex post facto* sanction to a completed surrogacy transaction and conferring full legal recognition on the social parenthood that has been established.

(d) The Structure of Parenthood in English Law

The above should indicate that, in law at least, parenthood is not a straightforward matter, corresponding simply to some "natural" phenomenon. But it becomes even

25 Human Fertilisation and Embryology Act 1990, s. 28.
26 N.2, above.
27 Human Fertilisation and Embryology Act 1990, s. 28(6)(a). Also, if the inseminated woman has no partner, the donor will be treated as the father unless licensed facilities were used.
28 Section 28.

more complex when account is taken of the concept of "parental responsibility" introduced in the Children Act 1989. Parenthood can, in fact, be broken into three distinguishable elements: biological parenthood, legal parenthood and the holding of parental responsibility.

(i) Biological parenthood

Although, as we have seen, there may be occasions when the law will not permit its ascertainment, biological parenthood will always be *theoretically*, and often *practically*, ascertainable. Agencies accepting sperm from donors are obliged to record the identities of the donors, although the information will be kept secret, even from the children produced from the sperm, at least until government regulations proclaim the contrary.[29] These men are fathers, but they are not legally recognised as fathers. If a mother hands over her child to a married couple and a court makes an order under section 30 of the Human Fertilisation and Embryology Act 1990, she ceases to be the legal mother of her child. The same holds true for parents whose children are adopted, although in this case, if the adoption took place after 1975, their identity may be revealed to the children.[30]

(ii) Legal Parenthood and (iii) Parental Responsibility

Normally, legal parenthood will attract "parental responsibility", turning it into a kind of "full" parenthood because "parental responsibility" is defined as "all the rights, duties, powers, responsibilities and authority which by law a parent of a child has in relation to the child and his property."[31] All mothers have "parental responsibility", as do married men over children of whom they are the legal father (although, as we have seen, they may not be the biological father). They retain parental responsibility as long as the child remains a minor (unless she is adopted, but then parents cease to be the legal parents too), although they lose it in everything but name if the child is taken into care on a care order. Each keeps parental responsibility even after divorce.

The father of a child born to an unmarried woman is the exception. He does not have "parental responsibility". Similarly, the unmarried partner of a woman who consents to her artificial insemination by the sperm of another will be "treated" as the child's legal father, but he will not have "parental responsibility". Like any unmarried father, he can acquire it through agreement with the mother or by court order.[32] But even without parental responsibility, as the child's legal father he may be ordered to pay child support, and the mother may be required to disclose his identity for this purpose.[33] His name may appear on the birth certificate if the mother agrees, or if a

29 See Gillian Douglas, *Law, Fertility and Reproduction* (London, Sweet & Maxwell, 1991) ch. 6.
30 Adoption Act 1976, s. 51.
31 Children Act 1989, s. 3(1).
32 Children Act 1989, s. 4.
33 Child Support Act 1991, sections 6 and 46.

court has awarded him "parental responsibility", or if he is ordered to support the child.[34] He is a "liable person" with respect to the child under social security legislation. If a local authority holds the child under an Emergency Protection Order, it has a duty to allow reasonable contact between him and the child (unless the order provides otherwise)[35] and, if the authority accommodates the child, it must endeavour to promote such contact.[36] As a parent, he may apply for the discharge of an Emergency Protection Order after 72 hours.[37] We have already seen that, in *re O.*,[38] an unmarried father was seen as having a special claim as against non-parents to the care of his child.

Parental responsibility can also be attached to a non-parent. It is tempting to think that this marks it off from legal parenthood, until we recollect that this too can be "detached" from a biological parent (as in the case of artificial insemination by donor), and even transferred from a biological parent to a social parent (as under section 30 of the Human Fertilisation and Embryology Act 1990). Nevertheless, the acquisition of parental responsibility by a non-parent will be much commoner than those instances. A local authority acquires parental responsibility through a care order. Anyone in whose favour a Residence Order is made will acquire parental responsibility:[39] the most obvious examples are step-parents and foster-parents.[40]

(e) A Rationalised Structure

The resulting structure of parenthood in English law is one of in which a medieval land lawyer would have taken pride. In its amplitude, full parenthood might be said to occur when biological parenthood, legal parenthood and parental responsibility coincide. But, as we have seen, these elements can be split and distributed between various people. Suppose a child is born from sperm donated by A to an unmarried couple (a woman, W, and a man, B) who jointly underwent the treatment from a licensed facility. If the couple subsequently separate and the mother marries another man (C), in whose favour a Residence Order is made, then, while W is the biological and legal mother, and has parental responsibility, A is the biological father, B the legal father (without parental responsibility) and C shares parental responsibility with W. Such fatherhood has little to do with nature.

Yet such social constructions can surely be defended. The social positions vis-a-vis the child of a sperm donor, an unmarried father who has never lived with the mother, or who has done so only fleetingly,[41] and a step-father who is bringing up the child are very different. It is a weakness of traditional continental European systems

34 See John Dewar, *Law and the Family* (London, Butterworths, 1992) p. 96.

35 Children Act 1989, s. 44 (13).

36 Children Act 1989, Schedule 2, para. 15 (1).

37 Provided he did not receive notice of the original application or attend the original hearing: Children Act 1989, s. 45 (8) & (11).

38 N.2 above.

39 Children Act 1989, s. 12 (2).

40 See Children Act 1989, s. 10 (5).

41 See Ruth Deech, "The Rights of Fathers: Social and Biological Concepts of Parenthood" ch 2 in Eekelaar and Sarcevic (eds), n.22 above.

that they fail to make appropriate distinctions of this kind. An example occurs in the so-called "false acknowledgement".[42] One of the few ways in which a step-father can acquire a parental relationship with a step-child is to make a "false acknowledgement" that the child is his (provided the child has not been acknowledged by another man). This is the converse of the situation (as in *re F.*[43]) where the law *denies* the opportunity to establish biological parentage because it will not be accompanied by social parentage, and its confirmation may disturb an existing social parentage.

But why should biological parenthood and social parenthood be linked in this way? The invention in the Children Act 1989 of parental responsibility, which can be detached from legal, and indeed, biological, parenthood, shows that they can be separated. Parental responsibility, broadly speaking, attaches to persons exercising social parenthood, such as those in whose favour a Residence Order is made. It could be described as the legal recognition of social parenthood. It may be granted to an unmarried father if, in the words of Waite J., "the association between the (parents was) sufficiently enduring", and the father by his conduct during and since the application to the court has "shown sufficient commitment to the children" to justify treating him in the same way as a married father.[44] Unfortunately, the concept is not treated *consistently* throughout the Act, largely because it also assumed an ideological perspective, designed to remind people that biological parents, not the state, were primarily *responsible for* their children.[45] Nevertheless, it can provide the basis for a more satisfactory analysis of the concept of parenthood.

In view of the near certainty with which biological parenthood can now be established, and the growing tendency of people to take their genetic origins seriously,[46] biological parenthood should now be legally recognised in all cases. The biological father, including the sperm donor, should be the legal father. Similarly, the genetic parents of a child born as a result of an embryo implant should be the legal parents. But the *incidents* of legal parenthood can vary according to the circumstances. If, for example, a donor gave sperm on the basis of anonymity, there are strong grounds not to reveal his legal fatherhood and to exempt him from financial responsibility for the child. On the other hand, in different circumstances, and for a variety of social reasons,[47] it may be decided that a legal father should be required to support his child financially even if he never enjoyed a social relationship with the child. In principle,[48] legal fatherhood should always be capable of being established even if another man is acting as social father, and the legal father would not so act.[49]

42 See J. Sosson, "The Legal Status of Step-Families in Continental European Countries", ch 26 in Eekelaar and Sarcevic (eds), n.22 above.

43 Note 23 above.

44 *re C (minors: parental rights)* [1992] 1 F.L.R. 1.

45 See n.5 above.

46 See, for example, Eriksson and Saldeen in ch. 5 of Eekelaar and Sarcevic (eds), n.22 above.

47 For example, in furtherance of a policy endeavouring to promote responsible social behaviour; or a policy to relieve the public purse.

48 That is to say, unless defeated by a stronger right in another that it should not be: see below.

49 An analogy may be drawn with the concept of legal *title* (or *dominium*), the incidents of which can be fragmented.See A.M. Honoré, "Ownership", ch. 5 in A.G. Guest (ed) *Oxford Essays in Jurisprudence* (Oxford, Oxford University Press, 1961). Like title, legal fatherhood should provide a basic identification of a child with its parents.

Parental responsibility, however, should in principle always be associated with the exercise of social parenthood. The assumption that this is exercised by married couples should be retained, but it might extend to longer-term cohabitees and step-parents, who might acquire parental responsibility automatically, as married parents do, or by simple administrative procedure.[50] It might presumptively continue if the parents separate, but should be related to the degree of involvement by the parent concerned in the child's life. Loss of such involvement should lead to loss of parental responsibility, but not of legal parenthood and any incidents that are appropriate to it in the circumstances. Similarly, where a child is taken into care, the logical effect should be suspension of parental responsibility, though not of legal parenthood.

Moral Duties and the Rights of Parents and Children

In this Part, I wish to complete an argument I began when addressing the question: "are parents morally obliged to care for their children?"[51] That argument was incomplete because, although it attempted to construct a moral basis for the duty to care for children, it did not deal with how this duty related to conceptions of rights, especially of children's rights.

(a) The Moral Duties of Parents

My argument advanced the propositions that

(1) moral principle by itself did not place a duty to care for his or her child on the child's biological parents; (put another way, biological parenthood of a child was not *necessarily* a source of moral obligation to care for that child);

(2) moral principle did, however, dictate a duty to promote human flourishing, including the flourishing of the newly born;

(3) the allocation of the duty to care for particular children was a contingent social fact; a person fell under a duty to care for a particular child as a result of a conjunction between social rules and the background moral principle.

On this argument, the *moral* obligation might be satisfied by caring for children over whom one has assumed social parenthood, even if they are not your own, and you have placed your own children out for adoption. Or you might assume social parenthood through step-parenthood, leaving your own children to be primarily cared for by another step-parent. Provided individuals participate in social arrangements which promote the well-being of the new members of the society, they are discharging the primary moral obligation.[52] The social and legal structure of parenthood adopted in a

50 See the suggestion by Gillian Douglas and N.V. Lowe, "Becoming a Parent in English Law" *Law Quarterly Review* 18, 1992, 414, p. 431.

51 See John Eekelaar, "Are Parents Morally Obliged to Care for their Children?" *Oxford Journal of Legal Studies* 11, 1991, 340.

52 These individuals need not be parents or parent-figures. Such duties may well be assumed by the wider community, including (perhaps especially) kin-groups. These are, however, socially determined practices.

particular society provides the mode through which that moral obligation is met. This does not amount to an assertion that the responsibility for caring for children falls (or should fall) on the state, or society, rather than parents but an observation that whether it falls on the state (or society) or on parents (or other individuals) is contingent on actual social practices, and is not a *moral* issue.

This structure can be analysed in terms of an interconnecting web of *rights* and *duties*. Before examining this further, however, it is necessary to clarify the sense in which I use the concept of rights.[53]

(b) Rights as Manifestations of the Choices, or Presumed Choices, of Individuals

I follow mainstream analysis in avoiding any naturalistic perceptions that rights are independent entities. I recall Feinberg's statement that "when we affirm that some person has a moral right to something whatever the local institutions, positive laws and established conventions may say, we are endorsing reasons derived (as we think) from wider principles that are applicable in other contexts, in support of that person's claim".[54] You think someone has a right, therefore, when you accept *grounds* that others should act in particular ways towards that person. I argue that the relevant grounds must be related to the *rightholder's standpoint*. As Finnis has declared: "In short, the modern vocabulary and grammar of rights is a many-faceted instrument for reporting and asserting the requirements or other implications of a relationship of justice *from the point of view of the person(s) who benefit(s) from* that relationship".[55]

I therefore deviate from Raz's formulation that "'x has a right means that, other things being equal, an aspect of x's well-being (his interest) is a sufficient reason for holding some other person(s) to be under a duty"[56] because this could be applied consistently with what I take to be an antithetical position to the holding of rights *viz*., where another has power to determine what my interests are. I therefore modify Raz's formulation thus: "if I say that 'x has a right' I indicate that, other things being equal, I think that the fact that x claims or may plausibly be thought to claim a specific outcome is a sufficient reason for holding some other person(s) to be under a duty to allow or to bring about that outcome". It may be possible for people to have rights without knowing it, but the concept of rights has content only if they would be likely to want them if they knew they had them. If people have no wish to achieve an outcome, or to have the choice to achieve it, or if it is implausible that they would have those wishes, then to give them the "right" to achieve or to choose to achieve the outcome is an empty gesture. So to give a devout Muslim the "right" to eat pork, or a rebellious population the "right" to join the army, is as devoid of content as would be the claim that a

53 This is set out in full in J. Eekelaar, "The Importance of Thinking that Children Have Rights" *International Journal of Law and the Family* 6, 1992, 221; also in P. Alston, S. Parker and J. Seymour (eds), *Children, Rights and the Law* (Oxford, Oxford University Press 1992) 221.

54 Joel Feinberg, "In Defence of Moral Rights" *Oxford Journal of Legal Studies* 12, 1992, 149, p. 168.

55 John Finnis, *Natural Law and Natural Rights* (Oxford, Oxford University Press, 1980) p. 205, emphasis in original.

56 J. Raz, "The Nature of Rights", *Mind*, 93 (1984), p. 194; reprinted in "Rights-based Moralities", ch 9 in Jeremy Waldron (ed), *Theories of Rights* (Oxford, Oxford University Press, 1984).

population is living under the rule of law if the law stipulates that whatever one individual stipulates to be law is law.

I argue that the well-known difficulty in the case of a child who is too young to make claims must be overcome by linking the outcome to an assumption that it is the outcome which such a child, when fully informed and mature, would be likely to have chosen. This construct views rights discourse as a mode of reasoning, so that, by thinking that children may have (certain) rights, a *process* is opened up which leads to a framing of certain questions in a characteristic way. Under this process, unless no other course is available, it is not enough to make a decision for a child on *nothing more* than the assertion that the decision is in the child's best interests. The "interests" demand explication, and the explication requires justification, *if possible*, in terms of the child's claims; or, what it may plausibly wish to have claimed for itself on the attainment of full information and maturity.

The process requires close analysis of children's actual claims, and this requires their evaluation in relation to children's development. Claims which are not *competently* made would not be adequate justifications.[57] Furthermore, a rights-based approach must impose a constraint in the form of an assumption that children would not wish decisions to be made which restricted their opportunities for exercising choices. Despite these necessary restrictions, the special orientation of rights-based thinking has the potential to influence outcomes by its sharp focus on the value of self-determination by the subjects of the decision.

(c) Morality and Rights

It is not claimed that we are morally bound to make decisions about children on this basis. The claim is only that decisions must be founded on this process if they are to be described as a realisation of the child's rights. Furthermore, Raz[58] and O'Neill[59] have argued that the identification of rights cannot provide a complete basis for determining the morality of the actions of others. Their main ground is that rights indicate only the *duties* of others, whereas morality ranges wider than such duties. Raz also argues that the individualistic nature of rights misses the wider values of some collective goods. If rights are seen as grounded in claims made by people (which is different from the view put forward by Raz), there is an even stronger reason why they cannot be a sufficient foundation for determining the morality of action. We cannot know in advance what people will claim. Unless some prior moral principle was to stipulate otherwise, the claims of the racist or the child pornographer would become a constituent element of morality.

So the extent to which we decide whether to accept claims (or presumed claims) as justifications for action, and, in particular, the manner in which we resolve conflicts between inconsistent claims, is a matter for an independent political or moral theory. It

57 See further, below p. 95.
58 N. 56 above.
59 See "Children's Rights and Children's Lives", *Ethics*, 98, 1988, p. 445; reprinted in *International Journal of Law & the Family* 6, 1992, 24; Alston, Parker & Seymour, n. 53 above, p. 24.

is not the purpose of this paper to examine or defend any such theory. However, it may be observed that such theories may be broadly conservative, favouring a static or slowly evolving application of a dominant morality; or they may be more dynamic, responding to an ethos in which greater weight is given to assertions to moral independence of individuals making up the society, thereby feeding new values into the dominant morality. Mackie argues in favour of the dynamic solution, seeing it as providing a core element of a theory of morality. "If we assume that, from the point of view of the morality we are constructing, what matters in human life is activity, but diverse activities determined by successive choices, we shall, as I have said, take as central the right of persons progressively to choose how they shall live."[60] Rights-based thinking is likely to contribute to a more dynamic scenario.

(d) Rights and the Structure of Parenthood

I now need to make good my earlier claim that the view we take of the respective rights of parents and children underpins the social organisation of parenthood. The notion that parents might have rights has recently come under a cloud. It has the uncomfortable ring of a proprietary relationship between parent and child, and courts have preferred the expression "responsibility".[61] Yet, since "parental responsibility" is defined in the Children Act 1989 as including "rights", there should be nothing shameful about thinking that parents have them. But what rights do they have? I do not intend to attempt a full classification.[62] I want to consider only two possible rights: the right to exercise social parenthood and the right to establish one's own biological parenthood (or "legal parenthood" on the classification suggested above). I shall then consider special cases of conflicts between parents' and children's rights.

(i) Rights of Biological Parents

In normal circumstances, the birth parents will wish to possess their child and this claim may be the foundation of a right. Happily, this will usually coincide with what we can plausibly take to be the hypothetical wish of the child. In a variety of less usual situations the coincidence may be less sure. There may be a likely conflict, as where the child would be at risk of serious harm if left with a birth parent. We must then choose between the two claims. Sometimes the child's hypothetical choice is just too speculative. Then we may fall back on the parental claim.

It was this claim which was recognised in *re O.*[63] as a right, although as if it was just a matter of following nature rather than social engineering. But the recognition of rights, and their enforcement, are social decisions. There is nothing "natural" in preferring the claim of an unmarried father to his child over those of strangers in blood

60 J. Mackie, "Can there be a Right-based Moral theory?", ch. 8 in Waldron (ed), n. 56 above.
61 See *re K. (a minor)* [1990] 2 F.L.R. 64; *re K (a minor: wardship: adoption)* [1991] 1 F.L.R. 57.
62 Which I once did: J. Eekelaar, "What are Parental Rights?" *Law Quarterly Review* 89, 1973, 210.
63 N.2 above.

who are acting as social parents, and for many years the law tended to favour the social parents.[64] In *J. v. C.*[65] the House of Lords held that even married parents did not have a preferred claim as against strangers in blood: the child's best interests determined the matter, and indeed this is the principle underlying Dutch law.[66]

A placement rule favouring a "natural parent" over a stranger in blood is just as much an expression of a social vision as a rule favouring a father over a mother (as used to be the case). It is the foundational social rule of our society. Unless there are strong grounds for departing from it, the biological mother and father are *entitled* to initiate the period of social parenthood over their child. The rule is so strong that it will not be overridden even by an agreement either may have made to hand the child over at birth to others. Their continued exercise of social parenthood re-inforces the foundational rule, though if it has been uncertainly exercised,[67] or not exercised at all, and social parenthood has been established with others, we become less sure about whether they should be entitled to take over social parenthood. We *might* hold that they are so entitled, and (as Butler-Sloss LJ suggested in *re O.*) allow them to assume social parenthood unless they suffer some serious deficiency. But we might prefer to allow the established social parenthood (with its accompanying parental responsibility) to prevail, leaving the natural parents with legal parenthood only. All these are social choices. They reflect a complex structure of rights and duties which runs deeply in our society. They have little to do with "nature".

(ii) The Right to Establish Biological Parenthood

Let us next consider those complex rules limiting the opportunities for "third-party men" to establish their parenthood over a child born to married woman. The consequence of a bar to such an action leaves the issue of the child's biological paternity in doubt, or entrusts the spouses with the discretion whether to reveal the truth (if they know it) to the child. These rules either reflect a prioritisation of the claims of the husband or wife, or a welfarist concern about protecting family harmony. If we are to ask what might be the child's rights in the matter, we should be forced to confront the question: what action would the child, assuming full information and maturity (that is, uninfluenced by possible parental pressures), be likely to have wanted to be taken? Greater awareness of such a perspective may explain why European systems have recently extended the circumstances in which a child may contest the paternity of a man claiming to be his father, although the opportunities are still limited.[68] If we think that a child is likely to

64 For a striking example, see *re E (P)* [1969] 1 All ER 323. Hence, even now, an unmarried father's consent is not a pre-condition for the adoption of his child. There is extensive literature: cf. eg Andrew Bainham, "When is a Parent not a Parent? Reflections on the Unmarried Father and his Child in English Law" *International Journal of Law & the Family* 3, 1989, 208.

65 [1970] A.C. 668.

66 See P. Vlaardingerbroek, "The Rights of Parents and Children in the Netherlands: Seeking a New Balance", ch. 31 in Eekelaar and Sarcevic (eds), n.22 above.

67 See the cases of "prevaricating" mothers of children placed out for adoption: see P.M. Bromley & N.V. Lowe, *Bromley's Family Law* (London, Butterworths, 1992) p. 430.

68 See P. Senaeve, ch. 6 in Eekelaar and Sarcevic, n.22 above.

have wanted her genetic parentage established in a way which did not, however, disrupt the social parentage she was enjoying as a child, we might favour routine establishment of legal parentage in such circumstances, without any implications for the exercise of the social parentage. And if we were to consider the *parent's* claims, we might find that these coincided with those of the child.

We have seen that in the case of artificial insemination, the principle of anonymity of the donor is widely maintained. This protects both the claims of the donor and of the social parents to conceal the nature of the conception. What, however, may be a child's "rights" in the matter? Is it plausible to assume that a person, thus conceived, and of full understanding and maturity, would choose either to live his or her life on the basis of deliberate deception as to his or her biological origins, or on the basis that the true origins would never be revealed? In the case of surrogacy, it seems plausible that a child born to a surrogate as a result of the implantation of an embryo derived from the genetic material of a couple who wanted the child would choose to be reared by that couple. If that is so, the presumption in favour of the birth mother for which Martha Field[69] argues could not be supported on a children's rights basis.

(iii) Conflicts between parents' and children's rights

We should distinguish between conflicts between the right a parent claims to decide what is best for a child and the child's own wishes, and conflicts between what a child wishes for herself and what a parent wishes for himself.

If either situation were to come to an English court, the child's welfare should be the "paramount consideration".[70] But in the latter situation this can hardly mean that the child's wishes (assuming that they coincided with the court's view of the child's welfare) should *always* prevail irrespective of the relative seriousness of the issues involved. No doubt the welfare principal gives added weight to the child's interests, but such conflicts must be resolved according to independent moral, or social, criteria. The more difficult problem arises where the parent seeks to insist on his "right" to determine the child's best interests over the child objections.

It had, for example, been thought that the House of Lords had established, in *Gillick v. West Norfolk and Wisbech Area Health Authority,*[71] that a child who had acquired sufficient understanding and maturity could make decisions about (among other things) his or her medical treatment independently of his or her parents.[72] The Court of Appeal has now truncated this right and stated the position to be that, while the child may accept such treatment against parental opposition, a parent may authorise a

69 See Martha A. Field, *Surrogate Motherhood* (Cambridge, Harvard University Press, 1988); also, ch. 14 in Eekelaar and Sarcevic (eds) n.22 above.

70 Children Act 1989, s. 1.

71 [1986] A.C. 112.

72 Andrew Bainham, "Growing up in Britain: Adolescence in the Post-Gillick Era", *Juridical Review* 1992, 155 points out that in most cases it makes little sense to talk of a parent's or a child's right to decide on medical treatment because doctors cannot be *compelled* to provide it. But issues of rights do occur where the doctor is willing to intervene but the parents, or the child, disapprove.

doctor to carry out medical treatment on his or her child against the child's wishes.[73] The decision was made in a case in which the court authorised treatment against her wishes of a 16 year-old girl who was suffering from *anorexia nervosa*. The court might have reached its decision by holding that that condition causes such a distortion of self-perception that the sufferer's decision-making capabilities are significantly impaired. But it did not do so. The key role is held by the doctor. If a doctor approves of providing the treatment, it may be given if *either* the child or the child's parents agree. If the child does not agree, and the action proceeds, the mode of justification reveals sharply the relationship between moral justifications and rights-based thinking. It may well be possible to find moral justification in imposing such treatment: it could be found in the duty of the medical profession to heal (whether or not acting together with the social parent), or in the duty of a social parent to safeguard the well-being of the child. But it would miss the central core of rights-based thinking to maintain that such action instantiates a right of the child. The right the child is claiming is to be free of the treatment. *If the integrity of her claim cannot be impugned*, to concede the child the status of a right-holder necessarily implies recognition of this claim.

But this does not concede to the child control over outcomes in all cases. The child must at least be "competent" to make a decision. Competence may be impeded through at least the following factors: lack of understanding through immaturity; distortion of judgement through illness or coercion and inexperience with social reality. But even if "competent" in that sense, we may wish to deny the child control if the decision would harm the child's self-interest in the narrow sense of keeping alive and healthy and promoting the capacity to formulate and pursue life-goals.[74] If self-interest were to be defined much more widely, it becomes harder to reconcile removing control over decision-making from a competent child with recognizing the child as a right-holder.

Similarly, where parents separate, allocation of the child is often effected on the basis of the "best interests" of the child concerned, and this may be defended on a rights basis as representing the outcome the child would have wanted. But too often the "best interests" formulation has represented *a priori* conceptions of *what adults deem a good outcome for the child to be*, rather than a sensitive appraisal of what the child in question *actually wants* or, taking into account the family dynamics and social context, it can be deemed likely later to have wanted. The mechanical rule of thumb now widely advocated in the United States, the "primary caretaker" presumption, similarly sidelines the child's perspective by presuming an optimal outcome follows from continuation of the dominant pattern of interaction and being in any case primarily designed to reduce litigation.[75] An approach more sensitively attuned to a child's claims would surely

73 *re R. (A Minor) (Wardship: Medical Treatment)* [1992] Fam. 11; *re W. (A Minor) (Medical Treatment: Court's Jurisdiction)* [1992] 3 W.L.R. 758.

74 For a discussion of competence of children, see John Eekelaar, "The Best Interests of the Child and Children's Wishes the Role of Dynamic Self-Determinism" *International Journal of Law & the Family*, 8, 1994.

75 See Bruce Ziff, "The Primary Caretaker Presumption: Canadian Perspectives on an American Development" *International Journal of Law & the Family* 4, 1990, 186; Marygold S. Melli, "Toward a Restructuring of Custody Decision-making at Divorce: An Alternative Approach to the Best Interests of the Child", ch. 22 in Eekelaar and Sarcevic, n.22 above; see Sanford N. Katz, "'That they may Thrive' Goal of Child Custody: Reflections on the apparent Erosion of the Tender Years Presumption and the Emergence of the Primary Caretaker Presumption" *Journal of Contemporary Health Law & Policy* 8, 1992, 123.

privilege an outcome which retained the child's most satisfying personal relationships (perhaps allowing, as a *subsidiary* aid, a presumption that these are likely to be with the individual with which the child has most frequent contact, at least at certain ages). In many cases a rights approach will yield no clear solution: the child may wish to be with both parents, or its relationships with each parent may be equally fruitful. These outcomes may not be achievable, but it does nevertheless provide a foundation upon which compromise solutions may be explored.

(e) Should Parents be under a Duty to Exercise Social Parenthood?

I have referred to the right of parents to establish social parenthood as a foundational social rule, which can be taken in most cases to coincide with the child's rights. But should it be a duty rather than a right? The Scottish Law Commission has recommended that a parent should have a statutory responsibility to his or her child, insofar as is practicable and in the interests of the child, to "safeguard and promote the child's health, development and welfare"; to "provide, in a manner appropriate to the stage of development of the child, direction and guidance to the child"; "if the child is not living with the parent, to maintain personal relations and direct contact with the child on a regular basis"; and "to act as the child's legal representative".[76] These responsibilities constitute the main elements of social parenthood.

Such provisions may be grounded in a concept of children's rights, for it is plausible that children would wish their legal parents to act as their social parents too. But they cannot be more than an aspirational statements. To be more would bring these claims into conflict with parental claims to autonomy: to have the right to leave home and lose contact with their children. The social cost of denying this right, even to the detriment of children, is too great. There is no practicable way of preventing a parent withdrawing. This is just one example of the hard fact that not all claims can be translated into legal rights. Hence the relevant enforceable rights in relation to social parenthood are those of the parents, and, indeed, the Scottish Law Commission sees parental rights as existing "in order to enable them to fulfil their parental responsibilities".

Conclusion

From the mists of time, human society has constructed elaborate social practices around the "natural" process of reproduction. This has been necessary in order to maintain social cohesion in the face of the potentially explosive nature of sexual behaviour[77] and the importance of social reproduction. There is nothing "natural" about courtship rituals, family and kinship structures or of marriage itself. The social and legal conception of parenthood forms part of these constructs. The employment of

76 See Scottish Law Commission, *Report on Family Law*, Scot. Law Com No. 135 (Edinburgh, HMSO, 1992): clause 1 of Draft Bill.

77 See Norbert Rouland, "Cultural Dimensions of Kinship", ch. 1 in Eekelaar and Sarcevic (eds) n.22 above.

concepts of rights is only one way of representing, and devising a critique of, such constructs. The process allows a set of social institutions to be scrutinised in the light of a powerful social idea. The people living within them will lead their lives in accordance with the practical and moral norms which guide every-day action.

Brenda Almond

Parenthood - social construct or fact of nature?

'There is nothing „natural" about courtship rituals, family and kinship structures or of marriage itself. The attribution of parenthood and child-rearing are part of these constructs.'
[J. Eekelaar 'Parenthood, Social Engineering and Rights'][1]

John Eekelaar's striking conclusion is remarkable in view of the history of family bonds in the story of the human race. It may well seem equally remarkable to anyone who has had direct experience of parenting and, in particular, of giving birth. These are purely contingent considerations, of course, but it must at the outset be conceded that philosophy alone is unable to provide a challenge to Eekelaar's claims, and that any challenge must involve at least some reference to the kind of facts that social anthropology and related disciplines can provide, as well as, perhaps, to some introspective reflection on one's own experience as child, parent, spouse or other kin relation.

It is clear, however, that very different assumptions have guided human thinking on these matters in the past. Some indication of this is to be found in literature, legend and folk-lore. In particular, there are those stories and traditions which centre on what might be called the Cinderella experience. In the familiar version, the not-biologically-related child is used and abused by step parent and step-siblings alike. Similar stories abound of wicked stepmothers – or fathers – as well as the more intangible but ubiquitous myth of the changeling. It is worth asking, what is the point of this myth? What *is* a changeling? The answer must be that it is someone who lives in an intimate situation with those who are, biologically-speaking, strangers or – from the other point of view, a stranger who invades a situation of close intimacy. Without any knowledge of the science of genetics, those who framed these stories had in mind a scarcely tangible web of connections and expectations – a sense or expectation that the absence of the biological link would mean an absence of what might be called psychic similarity: shared attitudes, appraisals, interests, tendencies; common qualities of character, a common *Weltanschauung* – a characteristic way of looking at the world. Of course, we all know that none of these things can be assumed, even where relationships are indisputable, but total breakdown or absence of common sympathies is regarded as extraordinary, and provides the stuff of tragedy and disillusion.

It is interesting to contrast the position Eekelaar defends with that put forward by Hegel in *The Philosophy of Right*:

> In substance marriage is a unity, though only a unity of inwardness or disposition; in outward existence, however, the unity is sundered in two parties. It is only in the children that the unity itself exists externally, objectively, and explicitly as a unity, because the parents love the children as their love, as the embodiment of their own substance ... a process which runs away into the infinite series of generations, each producing the next and presupposing the one before.[2]

1 Eekelaar, J. 'Parenthood, Social Engineering and Rights' p. 80.

2 Hegel (Part III, Subsection 1 C.173) *The Philosophy of Right*, trans. T. M. Knox (Oxford: Clarendon Press, 1952), p. 117.

The contrast between natural and artificial, biological and social, is starkly presented in these two different approaches. One explanation for Eekelaar's emphasis on the social, is that some relationships are indeed of the type he describes – that is to say, relationships by marriage. But even at the level of popular culture, there is recognition of the existence of relationships which are not merely social alongside those which are, and the responses these evoke are commonly quite different in quality. One may compare, for example, popular attitudes to mothers with those to mothers-in-law. Many societies, then, including both primitive cultures and complex modern ones, distinguish socially-created relationships from blood-relationships, seeing the latter as special and immutable.

In contrast, Eekelaar sees only one side of the matter, the double-sidedness of which is well described by Marilyn Strathern, an anthropologist with a particular interest in kinship networks:

> 'Family life', Strathern writes, 'is held to be based on two separable but overlapping principles. On the one hand lies the social character of particular arrangements. Household composition, the extensiveness of kin networks, the conventions of marriage – these are socially variable. On the other lie the natural facts of life. Birth and procreation, the inheritance of genetic material, the developmental stages through which a child progresses – these are naturally immutable.'[3]

One might add – although this is part of what is at issue here – even the changes made possible by new technologies cannot negate the essential *naturalness* of conception, pregnancy and childbirth, the relationships they create and those on which they depend. So why does Eekelaar think otherwise? Why does he deny what to many people will seem obvious – the deep importance of human kin connections?

Eekelaar's views, it would seem, rest on a double foundation. The first is his view of the role of law; the second, his view of the role of society in relation to the duty of care of the young. I will discuss his argument in relation to these two foundational points, before going on to say a little about the specific cases which he uses to illustrate his views.

The role of law

Eekelaar sees law as active, not a passive by-product of social change – as leading, not following, social convention. In this he follows the legal historian Roscoe Pound in rejecting the Hegelian thesis – later developed into a new and more general theory of law, ideology and society by Karl Marx – that law is a reflection of social progress and development.[4] From the point of view of moral philosophy, this theory could be said to run parallel to the emotive theory of ethics, which, in similar way, portrays *moral* language as dynamic rather than descriptive, as seeking to influence others rather than to inform them – as attempting to evoke action and alter attitudes. The term used by Pound to describe this dynamic or active function of law was 'social engineering' – a

3 Strathern, M. *Reproducing the Future: anthropology, kinship and the new reproductive technologies*, (Manchester: Manchester University Press 1992) p. 17.

4 Pound, R. *Interpretations of Legal History* (Cambridge: Cambridge University Press, 1923), pp. 151–2 cited by Eekelaar, *op. cit.* p. 4.

term which, as Eekelaar points out, is often used pejoratively today, although Karl Popper, in *The Poverty of Historicism*, used it with favourable overtones.[5] Popper's sympathetic perception, however, was based on a conception of social engineering as small-scale and limited in scope, and he chose it in order to point a contrast between the humdrum and unambitious goals of the engineer – a kind of social repairman – and the Utopian architectural blue-prints of totalitarianism. I suspect Popper would see attempts to change the natural structure and basis of the family by means of a pincer attack from medicine and law as having more in common with the latter than the former.

Eekelaar supports his general perception that law does in fact lead rather than follow in these areas by appeal to the legal ruling that a husband is presumed to be the father of a child, when it is born to a woman living in a marital relationship with him. (*Pater ist quem nuptiae demonstrant*). He speculates as to the reasons for this, in part interpreting historical attitudes by appeal to recent developments, for example, new legislation concerning surrogacy, and the recent refusal by a judge to allow DNA 'finger-printing' for purposes of establishing paternity. (It should not be overlooked, however, that it has become a well-established procedure in cases involving immigration applications). He concludes that these recent judgements, like the rules that have prevailed in the past, are to be understood as expressing the primacy of social over biological parenthood. Their implication is, he says, that parenthood is "socially engineered."[6]

This is to overlook, however, an important, indeed crucial, point as far as an appeal to past practice is concerned – that the capacity to establish parenthood reliably through DNA fingerprinting is an entirely new development which was quite simply not available to earlier generations. Previously unconceived-of possibilities now exist – take, for example, the remarkable capability of establishing the identities of bodies thought to be those of the Russian Tsar and his family by comparing the DNA to that of known descendants of the family. Indeed, in view of such possibilities, it could well be argued that both the recent legislation, (e.g., Section 30 of the Human Fertilisation and Embryology Act 1990) and the decision of the judge in the case cited, are actually ill-conceived. Whatever view one takes of the new legislation, however, it would be foolish to overlook the fact that the older approach to confirming paternity would of necessity have been based on pragmatic rather than theoretic considerations. In earlier times, conclusively establishing paternity would have been, in most circumstances, an impossible task – except, of course, in those cases that the law indeed recognised, in which the husband was physically apart from his wife for the relevant period. For clearly, under normal circumstances, the only way for a woman to be sure of the fatherhood of her baby would have been to have intercourse with only one man during her menstrual cycle. The law – or any outsider – would be obliged to assume that she *might* have had intercourse during this period with her husband, so there could be no *better* founded claim than his, even if there was evidence of a concurrent adulterous liaison. But to suggest that what must be legally presumed is the whole of the story would be to deny commonsense, which even in the past was prepared to cast a glance, whether jaundiced or ribald, at striking physical resemblances of children to persons

5 Popper, K. *The Poverty of Historicism* (London, Routledge, 1945).
6 Eekelaar, *op. cit.* p. 5.

outside the family circle. A legal convenience does not, then, require one to interpret the facts in such a way as to see the case of human procreation as totally distinct from reproduction in livestock or plants – a rose is a rose, not the alien stock on which it is grafted.

So while Eekelaar is no doubt right to suggest that law is not inevitably to be seen as merely following, or describing social convention, there are limits to its scope for creativity – for moulding the relationships between people by *flat*. Indeed, it is often the other way round. As Marilyn Strathern points out, the very notion of a parent in Western though evokes the idea of a social relationship. Moreover, such a conception of kinship has implicit within it an expectation of a closeness of understanding and empathy, a 'crisscrossing network of similarities' of character (to lift a metaphor of Wittgenstein's out of context), and an expectation of service and sacrifice which is, more often than not, actually forthcoming. It is these natural tendencies and inclinations, on the whole, that have provided the signposts which have supplied a direction for law to follow over its long evolution.

This is to place a considerable weight on kin relationships, but it is hardly surprising that humans should attach importance to these – particularly the parent-child relationship – when other species defend their young to the death and when, as has been claimed, event the organically simple tadpole is able to recognise differentially siblings, half-siblings and unrelated individuals. But evidence from the animal kingdom is not essential to this case. The Greeks, whose literature and philosophy has exercised so much influence over modern thought, saw blood relationships, particularly those between parents and child, brother and sister, as absolute and as morally exigent. It is interesting to note that the Oedipus story would lose its point, its sting, if social relations were regarded as primary – the whole point of that story is that social relationships were being impeccably played out amongst people whose biological relationship made this wholly inappropriate. To kill a father – even one you have never met before – was in inexpiable crime, as it was to violate a mother, even one who had never known or nursed her child.

Eekelaar, however, in a kind of modern updating of these Oedipal possibilities conceives of a case in which biological, legal and responsible (or caring) fatherhood are separated. He is concerned about an actual case, *re O*, in which biological fatherhood was preferred over social parenthood.[7] In his own hypothetical case, the biological father, A is an anonymous sperm-donor playing no further role; the legal father, B, is the man with whom the mother was living at the time of the birth, but from whom she has separated, and the responsible father, C, is the mother's new husband who has been granted parental responsibility. For Eekelaar, the significant person in this situation is C. Parental right and responsibilities should go to him for: 'Parental responsibility should always be associated with the exercise of social parenthood.'[8] He argues, therefore, that the Children Act 1989 is wrong in its underlying presumption that biological parents have responsibility for their children, and in its attempt to attach social and legal responsibility to biological parenthood.

7 1 FLR 77, cited in Eekelaar, p. 1.
8 Eekelaar, *op. cit.* p. 10

Eekelaar's view, in contrast, amounts to an assertion that biological parenthood is in itself negligible. But if this is what is being claimed, it has wide implications. To begin with, it involves endorsing a common but simplistic view of artificial insemination by a donor as a simple *medical* procedure. And secondly, it involves seeing as unproblematic developments in *in vitro* fertilisation which have led to the detachment of motherhood, too, from its biological meaning. Initially, the transfer of an egg from a willing donor to a woman desperately wanting to bear and raise a child may seem to raise few ethical difficulties, but technological possibilities do not stay tidily within the bounds of this relatively uncontroversial scenario. Instead, they open up a 'slippery slope' of devastating potential. Examples are not hard to find: the possibility of harvesting viable eggs from a foetus means that an aborted foetus could now be a genetic mother; eggs taken from women in their twenties have been successfully implanted and brought to term by women in their late fifties; while developments in intensive care have made possible the gestation and delivery of a baby to a dead woman whose womb and reproductive system have been kept artificially functioning. To regard any of these developments as of purely practical importance is to ignore the possibility of psychological and emotional effects as yet unknown. At a minimum, one might say, that to be born under such circumstances would indeed be to be an orphan in a sense previously unknown to human beings. It would be to be born already an exile from the kinship network.

These considerations suggest, then, that one should pause and look very carefully at what might be called the 'hard-headed' assumption that gametes are detachable, that genetic relations are negligible. Initially, this is to rely on an intuitive response, a sense of ethical affront – perhaps, even, as Mary Warnock described it, a feeling of 'outrage'.[9] But it is not hard to find practical arguments to lend weight to these reactions. To begin with, the consent of the donors, particularly of the young women who donated their eggs, or gave permission for use to be made of a foetus may well have been secured on quite different tacit assumptions about the destiny of those eggs or the use of the foetus. In view of the breadth of possibilities, therefore, there is a case for interpreting 'informed consent', quite strictly in this area. But secondly, the 'hard-headed' approach may be based on some unrecognised factual assumptions about the quality of care that can be relied on where purely social connections are involved. Indeed, I would suggest that there is a need for a new judgment of Solomon here. In the biblical tale, Solomon recognised that the true – i.e., the biological – mother, would prefer even to sacrifice her own rights and her relationship with the child if that was necessary to preserve the child's life, and that it was *for this very reason* that her rights and relationship should be preserved. I would suggest that things are not intrinsically different today, if one considers, for example, recent abuse cases connected with children's homes to which children have been taken, often on the grounds that this is necessary to protect them from possible abuse by their natural parents. Who can be trusted with children? Clearly parents cannot always be, and children must sometimes be removed from their care, but it is far from self-evident that other carers are less fallible.

9 Warnock, M. '*Do Human Cells have Rights?*' *Bioethics*, 1, 1987, pp. 1–14. She also defends the role of intuitive sentiment in 'The Artificial Family' in *Moral Dilemmas and Modern Medicine* ed. M. Lockwood (Oxford: Oxford University Press, 1985).

Role of society – the duty of care

But for Eekelaar, the problem is compounded by the fact that he does not attribute to the parent even a direct duty to care. Instead, he sees the responsibility for looking after children as falling on the state, or society in general. Everyone, he says, has a general obligation to 'promote human flourishing', and a specific obligation derived from that to care for the newborn. He concedes, however, that society may best fulfil this obligation by imposing a duty of care on biological parents. Thus, a natural duty is neatly inverted in Eekelaar's argument, to become a derivative social or indeed legal duty, rather than a primary ethical one. The immediate consequence of this is that society might well fulfil its duties in a number of different ways, any of which would be equally morally acceptable. These would include various kinds of social parenting.

For comment on this, we must once again turn to social anthropology. Eekelaar seems to be overly influenced by the fact that different societies may deal with the problem of child-care in different ways. For example, Eekelaar would probably find useful support in the fact that in some tribes a woman's brother is responsible for a child, not its natural father. Nevertheless, while variation in social arrangements is possible, and while, of course, there have even been societies ignorant of the connection between sexual intercourse and child-bearing, the idea of a blood-tie has on the whole been the idea of something immutable and non-negotiable. As I have commented elsewhere: 'A person's "sisters, cousins and aunts" – narrow-minded uncles, bad-tempered brothers or handicapped son or daughter – are part of the baggage of life.'[10]

Nor is it only the parent-child relationship that is involved. For where there are 'real', i.e., blood relationships, these have wider implications – something that Eekelaar's discussion, which remains narrowly focussed on parents and children, completely ignores. These connections are not isolated facts and their social relevance spreads out in a widening circle. Strathern writes: "In many cultures of the world, a child is thought to embody the relationship between its parents and the relationships its parents have with other kin."[11] She adds, 'Until now, it has been part of most of the indigenous cultural repertoires in Europe to see the domain of kinship, and what is called its biological base in procreation, as an area of relationships that provided a given baseline to human existence'[12] and 'It is an extraordinarily impoverished view of culture to imagine that how we conceive of parents and children only affects parents and children.'[13]

This was so widely taken for granted until recently that it came as a surprising discovery to our legislators a few years ago that grandparents had no status in British law. And yet, with the ubiquitous breakdown of marriages and *de facto* partnerships, it is to be expected that contingent relationships could assume greater rather than lesser

10 Almond, B. 'Human Bonds' *Journal of Applied Philosophy*, 5, 1988, pp. 3–16 rep. in Almond, B. & Hill, D. *Applied Philosophy: morals and metaphysics in contemporary debate* (London, Routledge, 1992), p. 61.

11 Strathern, *op. cit.* p. 31.

12 *ibid.* p. 34.

13 *ibid.* p. 33.

importance.

It is worth noticing, too, that social work practice and local authority provision in the past – together with 'community care' today – work on quite the opposite assumptions from those implied by the 'social construction' view. While certain philosophers promote the view that advanced reproductive medical techniques are to be welcomed as expanding choice – making it possible for any kind of relationship to be created or abandoned at will – social workers are routinely required to seek 'real' relatives and attempt to convince them of their moral and social obligation to change the whole pattern of their lives to accommodate sick, senile or disabled kin. And, of course, descent and lineage continue to be regarded as of crucial legal importance as long as inheritance is considered a just way of passing on wealth.

Eekelaar, in contrast, seems to see the primary family relation as confined within the duality of parent and child. He does, however, recognise that certain moral and legal concepts have a part to play in this relationship. Whilst rejecting any conception of rights as independent entities and describing them as 'intellectual constructs', he nevertheless recognises a complex of rights and reciprocal obligations involved in the parent-child relationship. In particular, he argues that children have rights, in the sense of what they 'when fully informed and mature, would be likely to have chosen.'[14] He distinguishes recognition of these rights from welfarism, which he defines as basing arrangements on some external judgement as to what is in the child's best interest.

I will not discuss Eekelaar's theoretical view of rights, since the central issues here do not depend on agreement on their analysis. I do, however, agree with him in dismissing the view – if anyone were to hold it – that morality can be based entirely on rights without appeal to other moral concepts. I agree, too, that it is not necessary to invoke children's rights in order to talk about parental duties. And thirdly, I endorse Eekelaar's insistence that the attribution of a right is not to be confused with someone else's judgement of one's interest. It is not for the football pools promoter, for example, to judge whether a prize-winner's life is likely to be ruined by his sudden access of wealth before deciding whether to award the prize. But I would also separate it from a person's *own* judgement of interest, noticing too, that there is a distinction to be drawn between what one wants, or would choose, and what actually *is* a benefit. So I would maintain that one can have a right to what is *not* in one's interest, and not a benefit. But of course it is true that one will only *claim* what one, at least in some sense, wants. (Though some people are perverse enough to claim or want something *only* because they conceive of it as their right and not because they have some independent reason for desiring it.)

Applying this to the case of a child in relation to a parent, I would go beyond Eekelaar in holding that there is a residual notion of a right not covered by the child's interest, benefit or even choice. I therefore agree that it is wrong to base judicial decisions concerning a child's care simply on the child's best interest as judged by a third party. To do this is, in any case, to ignore the question of *parental* rights. Eekelaar does concede something to the notion of parental rights, but sees them as qualified and provisional. I would argue, on the other hand, that parents have important and substantial rights, and that these are grounded in their duty to care for their children. This I suggest,

14 Eekelaar, *op. cit.* p. 13.

follows from the Kantian principle that 'ought' implies 'can'. In other words, society would be inconsistent to declare that there is a parental duty of care without conceding a parental right to do so. Unlike Eekelaar, but in common with the thinking he sees as underlying the Children Act, I believe that parents have a direct moral obligation to care for their children. If society does not permit them to care for their children, it prevents them from fulfilling that duty and thus violates their rights. A British judge, Lord Fraser, put the point like this: 'From the parents' right and duty of custody flows their right and duty of control of the child.'[15]

Other arguments may, however, be advanced for the priority of parental rights. Not without weight is the quasi-biological argument derived from Hobbes that there is at least some attenuated concept of ownership of children that is analogous to people's ownership of their own body.[16] Recognition of this claim can only be intuitive, for it can hardly be grounded on any extraneous considerations. Nevertheless, the biological argument need not stand alone. For it may be ranged alongside an argument of a political nature relating to the conditions necessary for cultural and religious freedom. Conceding parental rights, it can be argued, is the best and most effective way to limit the power of the state over the individual. Totalitarian projects, both philosophical and actual, have tended to encroach upon and limit parental control and family influence, while even under liberal regimes, where benign motives may be presumed, there is a continuing danger of the state usurping prerogatives.

Ferdinand Schoeman has added a moral argument to this essentially political one: that the right of parents to exercise power over their children is based on their own justifiable moral claim to a certain kind of intimate relationship. He writes: 'Why should the family be given extensive responsibilities for the development of children? Why should the biological parent be thought entitled to be in charge of a family? I believe that the notion of intimacy supplies the basis for these presumptions.'[17] Schoeman's argument, then, is that close human relationships require as their setting privacy and autonomy, and that a parent's right to this type of private relationship overrides even some limited cost to the child.

None of this is, of course, inconsistent with recognising the need for outsiders, or the state, to intervene in some extreme situations and it has to be admitted that some situations make a choice unavoidable. In situations which involve a conflict between adults' and children's wishes, Eekelaar proposes a solution based on recognising changing priorities at different stages. The question of who *initiates* social care, he suggests, may be settled differently from decisions about later arrangements, when he proposes that the child's own wishes should play a part.

There are, however, difficulties with both halves of this strategy. First, where an early choice by others is concerned, what of the wish a child might retrospectively have for its own (genetic) mother or father? Eekelaar's position seems to involve permitting early decisions which would in fact deprive the child of this, which may indeed later

15 *Gillick* [1985] 3 All ER 402.

16 See T. Hobbes, *Leviathan*, ch. 20. I have discussed this and the following points at greater length in 'Education and Liberty; public provision and private choice' *Journal of Philosophy of Education*, 25, 1991, pp. 193–202.

17 Schoeman, F. 'Rights of children, rights of parents, and the moral basis of the family' *Ethics*, 91, 1980, pp. 6–19, p. 14.

come to be seen by the child as the only and important option. Admittedly he says it should always be possible to establish legal parenthood, but he deprives this of all its natural 'care and contact' implications. As for the later choice, in which he recommends that the child should play a part, perhaps even being permitted to choose a new social family – something that has recently happened in the USA – it is unlikely that this could provide a stable base that lasts for life, generating responsibilities as well as benefits. What, one wonders, might become of the traditional network of expectations of kin – support later in life, particularly where there are adverse changes in circumstances? Would the 'chooser' child when adult accept a member of his or her 'socially chosen' family for expensive or self-sacrificing care? Would the socially chosen family, conversely, accept a child 'chooser' back to their care if adult life brings that child disability or hardship?

The inclination to answer 'no' to these questions is based on a perfectly sound and rational conception of the notion of choice. A 'chooser' on the whole, wants only what is pleasant and rewarding – that is the whole point of choice. But life, on the other hand, is a mosaic of darker and lighter patterns. And 'chooser' children are unlikely to volunteer for what is not personally satisfying. Indeed, there is a chance that the children Eekelaar has in mind will be unwilling to care for their elders even through social and community measures, whether taxes or charitable contributions – for they are apparently to be encouraged in 'individual assertiveness and self-discovery' rather than in care for others and the sacrifice of self.[18] Nor is the loss entirely on one side. For children, too, there is the loss involved in losing the possibility of a relationship with someone for whom their whole 'narrative' is familiar – those irreplaceable persons who have known them all their lives.

These are very general considerations. Their application may become clearer when set in the context of some of the practical issues touched on in the course of this discussion:

(i) Right to be informed of biological parenthood

In Sweden a child born by AID has a right (at 18) to know the identity of the semen donor, but the latter has no rights of legal paternity. In this country, as Eekelaar says, officially recognised agencies accepting sperm from donors must record their identities, but, as things currently stand, this is to be kept confidential, even from the child. He concedes nevertheless, that 'These men are fathers' though not legally recognised as such. My own view is that such donors should recognise that they are indeed fathering children, and that children should be guaranteed access to information about them. This said, it has, of course, to be recognised that the procedures involved are simple and in the end impossible to regularise or police. People might, however, be less willing to assist with 'irregular' donation if aware that this might have legal implications.

The issue of fatherhood, however, may seem straightforward when compared with the new complexities involved in the notion of motherhood. Sections 27 and 28 of the British Act defined mother as the 'carrier' of a child (whether or not that child is

18 Eekelaar, *op. cit.*

genetically hers. However, under Section 30, a woman who carries (gestates) a child but hands it over to a couple as a result of a surrogacy agreement, ceases to be the legal mother, just as in the case of adoption. This ambiguity is hard to resolve practically. In attempting to assess the relative claims of a genetic and a gestatory mother, I see the force of Raimond Gaita's view that it is inconceivable that a child conceived *in vitro* would have the same interest in seeking out his or her natural parent as one conceived in the ordinary way.[19] Nevertheless, I suspect that even in these circumstances the genetic connection might continue to exert some fascination – at a minimum, a kind of curiosity which has as its focus deep questions of personal identity. This unavoidable conflict between the claims of the genetic and the child-bearing mother should alert us to the unprecedented severing of links that may be a consequence of using such procedures. Eekelaar urges that biological parenthood should now be legally recognised in all cases, and I would support this as being an important step forward. On its own, however, the proposal is, I would suggest, too limited, for the 'legality' that Eekelaar recommends is empty and insubstantial.

(ii) Whose responsibility is to care for children?

Eekelaar asks: "Are parents morally obliged to care for their children?"

In general, he argues that parental responsibility should be associated with the exercise of social parenthood. It should also, he suggests, be extended to long-term cohabitees and step-parents. But he warns against giving long-term weight to the early claims of the mother. In particular, he strongly criticises the USA 'primary caretaker' presumption, for in the long run, he points out, the father's claims might deserve priority, as the child's preference changes with time. This is a useful warning; indeed, it could even be argued that modern European and N. American societies are moving towards matriarchy as a result of insensitive taxation policies which make little or no allowance for family responsibilities, and social provision which may actually be unintentionally destructive of family life – for the more provision is made for single parents, the less need there is for partnership between the sexes. A single mother in a recent interview remarked 'If it weren't for the help I get from my mother and grandmother, I don't know what I'd do.' – a remark that was revealing, in that it pointed to a demographic shift in the source of reliable support. It uncovers a situation that research might well show to be far more common than is generally acknowledged.

Conclusions

Variations in the traditional family are not unique to modern times. In particular, step-parents and step-siblings are no new phenomenon, although the reasons for their existence have changed. In the past women's high mortality, particularly in relation to childbirth, was the cause of remarriages and new relationships, while today the cause is more commonly divorce and remarriage, the breakdown of relationships, and an

19 Gaita, R. 'Parental rights and responsibilities' *Quadrant*, Sep. 1991, p. 42.

emerging but socially and emotionally unsatisfying pattern of 'serial monogamy'. It is worth noticing in relation to the contemporary situation that, for children, parental mortality would almost certainly have been a more acceptable reason for their own step-status than adults' choices, since these can be seen as a betrayal in a way in which a premature and undesired death is not. It is not surprising, then, if in some cases today's restructural families generate hostility within the home. This hostility may well be responsible for a variety of social ills, including teenage homelessness, truancy and youth crime; it may sometimes be connected, too, with abuse, particularly sexual abuse by an unrelated adult living in close domestic proximity to a sexually pubescent child.

In *Fertility and the Family*, Jonathan Glover recommends 'letting the future shape of the family evolve experimentally' – taking 'control of our own reproductive processes'.[20] But this is, I would suggest, a dangerous doctrine. Family bonds are the cement of social existence and are not subject to structuring and restructuring by something as fragile and volatile as individual choice.

I am, admittedly inconsequentially, reminded of the fact that 'Caesar divided Gaul into three parts'. We appear to be doing something of the same sort with parenthood, for I note that, in Eekelaar's paper, it has suffered three tripartite divisions. The first is the triple division of fatherhood – biological, legal and social; the second the tripartite notion of motherhood, as genetic, gestatory (or birthing) and commissioning. The third is the threefold division of parenthood itself: biological parenthood, legal parenthood, and the holding of parental responsibility.

This is, I believe, a dangerous process of fractionalisation, and I should like to suggest that developments in the area of reproductive medicine should not be endorsed by either law or social acceptance until some body of limited experience has been built up as a guide to the overall social implications. In these matters, in other words, it is foolish to rush in where even angels are justified in displaying a cautious conservatism.

20 Glover, J. and others, *Fertility and the Family* (London, Fourth Estate1989, p. 35).

Kenneth McK. Norrie

Medical Treatment of Children and Young Persons

Abstract

Since the *Gillick* decision the English courts have taken a different path from Scottish legislation in relation to medical treatment of children and young persons, but in both jurisdictions problems remain in balancing the various interests of the child, parent, family, state, and society. This paper examines the weight to be given to these different interests, attempts to explain the divergence between Scots and English law, and suggests that English law does not pay enough regard to the evolving autonomy of the young person below the age of 18.

Introduction

In examining the law's attitudes towards children and young persons, there is no better area of study than medical treatment. This is so for a number of reasons. First and most practically, the issue has generated a good deal of case law, including one of the most important family law decisions in recent years1. Secondly the important issues, such as the rights of the child, the responsibilities and rights of the parent, autonomy of the individual, the nature of the family, and the role and position of the state, all arise with unique sharpness. Thirdly, the resolution of the issues in relation to medical treatment is representative of the approach the courts are likely to take in other areas relating to the child, the family and the state and can therefore tell us much about the current position of children in the family and in society at large.

The *Gillick* Case

The starting point for any legal discussion of medical treatment of children and young persons has to be the decision of the House of Lords in *Gillick v. West Norfolk & Wisbech Area Health Authority*[2]. The legal point at issue in the *Gillick* case was relatively precise, being the question of whether it was lawful or not for a doctor to provide contraceptive or abortion advice or treatment to a girl under the age of 16 without the consent of her parent. As is well known, a bare majority of three to two in the House of Lords answered that question affirmatively, and thereby sanctioned the provision of all forms of medical treatment to *some* children on the basis of their own consent. However, the test to be applied in deciding which child or young person can determine her or his own medical treatment is by no means clear, because there is a stark dichotomy in the approaches taken by the majority judges[3].

1 *Gillick v. West Norfolk & Wisbech Area Health Authority* [1985] 3 All ER 402.

2 *Ibid.*

3 The differences between the judgments are more fully explained in Norrie, "*Gillick* Again: The House of Lords Decides" SLT (News) 1986, 69.

Lord Fraser pointed out that the case had a wider applicability than the precise issue involving contraceptive and abortion advice or treatment, and that, whatever the case decided in relation to these things, the principles had to be applied to all forms of medical procedure. The other majority judges did not disagree[4]. Lord Fraser went on to lay down a fairly extensive list of ethical and legal criteria that should guide the doctor; the focus of this paper is on the legal criteria only. Put simply, Lord Fraser held that a child under 16 could consent to medical treatment so long as she or he understood the nature and consequences of the proposed treatment. But he further held that the parental "right"[5] to determine the child's lifestyle survived the child's acquisition of capacity to consent, with the result that in a case of dispute between the parent and the child such dispute was to be resolved by having regard to the child's best interests (because parental "rights" are to be exercised in accordance with the child's best interests). In other words, in order for a child to be able to determine her or his own medical treatment the child must satisfy two tests: the mature understanding test, and the best interests test. The child must have a mature understanding of the nature and consequences of the proposed treatment, and the treatment itself must be in the best interests of the child.

Lord Scarman on the other hand took a fundamentally different approach, because he considered that the existence of parental rights has no bearing at all on the child's capacity to consent. He held that once the child acquires legal capacity to consent, any parental right to determine the child's medical treatment "yields"[6] to the child's right to make her or his own decision, and "terminates"[7] if and when the child achieves a sufficient understanding and intelligence to be able to give personal consent. Consequently, once the child has satisfied the maturity condition, there is nothing more that can be demanded of the child. In other words, in order for a child to be able to determine its own medical treatment the child must satisfy only one test: that is the mature understanding test, and the fact that the proposed treatment is not in the child's best interests is as irrelevant as it is in determining an adult's capacity to consent.

It is to be noted that the *Gillick* judgments were directed to the question of when a child can consent to medical treatment, and none of the judges addressed himself to the question of the child's legal capacity to refuse medical treatment. Nor do the judgments draw any distinction between medical treatment and medical procedure. In any event the law has developed significantly since 1985, both in England and in Scotland. The case of course was English, and therefore has little constitutional authority in Scotland, but it is fairly certain (at least to my mind) that the *Gillick* decision reflected Scots law at the time[8]. Since 1985, however, the two jurisdictions have taken increasingly divergent paths.

4 Only Lord Templeman was in favour or treating contraception as special and in some – unspecified – way different from other medical procedures.

5 English law no longer statutorily talks of parental "rights" (Children Act 1989), and in any event, for reasons discussed in the text later, the term was never jurisprudentially accurate.

6 [1985] 3 All ER 402 at p. 422.

7 *Ibid.* at p. 423.

8 See Norrie, *op. cit.*

English Law Since *Gillick*

Except on the precise point at issue (relating to contraceptives for the under 16 year old) the *Gillick* ruling left English law in a state of great doubt, because of the different judicial approaches described above. That doubt lasted for some years. Recently however the Court of Appeal has given unequivocal guidance as to how it believes the *Gillick* case ought to be interpreted, and it has done so in two highly significant cases. The issue in both cases involved not the young person's capacity to consent, but rather her or his capacity to refuse medical treatment.

The first case is that of *Re R (A Minor) (Wardship: Medical Treatment)*[9]. This case involved a 15 year old girl suffering from a psychotic disorder. During what was regarded as a lucid period, she refused consent to certain proposed drug therapy that the doctors considered to be in her best interests. The question for the Court of Appeal was whether it had the power to authorise the doctors to provide the treatment in the absence of the girl's consent. With little regret the court answered that question affirmatively. Founding on the fact that the treatment was in the child's best interests, the Court of Appeal effectively adopted Lord Fraser's approach in *Gillick*. The girl could not prevent the treatment being given because, although she was *ex hypothesi* mature enough to understand, her decision did not satisfy the welfare test. Lord Scarman's speech in *Gillick* was explained away by the Master of the Rolls, Lord Donaldson, who drew what to my mind is an unconvincing distinction between the right to consent to medical treatment and the right to determine medical treatment, and he said that Lord Scarman was not holding that the parents lose their right to consent, but only their right to determine medical treatment when the child attains capacity to consent. This decision followed an earlier case in which a 15 year old Jehovah's Witness boy had refused consent to a blood transfusion, and the court had authorised the treatment on the basis of the child's best interests[10]. Now, legally it is possible to explain away these decisions by pointing to the fact that they were both wardship cases, and the wardship court is obliged to protect the interests of its wards. But that avoids what is, of course, the real question, being what interest – or right – does the court, representing the state, have in the unwanted welfare of its citizens? I shall return to that question shortly.

The second significant English case went one step further, not least because the child was not a ward of court. In *Re W (A Minor) (Medical Treatment)*[11] a 16 year old girl suffering from anorexia nervosa refused treatment that the doctors deemed necessary to preserve her life. The Court of Appeal authorised the treatment, notwithstanding that the girl had statutory capacity to consent to her own medical treatment under the Family Law Reform Act 1969[12]. Clearly it was easy to distinguish *Gillick* on its facts. The House of Lords were concerned with capacity to consent, not to refuse, as in *Re W*;

9 [1991] 4 All ER 177.
10 *Re E (A Minor)(Wardship: Medical Treatment)* [1993] 1 FLR 386.
11 [1992] 4 All ER 627.
12 Section 8(1).

the House of Lords were concerned with the power of the parent to determine a child's treatment, not the power of the court. But distinguishing *Gillick* does not in itself answer the question of whether the court could override a refusal of treatment, nor upon what basis it should if it could. The Court of Appeal held that it could override a refusal, and the basis was the best interests test as suggested by Lord Fraser. Again, the approach of Lord Scarman in *Gillick* was rejected, Lord Donaldson MR doubting whether Lord Scarman had really meant what he said.

The court in *Re W* overrode the girl's own wishes, and held that a court could protect a 16 year old from her own decisions, legally because the inherent powers of the court under its *parens patriae* jurisdiction are theoretically limitless, and practically because the court was unwilling to sit back and let a minor act in such a way as would lead to her own death. The stated justification for the decision was, once again, the child's best interests.

Now, both *Re R* and *Re W* might have been explained by the fact that in both cases there was clear doubt about the patients' mental capacity. In *Re R* the girl was suffering from a psychotic illness, and in *Re W* it was found in evidence that her eating disorder affected her mind and her attitudes. It would be dangerous for a court to hold that a willingness to die needlessly is indicative of mental incapacity, and to the Court of Appeal's credit it did not do so. The road to totalitarianism is paved with the belief that those who do not wish to conform are necessarily and by definition insane. But that leaves the decisions as authority for the view that English law will permit the overriding of the wishes of young persons who have sufficient understanding to come to a competent and rational view of what their own medical treatment should be. That in itself suggests that autonomy in medical decision-making is not achieved by a child who achieves the capacity for mature understanding before reaching the age of 18. But then Lord Fraser never thought that she or he did.

Scots Law Since *Gillick*

Scots law has taken an entirely different approach, which reflects the traditional freedom enjoyed by Scottish young persons, which has always been much greater than that enjoyed by English young persons[13]. Parental rights last in Scotland, basically, until the age of 16[14], and since 1991 children and young persons aged 16 or more have effectively had full legal capacity[15]. For the child below 16 there are a number of situations in which legal capacity is recognised including, importantly, consent to medical treatment. Section 2(4) of the Age of Legal Capacity (Sc) Act 1991 provides as follows:

13 Many factual examples could be given to illustrate this freedom and recognition of maturity, but perhaps two will suffice. First, it has long been a rule and is now contained in the Adoption (Scotland) Act 1978, s. 12(8), as amended by the Age of Legal Capacity (Scotland) Act 1991, s. 2(3), that an adoption order cannot be made in relation to a child who is 12 years of age or more unless with child consents thereto. There is no equivalent rule in the English Adoption Act 1976. Secondly, Scots law contains no rule requiring parental consent to the marriage of a 16 or 17 year old.

14 Law Reform (Parent and Child) (Scotland) Act 1986, s.8.

15 Age of Legal Capacity (Scotland) Act 1991, s. 1(1)(b).

"A person under the age of 16 years shall have legal capacity to consent on his own behalf to any surgical, medical or dental procedure or treatment where, in the opinion of a qualified medical practitioner attending him, he is capable of understanding the nature and possible consequences of the procedure or treatment".

There is only one test here, and that is the mature understanding test. The subsection applies to all treatment and procedures[16], and it does not require satisfaction of the "best interests" test. Indeed, the Scottish Law Commission[17] who drafted the legislation expressly rejected welfare as relevant, and adopted instead the approach of Lord Scarman in *Gillick*.

It would be pleasing to be able to say that Scots law has simply and elegantly legislated away all the problems faced by the English courts, while at the same time reflecting a view of children's rights that is both consistent with international obligations[18] and the traditional approach of Scots law[19]. Unfortunately, that is not true. The subsection quoted above leaves unanswered many of the questions raised by the English cases. For example, in its terms, s. 2(4) confers capacity to consent and says nothing about the capacity to refuse. In my view that really cannot make any difference, for I see capacity to consent and capacity to refuse as being essentially different aspects of the same thing – that is, capacity to determine one's own medical treatment. The English Court of Appeal do not see the issue in these terms, and has distinguished consent from refusal by analysing the doctor's need to obtain consent solely as a mechanism by which the doctor obtains her or his defence to an action for assault or trespass to the person. But that surely cannot be right. The effect of consent is indeed to provide a defence, but that is not its *purpose*. Its purpose is to protect the patient's right of choice, or as it might be put, the patient's autonomy. The only point in a doctor asking a patient to consent to proposed treatment is to give the patient the opportunity to say no, that is to refuse.

Another problem with the 1991 Act – and again the problem is familiar to the English lawyer – is that it fails to address the issue of the parent's rights. Under earlier legislation[20] a parent with parental rights[21] has the right to consent to or to refuse medical treatment until the child reaches the age of 16; the 1991 legislation allows some children the right to consent to (and, surely, to refuse) medical treatment before then. The Scottish Law Commission intend to deal with parental rights later, but until they do it cannot be said with certainty whether or not the parental right to consent or refuse survives the acquisition by the child of that right. I should like to think that, since

16 *Cf.* the English Family Law Reform Act 1969, s. 8(1), which is limited to "treatment".

17 Scot. Law Com. No 110, Report on the *Legal Capacity and Responsibility of Minors and Pupils*, 1987, at para 3.77, citing Lord Scarman's speech in *Gillick* and my own comments thereon in SLT (News) 1986, 69.

18 See the UN *Convention on the Rights of the Child* 28 I.L.M. 1448 (1989), art 12 (right to express views), art 13 (freedom of expression), art 14 (freedom of thought, conscience and religion), art 16 (right of privacy).

19 See generally Wilkinson & Norrie *The Law of Parent and Child in Scotland*, Greens, Edinburgh 1993.

20 Law Reform (Parent and Child) (Scotland) Act 1986, s. 2 and s. 8.

21 i.e. the mother in all cases and the father if he is married to the mother or has been granted parental rights by the court.

Lord Scarman's philosophy is so clearly behind the drafting of s. 2(4), his view that the parental right "yields" or "terminates" when the child acquires capacity will be the view that prevails in the Scottish courts.

Analysis

So, put simply, the law in England is following Lord Fraser, while the law in Scotland is following Lord Scarman. What does this tell us about the position of the child in Scotland and in England? In Scotland traditionally a child has been an individual free from the constraints of her or his parents from 12 or 14 respectively and latterly from age 16[22]. Scots law had no difficulty in accepting that even before the age of 16 children can act as free agents[23]. The right to give personal consent to medical treatment is a right that includes the right to determine one's own lifestyle, and this is so not only in relation to contraceptive and other family planning treatment, but also in relation to treatment determined by one's own religious beliefs. If a child of 15 in Scotland firmly believes that blood-transfusions are evil and she or he has the maturity to have come to that conclusion independently, then that child is free to adopt the lifestyle that entails, and is free to accept the consequences: I do not see how, legally, this can be prevented.

In England on the other hand children have always been subject to greater control, and for longer. A minor is a minor until the age of 18, and remains until then a sort of protected species (though the analogy of the listed building is probably better). A child has less freedom to determine her or his own lifestyle, and even the 16 or 17 year old is not free to adopt a religious or other lifestyle practice that is grudgingly accepted for adults. A person under 18 is free in England to do only that which does not go against her or his welfare, and is not free to determine matters relating to lifestyle or even to life itself. Other examples of differences between Scots and English law can be found. Section 8 of the English Family Law Reform Act 1969 gives 16 – 18 year olds power to consent only to medical treatment, not to medical procedures, and Lord Donaldson MR in *Re W* has said that organ or blood donations are not treatment[24]. The Scottish statute is drawn far more widely and allows those under 16 to consent to any procedure or treatment so long as the nature and consequences are understood. A 17 year old person in England cannot donate blood (without parental consent); a 14 year old child in Scotland might sometimes be able to donate a kidney.

What is English law trying to do? Or to put it another way, how can English law justify forcing treatment on an unwilling person who is mentally mature enough to make up her or his own mind? The case law has, perhaps unsurprisingly, used as its justification the best interests test. But that test would not be regarded as sufficient in relation to competent adults, where its use to overrule patients' decisions would be described as paternalistic, dogmatic, and totalitarian. Why is it not regarded so when dealing with children and young persons? The problem with case law is that decisions

22 Age of Legal Capacity (Scotland) Act 1991.
23 See for example Age of Legal Capacity (Scotland) Act 1991, s. 2(1).
24 [1992] 4 All ER 627 at p. 635.

are given within the context of a particular fact situation, which may not be capable of giving general rules. The *Gillick* case is a perfect example: the policy of the majority judges in that case is quite clear (indeed is the only thing all three agreed upon), that is the need to encourage sexually active girls under 16 to seek protection from pregnancy. That is a valid social policy, and one which only the naive or emotionally autistic would fail to support. But it is much more difficult to identify a valid policy when the state, through the courts, tries to impose its own views on people who do not accept them, either for rational but objectively unsound reasons (such as the Jehovah's Witness refusing blood transfusion) or for entirely irrational reasons (such as the anorexic wanting to starve herself).

There are a number of interests which the law tries to protect, but which may be in conflict, and *Re R* and *Re W* can really only be understood in terms of the judges' reactions to the tensions these conflicts create. The immediately identifiable interests – and there are doubtless others – are as follows.

First there is the principle of autonomy, or the right to self-determination. This is an interest that, with adults, the law goes out of its way to protect and indeed to enhance. But it is important to be aware of the consequences of autonomy. Certainly it allows us to determine how to lead our own lives, and to make decisions about ourselves, but there is no doubt that it is not an unlimited principle. However, definitional of the principle of autonomy is the right to do things which our friends, relatives, society, the state, and even ourselves may regard as contrary to our own best interests. Autonomy is about free choice and that necessarily includes the right to choose to do things harmful to ourselves, like smoking, or having frequent unprotected casual sexual intercourse, or refusing consent to lifesaving medical treatment. Our ability to choose to do these things is the litmus test of whether we live in a free or in a totalitarian state.

Of course in order not to infringe other people's autonomy our own autonomy is limited, and there are other interests which the law recognises, and which might be used to overrule personal decisions in cases like *Re R* and *Re W*. Parents for example have interests which the law recognises, and the move away from the language of rights to the language of responsibilities does not alter the fact that the law recognises a parent's power over her or his children, a power which can be exercised even when this is not in the interests of the child (e.g. the determination of the form of education the child is to receive, or the religious upbringing she or he is to be subjected to) or is even mildly detrimental (e.g. refusal to innoculate against disease, and consent to neonatal circumcision for non-therapeutic[25] reasons). The law will interfere in the exercise of parental power only when the parents disagree or when the child or someone else can prove that the exercise is positively harmful to a significant degree.

Another interest, or possibly duty, is the state's interest in the preservation of life. This may well be considered important in times of war when the state requires ablebodied men to kill on its behalf. Rather more plausibly any case that comes before the English court under the wardship jurisdiction must be decided on the basis of the best interests of the ward, for that is the constitutional extent of the wardship court's

25 Or even social?

powers. But sometimes death may be in the best interests of a person[26]. It might be noted here that Scots law has never regarded itself as the preserver of life at all costs, and there has never been an equivalent to the bizarre notion that suicide or attempted suicide is a criminal offence[27].

The notion of family autonomy is sometimes mooted as an interest that requires protection[28], and this seems to be based on the notion that an interest lies in the group of individuals whose lives are significantly affected by one's decisions. This, I think, lies behind the comments in the second part of John Haldane's response to this paper[29]. However, for the reasons spelt out clearly in Bob Brecher's paper "What is Wrong with the Family"[30], I find this an implausible – and dangerously loose – justification for limiting a young person's right to self-determination. Everyone's acts have consequences for other people.

I should like to suggest that there is really only one justification for overruling a young person's health care decisions, and that is the need for protection. No-one would deny that some individuals require protection, and the very young clearly come within that category. But we have to be very clear why the law grants its protection. With young children the law correctly allows others to make decisions on their behalf: this is correct because the child is unable to come to proper conclusions about how to lead its own life, and it is that inability, I submit, that justifies the state's interference.

But when the child attains the physical and mental ability to come to proper conclusions about how to lead her or his own life, the need for protection disappears, because we are protecting against the consequences of inability. A child who can understand is a child who does not need protection from lack of understanding. English law does not give effect to this conclusion, and it allows the protection of the law (or the prohibitions of the law) to interfere with a young person's personal liberties in ways that would be entirely unacceptable for adults.

How does it justify this? Well for one thing a minor in English law is subject to parental control, weakening admittedly as time passes but still extant until the age of 18. The movement in English law has been to restrict full parental control of children downwards from 18. In Scotland on the other hand the movement has been to extend legal protection for children upwards from age 12 and 14. A residual feeling exists in England that parents can control their children: it is, in other words, a power game in which the balance of power rests with the parents. This has little to do with protection of the young person, and more to do with control.

This of course does not explain the role of the courts, for while the English courts like to claim that they act only in the way that reasonable parents act, in reality the court's powers are much greater: in *Re W* the *parens patriae* power of the court was

26 See *Re B (A Minor)* [1981] 1 WLR 1421; *Re J* [1990] 3 All ER 938; *Airedale NHS Trust v. Bland* [1993] 1 All ER 821.

27 The English Suicide Act 1961 abolished that offence, but s. 2(1) makes it a crime to aid and abet that which is not criminal.

28 "Family autonomy may be regarded as a hallmark of a democratic society": Thomson *Family Law in Scotland*, (Butterworths, Edinburgh 1991); "the independence of the family is the basic building block of a free and democratic society": Lord Mackay, L.C., (1989) 139 N.L.J. 505 at p. 508.

29 See *post* at p. 118.

30 See chapter 3.

described as "theoretically limitless"[31]. The state, through the offices of the court, is not willing to allow persons under 18 to determine their own lifestyles to the extent that they will effectively kill themselves before attaining that age. For the sake of freedom of course on the attaining of your 18th birthday, the state will wash its hands of you. Why does the court interfere when, ex *hypothesi*, the young person is mentally mature enough to make proper and valid decisions? Any explanation is lacking if it does not explain why there is a difference between the mentally mature 17 year old and the 18 year old. A presumption in favour of life may for example explain the legal position, but autonomy is held to override that with the 18 year old and we must discover why autonomy does not override that presumption for the 17 year old. The reason I should like to suggest is that autonomy is seen by the English courts as a concession by the state, and the state thinks it has an interest to limit those to whom it grants autonomy. The state by definition likes to control people, and though it cannot control adults fully, it retains its control of minors. The consequence of this is that children and young persons in England and Wales live within a totalitarian regime which we as adults would find intolerable.

31 per Lord Donaldson MR [1992] 4 All ER 627 at p. 637.

John Haldane

Children, Families, Autonomy and the State

Abstract

The present paper is a response to Kenneth McK. Norrie's "Medical Treatment of Children and Young Persons", and is concerned principally with two aspects of Norrie's discussion: first his claim that the state seeks to control people; and second his contention that the role accorded to the courts in English law in cases of conflict between the wishes of parents and of their children is unacceptable. After rejecting his thesis about the nature of the state I turn to consider the issue of autonomy and question the conception of this which I take to underlie Norrie's claims.

Introduction

Kenneth Norrie believes he detects something oppressive in the behaviour of the English courts with respect to the rights of minors. Asking why it is that a competent 17 year old can have his decisions concerning medical treatment overridden, while those of an 18 year old are respected, he writes:

> The reason I should like to suggest is that autonomy is seen by the English courts as a concession by the state, and the state thinks it has an interest to limit those to whom it grants autonomy. The state by definition likes to control people, and though it cannot control adults fully, it retains its control of minors. (p14).

When he remarks that the state believes it has "an interest to limit those to whom it grants autonomy", I take it he means an interest in limiting their number, rather than in imposing limits on those to whom it has conceded autonomy – though given the general drift of his argument I suspect he would claim that it seeks, by other means, to do the latter also. Assuming this interpretation, then, the concluding argument seems to runs as follows:

1. By its very nature the state likes to control people.
2. The state's capacity for control is limited and it has to grant autonomy to adults – thus it yields to the competent decisions of the 18 year old.
3. In respect of those whom it deems minors, however, it is able to retain its power – hence the coercion of the 17 year old.

Two questions suggest themselves in response to this: first, is the general claim about the state true? and second, are the further claims and explanations that are presumed to follow from them plausible? I distinguish here between truth and plausibility, for while I take it that there are indeed very interesting socio-empirical questions, to be addressed by inductive enquiry, about the motivation and circumstances of the legal behaviour of particular states towards adults and minors, the former is the more significant claim, concerning as it does the very nature of the state and the legitimacy of its use of coercive power. Also I presume that in this regard Norrie is not simply making an observation about the contingent inclination of a given political order; rather when he says "the state by definition likes to control people", he means what his words suggest – at any rate to a philosopher – i.e. that it is of the essence of states, as such, to seek to control their members (Norrie has subsequently confirmed my initial supposition that "likes to" is just a rhetorical flourish).

Legal Practices and Purposes

I will return to these issues, but first let me recall Norrie's route to his conclusions. In 1985 the Lords decided in favour of a health authority that it was legal for a doctor in its employment to provide contraceptive advice and treatment to a minor with her consent but without that of her parents. This decision in the Gillick case has more general implications for the treatment of young persons and Norrie discusses some of these; but the continuing focus of his interest is the set of conditions taken to establish legal warrant for such treatment. Here he makes the interesting observation that while the Lords Fraser and Scarman agreed that a necessary condition is that the minor's consent should issue from an understanding of the character and consequences of the treatment, Lord Fraser added that where the parents did not consent the minor's decision should only be respected if it could be shown to be in his or her best interests. Adapting the phraseology slightly, I shall term these the "mature understanding condition" and "the best interests condition" respectively.

Norrie's next descriptive point is that developments in England and in Scotland have been divergent inasmuch as England has followed Fraser in requiring the satisfaction of both conditions, whereas Scottish law has restricted itself in allowing that for a minor to determine his or her treatment it is sufficient that they give mature consent. Moreover, Norrie informs us that this difference results from a conscious decision on the part of the drafting agency – the Scottish Law Commission – to reject welfare as a relevant requirement; a decision issuing, Norrie believes, from different traditions regarding the relative autonomy of children and young persons. In brief, Scots law recognises wider scope for legal capacity prior to majority, whereas its English counterpart has sought to exercise greater control over children, and to do so for a longer period.

So much for the facts. The passage from these to the suggestions about the state is made in response to the question "What is English law trying to do?". Norrie allows that it is a legitimate function of law to protect interests, and recognises that relevant interests – those of parental concerns and of children's claims – may conflict. He further allows that when a child is incapable of directing its own life a parent, or the state, may interfere. The principle is one of legitimate protection. Scottish and English Law both recognise this, but the latter fails to acknowledge that as well as *warranting* intervention this condition is also *limiting* of it. Here it is not so much that English law is blind as that it sees itself empowered by the state to exercise control wherever it can.

In the previous section I took it that Norrie's claim about the directive interests of the state is an analytic one, in effect a claim about the nature or essence of the state. However, the fact that it emerges from a contrast between English and Scottish jurisdictions might suggest to some readers that he may after all be proposing it as a socio-empirical thesis. As such it has an interest, but not as a piece of philosophy. I do not mean by this that it might not be morally significant, and it is clear that it is has at least a normative aspect. I remain somewhat unsure, however, as to which precisely, if any, of the following theses Norrie wishes to advance.

1. All states, by definition, like to control people and use law to do so. However, some jurisdictions are less coercive than others. Scotland's is less and England's is more so.
2. All states, by definition, like to control people. However, legal systems may be more or less resistant to this tendency. Scotland's is more and England's is less so.
3. Some states or societies like to control people. England is more disposed to this than Scotland, as witness to which are the greater powers of intervention in the former jurisdiction.

My original guess was that 1. comes nearest to Norrie's view and in subsequent correspondence he has confirmed this ("1. is closest to my view and 3 is furthest"). At any rate he obviously believes that Scottish law allows greater space for self-direction and he regards this as a good thing. Let me, therefore, turn now to the nature of the state, individual freedom, autonomy, children and the family. Of necessity I shall be brief.

The State and Legal Power

Is it the case that by definition the state likes to control people, or at least that it seeks to do so? I think the answer is no, or at any rate not in the sense that Norrie seems to have in mind. Of course it is a matter of theoretical dispute what defines a state. But on anybody's view it involves at least the legal organisation of a group of people. In an interesting essay on the "Source of the Authority of the State"[1] Elizabeth Anscombe worried away at the question: how can the state be justified? She was concerned with the difference between the control of a region and population by a gang of bandits, and its authoritative control by a government. Her conclusion was that the latter administers a system of justice answering (well or badly) to the need for laws, trials and punishments, a requirement which itself is geared to the social need for systematic protection. This is an old, familiar and plausible idea. It is compatible with but neither presupposes nor requires the contractualist assumption that members of the state voluntarily hand over prior rights to self protection in exchange for just and effective government. Contracts, covenants, democratic control are further features *additional to* the core fact that a political state is, or proclaims itself to be, an organised, authoritatively governed community.

This account might already seem to support Norrie's general claim. However there is a long way to go from affirming that all states exercise legal power to regulate the behaviour of their members, to allowing that they all seek to control people. For one thing, it is conceivable that the regulative laws of a society might all be enabling ones, constituting a system of permissions. Norrie might respond that permissions require protection and that this necessitates coercive laws. Thus if a law is passed allowing the

1 "On the Source of the Authority of the State" *Ratio*, Vol. 20, 1978, reprinted in G.E.M. Anscombe *Collected Philosophical Papers*, Vol. III (Oxford: Blackwell, 1981).

grazing of cattle on certain categories of land this will involve complementary legislation prohibiting interference with this practice. Certainly it is not difficult to see how such complementary legislation, whether specific to the entitlement or more general, might come to be passed. However, permissions do not logically entail restrictions, and they may not even require them in practice. Where law turns in the direction of control the question to ask is what is the purpose of this? and very often the reply will be that it is to protect the individual's right to act in ways either permitted by or outwith the scope of law. Regulation in the sense of a rule or law is simply not the same as control in the sense of direction and restraint. Of course, some states do seek, and perhaps even 'like', to control people; but if they do that is not simply in virtue of their being states.

The Scope of State Control

This much said, there is also the question of whether when a state does control its members this is necessarily a bad thing. I just allowed that enabling law might be supported by specific or general prohibitions. Since Norrie thinks that autonomy is a good thing he also concedes that it is sometimes proper for governments to protect it from threats of interference. Indeed he seems to believe that it may be legitimate for the state to act so as to *promote* autonomy and for the courts to uphold this. He writes: "Autonomy or the right to self determination ... is an interest that, with adults, the law goes out of its way to protect and indeed to enhance" (p. 11); and prior to this he appears to allow welfare interests as legitimate grounds for law.

> [T]he policy of the majority judges in that case is quite clear (indeed is the only thing all three agreed upon), that is the need to encourage sexually active girls under sixteen to seek protection from pregnancy. That is a valid social policy, and one which only the naive or emotionally autistic would fail to support. But it is much more difficult to identify a valid policy when the state, through the courts, tries to impose its own views on people who do not accept them, either for rational but objectively unsound reasons (such as Jehovah's Witness refusing to give blood transfusion) or entirely irrational reasons (such as the anorexic wanting to starve herself). (p. 10).

So it seems that the state may protect and promote autonomy, and act to advance welfare interests. To judge from what he says in the following discussion he also allows that the state may legislate to prevent unwarranted interference. Moreover some element of paternalism is taken to be acceptable:

> "No-one would deny that some individuals require protection, and the very young clearly come within that category ... the child is unable to come to proper conclusions about how to lead its own life and it is that inability, I submit, that justifies the state's interference". (p.13).

It is surely clear that far from being an implacable opponent of state control of people's lives, Norrie is a defender of both enabling and restrictive legislation. The point then, it may now seem, is not that he is against control; but rather that he is against control on grounds other than protection. But that is not quite right either. He thinks that protection from unwarranted interference by others provides extensive (if not sufficient) grounds for legislation, but that protection from oneself is only a legitimate ground when the threat to self arises from an inability to arrive at informed judgements or, in the earlier phraseology, to satisfy 'the mature understanding condition'.

Here it is assumed that there is a clear distinction between disqualifying ignorance or deliberative immaturity, such as is exhibited by a young child or someone mentally retarded, and the possession of unsound or irrational reasons, as in the cases of the Jehovah's Witness or the suicidal anorexic – a feature which does not of itself constitute a failure to satisfy the mature understanding condition. However Norrie needs to do rather more to support this distinction and its uses if it is to bear the considerable weight that his policy discriminations place upon it. "Self-determination" is a term of art in need of explanation. In advance of that being provided, and presuming no question-begging definition, one might at least wonder whether acting against one's best interests for 'entirely irrational reasons' may not constitute a failure of self-determination and hence be something protection from which constitutes a 'valid social policy'. And if that is so in the case of the suicidal anorexic what of the under-age patient seeking treatment at variance from what her parents judge to be in her best interests? Setting aside parental *rights of control* with respect to their children, there is also a question of the state's duty to enable parents to discharge their *duties of care*. Failure to take note of this may lead one into a position in which all judgements of disqualifying ignorance, and resulting restrictions of conduct, are reserved to the state. That in turn threatens the integrity of family life and indeed that of any form of sub-civic association in which authority is exercised by some for the sake of the good of others. It would be ironic, but not unheard of, if in the name of advancing universal autonomy one laid the foundation for an intrusive tyranny.

Autonomy, the Family and the State

These latter remarks turn in the direction of law and the family – the general theme under which the present discussions are offered. Let me conclude, therefore, by saying something about autonomy in the context of family life. Just as, in *some* sense, it is probably true that 'we are all liberals now', so and for related reasons it may be said that we are all believers in autonomy. Indeed, given the connections between action, intention, deliberation and responsibility, it would be difficult to construct an account of reflective agency in which some notion of self-determination did not feature. But that leaves almost everything still to be said, and as in the case of liberalism there is room for a range of contrasting views. These might differ in several respects, but an obvious dimension along which accounts of autonomy might be ranged (and again this point has its parallels in respect of liberalisms) is one definable in terms of conditions that are entirely self-originating and internally validated, and of alternatives that are other-derived and externally confirmed.

There is a marked tendency in contemporary thinking about autonomy to regard it as originating and residing wholly in the individual agent.[2] This strongly agent-centred view might be described as 'methodologically solipsistic' in as much as it regards the social context in which the agent's autonomy develops as extrinsic to it; at most the relation between the latter and the former will be one of partial and contingent

2 For a range of opinions see the essays in J. Christman (ed.) *The Inner Citadel: Essays on Individual Autonomy* (Oxford: OUP. 1981).

dependence. Set against this extreme is another, of Hegelian 'aroma', according to which what we think of as an individual's autonomy is in reality a non-localised collective condition of deliberative maturity, or some moralised version of this. Between these extremes stand a range of positions which I cannot even begin to explore. Let me suggest, however, that when Norrie writes of autonomy he thinks of it in ways that are close to the methodologically solipsistic variety; whereas I believe there are reasons for favouring a more socially-situated version.[3]

Here it will be as well to take note of an issue, which is apt to turn into a merely terminological dispute, as to whether anything that is not an individualistic doctrine of self-determination can be described as an account of *autonomy*. Someone inclined to this thought might then say that the opposition I am concerned with is between views of agency that include *autonomy* as an important element and others which put in its place some other notion such as *moral actualisation*. This move, however, achieves no significant advance towards resolving the substantial issue and is based on a misconception. It might be claimed on the basis of its etymology (*autos-nomos* = self-rule) that the idea of autonomy is necessarily individualistic; but this just begs the question as to whether all ideas of *selfhood* are essentially individualistic (in some relevant non-trivial sense). Anyone who insists that they are had better produce a plausible argument to that effect, or else stand charged with the attempt to define opposing possibilities out of existence. Far wiser then to allow that ideas of the self and of autonomy can come in individualistic and communitarian variants, and then to try and show the superiority of one version over another. I claim, therefore, that there is indeed an issue to be settled between opposing individualist and communitarian views about the correct account of autonomy.

Rather than debate the case between these contrasting views, however, I want to observe how the difference between them bears upon the issues of Norrie's paper. He invites us to consider the unacceptable circumstance of a young person who has satisfied the mature understanding condition having their consent to treatment overridden by their parents. This he regards as infringing their right of autonomy. If, however, one thinks of autonomy as deriving from one's development in a normative social environment and as involving reflective evaluations, the standards of whose correctness are at least in part externally located, then one will be more inclined to see in the judgements of parents, and of the courts in favouring these, expressions of legitimate sources of constraint (but not thereby necessarily sound judgements) on the young person's decisions. If autonomy is an acquired attribute all or many of the sustaining roots of which lie outside the individual, then reference to these sources and respect for their inclinations will be more appropriate than Norrie allows.

Relatedly, decisions which he thinks of as being the proper business of the individual alone will be seen as having to defer to the authority of the more mature minds to which that individual is indebted for its evolving autonomy. Usually the immediate source, and that which concerns us here, is the family. The implication of the present line of thought is that in considering the question of medical treatment it is

3 For some consideration of issues related to this see John Haldane, "Political Theory and the Nature of Persons", *Philosophical Papers*, XX, 1991, and "Identity, Community and the Limits of Multiculture", *Public Affairs Quarterly*, 7, 1993.

not enough to ask whether the young person consents to it. Rather there are two forms of family involvement to be taken account of. First, there is that I have been discussing, i.e. the dependence of the reflective agent upon the immediate moral environment; but second, there is the family considered now not as a source of moral consciousness but as a community whose well-being is partly constitutive of one's own interests. The most important relation here is again an internal one. It is not simply that the child should be brought to realise that its actions have effects on other people, in particular family members; but more profoundly it needs to see that its identity is, in certain of its aspects, inseparable from that of the family and that effects on the whole are *ipso facto* effects on it *qua* part of that whole. Put more directly, a minor who seeks to act in opposition to the deepest moral convictions of his or her parents, convictions that shape the moral sensibility and actions of the whole family (the dissenting child not excepted) does damage to that family and *ipso facto* to him- or herself. Save in the most extreme situations that is something to be avoided, and something which the state, if it respects the integrity of the family, will not wish to bring about.

In his paper Norrie refers to my arguments on behalf of the family and speculates that what lies behind them is concern for an interest which resides "in the group of individuals whose lives are significantly affected by one's decisions.". He continues:

"However, for the reasons spelt out clearly in Bob Brecher's paper 'What is Wrong with the Family?', [see this volume pp 00–00] I find this an implausible – and dangerously loose – justification for limiting a young person's right to self-determination. Everyone's acts have consequences for other people". (p. 12).

Here two brief responses are in order. First, it is simply a mistake to suppose that my argument turns solely, or even primarily, on the possible consequences of one's decisions for other people. Of course that is a consideration, but as Norrie observes it is too loose a one to constitute a major constraint on the scope of individual decisions. My points, though, were different in character. If, as by implication I have claimed, we owe our moral identities to social groupings of which we are parts, then to act at variance with the mostly deeply rooted values of these groupings, in this case families, is to cause damage to the sustaining sources of one's moral life and thereby to inflict damage upon oneself.

Second, Brecher's paper consists of a series of broadsides in part aimed against arguments in favour of family life, and in part targeted directly at the family itself – this latter attack being motivated by the interesting thought that what is wrong with the family is that it is "inimical to socialism and thus to feminism.". I am not sure as to which salvo or salvos Norrie is referring when he writes of "reasons clearly spelt out in Bob Brecher's paper", but given the context I suppose he is thinking of those sections which consider the claims that the family is a bulwark against rampant individualism and against the incursions of the state. To these Brecher responds that the family is in fact an ideological implement of capitalist control:

"[T]he values and requirements of the market, of the public world of arms sales, unemployment, lies and the rest of it are justified by their being said to offer the best possible support for the private, family world of 'nurturing, enduring and noncontingent relations governed by a feeling of morality.'"[4]

4 See Brecher, "What is Wrong with the Family", section IV, p. 63. The concluding phrases are quoted from Barrie Thorne, *Rethinking the Family: Some Feminist Questions* (New York: Longman, 1982) p. 18.

These are unargued assertions, but I am less concerned to refute them than to point out that even were a connection to be established between the institution of the family and the values of "late capitalism" much more would need to be done to show that this undermined the moral and social values of the family. For in my account these are not all external goods but include ones partly constitutive of the realisation of a worthwhile form of personal life. The point may be made by analogy with the institutions of fine art. It has often been said, for example, that portraiture and landscape painting belong within a class ideology that is socially oppressive. Even were that controversial claim to be made out, the particular social critique of which it is part also needs to show that this is not a merely contingent feature of these art forms; and even then it would have failed to demonstrate that there are no values *internal* to the practices of making and viewing such paintings which justify their existence. The case for the family with which I have been concerned is based upon its roles as a central factor in the moral formation of young persons, and as a continuing locus of their deepest concerns. This case is not refuted by such claims as that there is often abuse within families or that the institution itself may be used for other ends whose value is open to question. That bad things happen in and to families is no more reason for concluding that the institution should be dissolved than is the fact that hearts fail a reason for supposing that we would be better off without them. Of course we would be better with failproof hearts and with failproof families but let not the pursuit of perfection blind us to the value of what we have already.

Age: A Principled but Arbitrary Criterion

Before concluding let me offer a comment on Norrie's concern that the mere fact of a birthday should be taken to govern the state's respect for a person's autonomy. He writes: "any explanation [of the court's interest] is lacking if it does not explain why there is a difference between the mentally mature 17 year old and the 18 year old". The difference is surely obvious. If one takes issues of persons' maturity and competence to be relevant to the court's right to act on their behalf then one needs a criterion to mark the lower boundary of these attributes. Age is of course an imperfect criterion since it is not invariably correlated with them. But it has the merit of being a clear and impersonal one, involving no contested norms; and it is undisputedly the case that there is a general correlation between age, maturity and autonomy. That being the case, the possibility of an age criterion, and then the necessity of marking it clearly, become apparent. Of course any proposed age boundary will be arbitrary, but it need not on that account be unprincipled.

Conclusions

The state does not as such seek to control the lives of its citizens; though it is of its essence to be concerned with administering a system of law. To repeat, however, regulation in the sense of rule or law is not the same as control in the sense of direction and restraint. That said, there is state control of the lives of individuals and this raises specific questions of legitimacy. Where family life is concerned the state should be cautious and respectful of its role in the formation of young persons. Doubtless there will be occasions when the state should protect the choices of a minor against the demands of his or her parents, but that is something generally to be avoided. Interestingly, this last conclusion is one with which, I think, Kenneth Norrie may well agree.

Sandra Marshall

Whose Child Is It Anyway ?

> The line is immaterial Mr Worthing. I confess I feel somewhat bewildered by what you have just told me. To be born, or at any rate bred, in a handbag, whether it had handles or not, seems to me to display a contempt for the ordinary decencies of family life that reminds one of the worst excesses of the French Revolution. And I presume you know what that unfortunate movement led to.
>
> I would strongly advise you, Mr Worthing, to try and acquire some relations as soon as possible, and to a definite effort to produce at any rate one parent of either sex, before the season is quite over... [1]

For Lady Bracknell, and for assorted communitarians one might think, being the product of a handbag and lacking parents and a family, is to lack a proper identity. The identity which is lacking is both social and psychological. Without at least one parent poor Mr Worthing could not enter properly into society and marry Gwendolen; and those who do not know their parents, who, like Mr Worthing, lack a family, often speak of wishing to find their parents, in order to know who they themselves are; to become proper selves, so to speak. The social and psychological aspects of the self are so intertwined that it makes no sense to try and pull them apart.

Lady Bracknell is, of course, admirably clear about what constitutes parents and family and not even a whole set of matching suitcases could substitute for them. Developments in embryology and in *in vitro* fertilisation may have changed all that, for such developments will lead, if they have not already done so, to a different concept of parenthood and consequently of family. Whether such changes are good or bad is not the question, nor are the changes a consequence simply of these scientific developments, social changes have their effect too. So, we speak of one-parent or two-parent families, or even of families where there are three or four parents. A person who is adopted will have both natural and adoptive parents. Such an individual may wonder who to count as the 'real' parents. This question itself is interesting but unanswerable, which is to say that it may not be a real question. What is interesting is what prompts someone to ask it. It also brings into focus different facets of the concept 'parent' which do not usually cause us problems. 'Parent' may be taken simply in a biological sense, though even that is not entirely straightforward; or it may be taken in a social sense, and for most people it is still the case that those who fufill the social role of parent, characterised in terms of responsibilities and rights, are also the biological parents. In these cases there is no tension between these two aspects of parenthood. It is the unusual cases which introduce the tensions and most recently it is the developments in reproductive technology with respect to the treatment of infertility which have raised the questions.[2]

1 Oscar Wilde, *The Importance of Being Earnest* (London: Collins, 1948).

2 These developments are not the only ones to raise questions. Attempts at the legal enforcement of particular regimes during pregnancy as a result of greater knowledge of foetal development and the management of the whole process of birth are not insignificant.

ARSP-Beiheft 57. Derek Morgan & Gillian Douglas (eds.)
Constituting Families.

What I am particularly concerned with here is the discussion which these developments have prompted about surrogate motherhood.

"Surrogacy is the practice whereby one woman carries a child for another with the intention that the child be handed over after birth".[3] From this way of describing a practice of surrogacy it will be clear that such a practice does not depend upon technological innovation since it is perfectly possible for one woman to carry a child for another without any such intervention. However, technological developments make possible something which might be thought desirable and not otherwise possible, namely that one woman can carry a child for another without the necessity for sexual intercourse between the surrogate and the genetic father, whoever he might be. Moreover, and this is probably the most significant point, the technology makes it possible for there to be no genetic connection between the surrogate and the resultant child since the commissioning woman can be the genetic mother and the genetic father will be either her partner, or a donor. The attraction of such an arrangement would be that, given certain assumptions about what constitutes being a parent, an infertile woman could end up with a child which is 'hers' and an infertile couple with a child which is 'theirs'. The scare quotes here indicate that this way of putting the matter is likely to be too simple, for whose child it is might be just what is in question.

Whether there is or has been a widespread practice of surrogacy unassisted by technology I do not know, but the point is that technological developments have removed an obstacle to surrogacy, thus making it a more attractive option for the infertile than hitherto. It is this which made it a live issue for the Warnock committee and seemed to it to require legislation. It may no longer be such a live issue, partly because of the subsequent legislation to which there seemed to be relatively little opposition. It is, on the other hand, still matter of considerable academic debate.[4] One obvious reason for this is that surrogacy raises questions which go far beyond the rather limited characterisation of the issues given in the Warnock report. The interest in these debates lies not simply in what they have to say about surrogacy but in the presuppositions which lie behind the arguments. Indeed, I might go so far as to say that the really interesting questions are not so much the ones about surrogacy but the ones which we need to see as part of the background to surrogacy : in particular the question about what sort of problem we take infertility to be, such that biotechnology seems a suitable way of dealing with it. There is no space to even begin to address this question but it is the question with which my discussion ought to end.

The Warnock characterisation of surrogacy covers at least two kinds of surrogacy practice. One of these, the commercial practice, has given rise to much significant debate, the other, which I shall call 'sisterly surrogacy' has had relatively little attention. Whilst I shall likewise devote most of my discussion to the commercial practice, it is worth making a brief excursion into the other in order to bring out a number of ways in which the Warnock description above is unhelpful in its simplicity, to the point of being vacuous. The point must be that there is no *one* way of seeing the practice, no fact of the matter which different practices in the end must come to.

3 *Report of the Committee of Inquiry into Human Fertilisation and Embryology 1984*. (Cmnd 9341, London, HMSO, 1984) Hereafter the Warnock Report.

4 In, for example, recent volumes of *Philosophy and Public Affairs*.

Sisterly surrogacy will involve something like this: one woman out of love, friendship, generosity, carries a child for another and hands the child over as, one might say, a gift. Such a practice may not be widespread but it fits in with a more general way of seeing a child as a gift. So, parents may speak of their child as a blessing, a gift from nature perhaps. We might imagine too that even where the pregnancy is through technological intervention the idea of a gift can be retained.[5] We might imagine that where one woman carries a child for another in friendship both might see themselves as engaging in a joint enterprise – not dissimilar perhaps from the way in which, for want of a better expression, the ordinary way of producing a child might be seen as a joint enterprise. Recent cases of mothers bearing a children for their infertile daughters might be seen in this way. And, given that we recognise that pregnancy and childbirth involve inconvenience, discomfort, not to say pain, we might well find such generosity on the part of one woman towards another admirable. In much the same way we admire the person who gives a kidney to save the life of a relative. In neither case would we approve the public encouragement of such acts. We would not, for instance approve of posters in doctors' surgeries urging us to 'Give a kidney today and save a friend'[6].

We might imagine, nonetheless, that sisterly surrogacy become more widespread without public encouragement, and given the developments in techniques for prolonging women's fertility.[7] Women who no longer have an interest in bringing up children, having done enough of that already, might be happy to bear a child for a younger infertile woman, or indeed for a fertile one. There is no reason that I can see why surrogacy should be limited to the alleviation of infertility; this is to say that I can see no reason why infertility should be taken as the only serious reason. The point is, however, that it would be mistake to suppose that sisterly surrogacy is acceptable simply because it is done from friendship and affection. Many things done from affection can be objectionable, and friendships can be exploitative. The arguments against commercial surrogacy cannot then depend just on the fact of the commercial nature, as if without that the practice would be unobjectionable. Indeed, it will be part of my argument that many of the objections to commercial surrogacy are in fact also arguments against sisterly surrogacy.

So, it might be said that even sisterly surrogacy is wrong because it treats the child as an object. This might be implied by the idea of the child as a gift, although there is more than one way of taking the idea of a gift. This requires us to think more carefully about how we might describe sisterly surrogacy and to think more carefully about what is involved in the idea of one woman bearing a child for another. One thought might be

5 Much will depend on how the people concerned see science. Some see it with a sense of wonder in tact, for others it holds no mystery at all. By this I do not mean that *they* understand it where the others do not. Scientists themselves may retain the sense of the mystery of science because of their understanding, not in spite of it.

6 For a similar point see Bob Brecher, "Surrogacy, Liberal Individualism and the Moral Climate", M*oral Philosophy and Contemporary Problems,* J D G Evans (ed), (Cambridge University Press, 1987), p.195. There is room for argument here about why this should be so, but these go beyond the scope of this paper. It is not, however, simply that these are acts of supererogation but it has to do with the kinds of relationship which inform them.

7 These developments are not, of course, uncontentious.

this: what constitutes the 'gift' is not the child but the woman's 'reproductive labour'.[8] The child is not given away since the child is already, in some sense yet to be made clear, the recipient's own child. In the kind of case which I mentioned earlier a mother may be said to give birth to her daughter's child. The child already belongs to the daughter. What the mother gives to her daughter is all that labour which goes into the whole process of pregnancy and childbirth. It is, one might say, a service which she renders.[9] This argument seems most plausible in the case where the recipient is the genetic mother. But even here matters are not quite that simple. Consider an analogy, which is not intended as a complete one. I am quite incapable of making a decent souffle, though for all sorts of reasons, which need not be frivolous, I long to be able to do so. My friend is a person for whom the making of a perfect souffle is, if not a mere bagatelle, at least something which she always manages to do with relative ease. She is also generous enough to be prepared to produce souffles for her friends, so she is willing to come and make me a souffle to serve on an important occasion. She puts the effort into the production of this wondrous thing and I provide all the ingredients. Is the resulting souffle mine? My friend says, as she whips it out of the oven, "Here's your souffle S, and its a beauty." Some guests all say "S's souffle was quite splendid, did you know W made it for her?" But then some say, "Had a great souffle at S's dinner party the other evening. Of course, the souffle wasn't really hers." Certainly it would be the end of a beautiful friendship if my friend were to say, "Wow, this souffle is a real cracker, I think I'll just hang on to it myself." But is that because the souffle is really mine? Certainly the ingredients were, but the mixing of those ingredients includes the mixing of her labour with them. Does that substantially alter the picture ? Or is it that it is mine because she agreed to do it for me? Suppose I had just given her some ingredients and said, "Make me a souffle one of these days when you get a chance," and then I discover that she used these ingredients to make a souffle for sick friend; could I then complain that she had given away my souffle? I am not concerned here with what would be said if I were to sue her in a court of law, but what we might ordinarily say.

Suppose then we imagine the souffle scenario a little differently; to get the very best souffle you need the very best ingredients, I can get some of these ingredients but I cannot get the right kind of eggs. My friend who will make the souffle for me will also provide the eggs which are of the very best kind, and of course a souffle is mostly eggs. Does this make a difference to whose souffle it is? Would we think that W had run off with my souffle or just that she was a bit mean not to give me the souffle after she had agreed to make it for me? Now while it is quite clear that children are not just like souffles the analogy helps to show that speaking of what belongs to someone, as 'hers' or 'mine' is not necessarily a simple matter and neither is the idea 'service'. The 'service' is not here so easily detached from what is produced, and one might think that

8 I have my doubts about the efficacy of this term; it is quite rightly used to draw attention to the important fact that childbearing is something which women do and not simply something that happens to them, and that what they do has an important economic status. It can also be something of a double edged sword, as my subsequent discussion will, I think, show.

9 cf. Martha Hall, "Rights and the Problem of Surrogate Parenting" *Philosophical Quarterly* 35, 1986, for just one of many arguments of this kind.

in the case of producing a child nor should it be. If we are to speak of reproductive labour it will be important how we fit that into the wider context of labour and service.

What hangs on this is a way of seeing a set of relations between parents and children and how we see the whole activity of childbearing. It is important to see here that an appeal to a genetic relationship does not settle it. We can certainly understand motherhood as simply a genetic relationship, and we do not make a mistake if we do so, but that relation is no more fundamental to the concept of motherhood than any other. There is no *a priori* reason for supposing that a child belongs to the genetic mother than to the birth mother. It is of course true that in many of the cases of surrogacy that have come to public attention it looks as of what the commissioning parents want is a child which is 'theirs' in the sense of being genetically theirs but careful attention to the ordinary case of motherhood will also show that what is involved is something more than just the genetic relation. This 'more' is what comes under the heading of reproductive labour. To claim that the core of parenthood is the genetic relation ignores the way in which, even in the ordinary case, this genetic relation is part of a more complex relation and not the foundation of it. It is in this context that I now want to consider the debate about a practice of commercial surrogacy.

Central to commercial surrogacy is the idea of a contract, so I shall follow Debra Satz and call it contract pregnancy.[10] A contract pregnancy involves the contract mother who is "commissioned and paid to undertake the labor of pregnancy in order to produce a child that will be delivered to the commissioning parties [or party], who will raise the child as their own and will hold all parental rights."[11] One should also add that they take on all the parental duties. Commercial contracts of this kind were precisely what the Warnock report and the subsequent legislation ruled out. Why? The report is firm but a touch vague,

> In the first place we are all agreed that surrogacy for convenience alone, that is, where a woman is physically capable of bearing a child but does not wish to undergo pregnancy, is totally ethically unacceptable. Even in compelling medical circumstances the danger of exploitation of one human being by another appears to the majority of us to far outweigh the potential benefits in almost every case. That people should treat others as a means to their own ends, however desirable the consequences, must always be liable to moral objection. Such treatment of one person by another becomes positively exploitative when financial interests are involved. It is therefore with the commercial exploitation of surrogacy that we have been primarily, but by no means exclusively, concerned.[12]

There is much in this passage that one might take issue with. For example, the concern with a person treating other people as means to their own ends makes nothing clear since what such treatment amounts to is opaque. It looks as if this is some sort of Kantian requirement, but Kant himself was hardly a model of clarity on this matter. What is more central to my concern here, however, is the unclarity of the remarks concerning exploitation. Is it that surrogacy is itself exploitative, or that in some circumstances it might be, or that it is the commercial aspect which is necessarily

10 Debra Satz, "Markets in Women's Reproductive Labor" *Philosophy and Public Affairs 21*, 1992. It is also worth noting that the discussion here has also to be seen in the wider context of a debate about market liberalism and the conception of the self which informs it.

11 Richard J Arneson, "Commodification and Commercial Surrogacy" *Philosophy and Public Affairs* 21, 1992, p.132.

12 Warnock Report, p.46.

exploitative? Market liberals can deal easily with the second variation, at least at the theoretical level, since all that is then required is a form of contract which avoids the contingent features which constitute the exploitation. It is the first and third cases which the real argument is about.

Before getting down to the details of this debate there are two arguments which are sometimes raised, which have minimal force and which I shall deal with in a cavalier way. The first is rather more minimal than the second and it is that any law of contract in this area would be very difficult to draw up and difficult to enforce. Judges might be unwilling and the law complex. Now it has to be said that this might be more of a lawyer's objection since complexity and unwillingness on the part of others have never worried philosophers. (Quite the reverse, some might think.) So the answer I offer to this is that if we were to balk at introducing new legislation on these grounds in general, we should hardly ever get round to new legislation at all.

The second argument is perhaps a little more sensitive and my cavalier treatment of it may well give rise to some unease. It may be argued (and this may be part of the Warnock objection) that the women most likely to become 'contract mothers' are poor women.[13] The Baby M case and subsequent statistical evidence from the United States seems to bear this out. In any case it surely seems entirely plausible that, given the demands of the job, as it were, a woman would have to be pretty hard pressed to be willing to do it. Nonetheless I do not think that this argument, just by itself, carries very much weight as an objection to contract pregnancy. (Which is not to say that it carries no weight at all.) There are a great many jobs which are tedious and unpleasant and which we pay people to do. It is also true of these are jobs most likely to be done by the least well-off. The liberal only needs to answer here that such jobs, including contract pregnancy ought to be better paid. Suppose that contract pregnancy were to attract a relatively high remuneration, and suppose that it also for that reason became popular among the Sloane Ranger set, would there still be objections to it? The reason why this seems such an absurd scenario is not that it is difficult to see it being highly paid but that there is something about the nature of the enterprise which makes it seem unlikely that it would ever be popular amongst those who are relatively well-off. But there has to be more to it than that it is just hard or unpleasant.

The arguments which I want to focus on are intended to show that contract pregnancy corrupts or distorts women's reproductive labour in such a way as to alienate that labour. There are different versions of these arguments but I shall call them, in a rough and ready way, the affective and the identity arguments. Elizabeth Anderson puts the affective argument in this way:

> The application of economic norms to the sphere of women's labour violates women's claims to respect and consideration in three ways. First, by requiring the surrogate mother to repress whatever parental love she feels for the child,these norms convert women's labour into a form of alienated labour. Second, by manipulating and denying legitimacy to the surrogate mother's evolving perspective of her own pregnancy,the norms of the market degrade her. Third, by taking advantage of the surrogate's non – commercial motivations without offering anything but what the norms of commerce demand in return, these norms leave her open to exploitation. The fact that these problems arise in the attempt to commercialize the labour of bearing children shows that women's labour is not properly regarded as a commodity.

13 Brecher, p.195 and Arneson, p.155, consider arguments of this kind.

The key to understanding these problems is the normal role of the emotions in non commercialized pregnancies. Pregnancy is not simply a biological process but a social practice.[14]

There can be no denying that the whole activity of child bearing and rearing ideally involve an affective relationship between parents and children. Which is not to say that every family embodies that relationship in the same way and to the same degree. So the first question we might ask is what this 'parental love' is which the contract mother is required to repress. Secondly we need to understand how the contract makes such repression a r*equirement* . As Debra Satz points out[15] it looks as if what Anderson has in mind here is what is sometimes called 'bonding' between a mother and her child-to-be. In contracting to give up the child the contract mother will then have to be prepared to break this 'bond'. Thus, the bond in the normal case, seen as something essential to the pregnancy, becomes quite unnecessary and even undesirable. Why does it require repression though? Anderson does not make this very clear but the idea might be that the breaking of the bond, which giving up the child involves, is likely to be a painful experience. It might then seem to be to the contract mother's benefit if she could avoid developing such bonds altogether. The talk of repression suggests that Anderson thinks of this 'bonding' as in some sense 'natural' so that it is not for the contract mother simply to view the child in a different way.

Certainly the idea of this 'bonding' between mother and child has become quite popular in recent years, together with the claim that children who are not thus super-glued to their mothers at birth will suffer from all manner of problems, from having ill-developed brains to unpleasant social habits. But it is also true that some women, perhaps many, do not 'bond' with their children in this way, do not develop that picture of their pregnancy and have to develop their relationship over a long period of time and some may never come to manage it at all. It does not follow from this that they cannot care for their children in other ways. It might be argued, indeed, that women should resist the kind of essentialism which this talk of 'bonding' implies and give more recognition to the range of affective relations which parenthood can involve.

Suppose we were to grant that a contract mother might form an affective bond with the child she carries, does the contract, in requiring her to break this bond alienate her labour?[16] Compare it with this : I commission a piece of jewellery from a master craftsman. He designs the piece just for me, the fine stones are selected just for me and are suited exactly to the design. The resulting piece of jewellery is also a work of art. My artist/craftsman brings to his work a concern for what he is doing which goes beyond the idea that this is just a matter of making something for money. He has a regard for his materials which means that he cuts the stones in ways which will not damage their integrity, he will use only the best materials for the design and he will not incorporate into his design elements of bad taste, even if I were to want them. In the end

14 Elizabeth Anderson, "Commodification and Commercial Surrogacy" *Philosophy and Public Affairs* 19, 1990, p.81. I shall take this paper as my paradigm example for arguments of this kind.

15 Debra Satz, pp.115-116.

16 It is not obvious that a contract need require her to break the bond – there can be more than one kind of contract. Still, if one reflects upon the reasons why the commissioning parents would want to enter into such a contract arrangement it seems more than likely that they would not want to continue contact with the contract mother after the birth. Such contact would not accord with the desire for a child which is 'theirs'.

he may become attached to the piece and experience a pang of regret at having to part with it. Sometimes he makes non-commissioned pieces which he decides to keep for himself, even though he gets good offers for them. Now this kind of regard for what he produces is an important aspect of his craft and I recognise that it is part of what I pay for when I pay for the piece which I commission. Is his labour alienated therefore? If it is, then it is difficult to see how any paid labour which demands some affective engagement will not also be alienated labour, and that will include teaching philosophy for a living. It would certainly not be incoherent to hold such a view but it does require the kind of background theory of labour to make sense of it which does not feature in any obvious way in the debate which I am considering here.

The analogy which I drew with the jeweller/artist points to a slightly different argument which might be connected to Anderson's third objection. Contract pregnancy, she argues, exploits the contract mother's 'non-commercial' motivations. How does it do this? Anderson claims that,

> A kind of exploitation occurs when one party to a transaction is oriented toward the exchange of "gift" values, while the other party operates in accordance with norms of the market exchange of commodities. Gift values, which include love, gratitude, and appreciation of others, cannot be bought or obtained through piecemeal calculations of individual advantage. Their exchange requires a repudiation of a self-interested attitude, a willingness to give gifts to others without demanding some specific equivalent good in return each time one gives. The surrogate mother often operates according to the norms of gift relationships......This situation puts the surrogate agencies in a position to manipulate the surrogate mothers' emotions to gain favourable terms for themselves. [17]

There can be no denying that what is elaborated here is a form of exploitation. What is not clear, however, is that this is what a practice of contract surrogacy *must* amount to. The argument suggests that the motivations which inform the practice are those associated with 'gift' values and that these are exploited by others who do not see it in that way. But even if we suppose that the proper motivations for entering into such a contract must be altruistic ones it does not follow at all that they must be based on gift values. A wish to help others who one sees as needy in one way or another does not commit one to thinking of the help one gives as a gift. Nor does it follow that, because someone is motivated by altruistic concerns, they are exploited if they are paid to do what they do.

Anderson's arguments depend upon taking a very limited view of the range of affective relationships which parenthood and pregnancy can involve and a very limited view of what can constitute an altruistic motivation. Her argument works, in part, because she shifts between claims about what is sometimes in fact the case and what must be the case for a practice of contract pregnancy. More argument is needed to show that the practice *could not* be otherwise than as Anderson portrays it.

Yet, there is something right in the argument that Anderson offers. What the commissioning mother/parents enter into is an agreement which requires the contract mother to stand in some affective relation to the child she carries. (At least, if this is not what they require then it looks as if they are prepared to treat her as no more than a substitute for a technological handbag, one might say. So that were the technology available they would prefer to have the child develop in an artificial uterus, something

17 Elizabeth S Anderson, p.84–85.

like a plastic bag perhaps.) Commissioning parents presumably want the child who will become theirs to have as normal a development as possible. Part of this development involves the affective participation of the gestational mother. She must have a concern for its welfare, see it as a developing child and not just as an increasingly large blob of protoplasm. She will want it to be fit and healthy, indifference to the developing child will be no more appropriate in the contract pregnancy than it is in a normal one.Which is not to say that ordinary mothers are never indifferent to the children they carry, nor that such indifference can never be understandable. The contract mother is not required to develop just the same affective relationship to the developing child as a normal mother ideally does, nor as the commissioning mother might expect to do. That is to say that she is not required to regard the child as 'hers' and to love it as 'hers'. This does not mean that there can no sense in which affection or concern for it is appropriate. The concern which I suggest is appropriate to contract pregnancy certainly requires a kind of detachment but is this objectionable? Only if, I suggest, we suppose that there is only one kind of affective response which is either possible or proper to pregnancy. I can see no reason why this need be so. It might be said, and I think this is something which Anderson is inclined to argue,[18] that many women will be unable to develop this kind of affective relation with the child they carry and will suffer badly if they enter into such pregnancy contracts. This may well be true and may provide a powerful argument against encouraging the practice, even if it is not, by itself, an argument against allowing such contracts at all.

One might suspect, however, that Anderson would object to any kind of contract pregnancy just on the grounds that it involves any affective relation under any description, so long as it can be seen as a part of a parental relation. Thus, she says,

> Hence, as in all putting-out systems, the surrogate industry faces the problem of extracting the final product from the mother. This problem is exacerbated by the fact that the social norms surrounding pregnancy are designed to encourage parental love for the child.The surrogate industry addresses this problem by requiring the mother to engage in a form of emotional labour.[19]

This form of argument will surely have implications which go beyond a practice of surrogacy.

If it is wrong to encourage 'parental love' for the child, as Anderson argues here, then we might wonder now where that leaves the practice of foster parenting. Foster parents are certainly expected to provide for the children they foster an environment as nearly like a home as is possible. They are expected to develop an affective relation with the child which is one might suppose parental, but which does not require them to think of the child as theirs. One aspect of the arrangement into which they enter is that at some point, wherever possible, the child will return to its parents. Sometimes, no doubt, foster parents find it very hard to return the child but we do not therefore regard the emotional involvement as distorting or alienating. It is worth bearing in mind also that foster parents may have the child in their care for longer than the nine months which a contract mother has the developing child in her care. Indeed, if the fostered child is quite young much of its early development, intellectual and emotional will be the responsibility of the foster parents. So, what one might call, for the sake of the

18 Elizabeth S Anderson, p.85.
19 *ibid.*, p.82.

analogy, their labour in rearing the child, can be considerable. There might be a sense too in which we could say that the child is 'theirs', but we do not on this account think that their labour has been alienated or exploited just because they have entered an agreement which requires them to return the child at some point. (But perhaps my argument serves only to show that we are mistaken here and that indeed their labour has been alienated.)

It might well be, then, that the best way to think of contract pregnancy is on the model of fostering. This will then make a difference to the kind of practice which is allowed to develop; for one thing is clear, although foster parents do receive remuneration for what they do, ie.they do not bear the cost of looking after the child themselves, nonetheless they do not, or should not, make a profit out of what they do. Here we may be able to pull apart the idea of a commercial practice the point of which is to make a profit and a practice in which there is a binding contract to do something and receive money for doing so. If there is a need for an agency to bring the contracting parties together then we may think of such agencies as similar to fostering agencies which do not operate with a view to making a profit either. These agencies could well be state-run agencies which operate in the context of state welfare provision. Anderson has objections to this which once again depend upon seeing the affective relation between the gestational, contract mother as just the same as that of ordinary parents. Since we do not see the relation between foster parents and the children they foster in this way there seems to be no reason why we should insist on seeing the relation between the contract mother and the child in this way either.

The response to this argument might be that there still is something about pregnancy which makes this analogy with fostering quite implausible and which will show that paying for someone's reproductive labour is *necessarily* alienating. Anderson takes it throughout her argument that the contract mother is required to hand over a child which is *hers* and the kind of gestational, affective ties which she insists are fundamental to pregnancy are what ground this state of affairs. But given a different view of the kind of affective tie which is necessary to contract pregnancy, a tie more like that between foster parents and fostered children, the claim that the child is hers is no longer so obvious. But suppose the argument is that there is something about the sheer *physical* facts of pregnancy which make the difference. A version of this argument is what I call the identity argument.

The term 'reproductive labour' was introduced as a way of emphasising the fact that childbearing is an activity and not simply a biological process. No doubt it is also a rhetorical device used to draw attention to the way in which childbearing along with the rest of the domestic sphere of women's work has been relegated to the private sphere and left out of account of the public sphere of work and economy. The use of this term makes more plausible the analogies with other kinds of labour which I have drawn on here. This may not, however, be entirely an advantage for it makes it easy to then ignore some features of pregnancy and childbirth which are central to them. Reproductive labour, for all that it can involve the kind of affective elements which I have discussed, is also a process which goes on within a woman's body and over which, short of termination, she has little control. This process is bound up with the body in a very intimate way. So Carole Pateman,[20] among others, argues that reproductive

20 Carole Pateman, *The Sexual Contract* (Oxford: Blackwell 1988)

labour is peculiarly integral to a woman's identity as part of the relation between sexuality and identity. Arguments of this kind are extremely difficult to give a clear content to but we might begin with the idea that being embodied is fundamental to our identities as human beings at all. (This seems obvious enough, though not if you are Descartes.) By now the criticisms of standard liberal theory on this score are familiar enough: the attempt to characterise the self as if it were a neutral matter ignores our embodiment, ignores the fact that our bodies are sexual bodies. In this way our bodies, and thus our sexuality, are part of our selves. Selling sexual services is selling the self. This is the merest sketch of an argument and it requires a great deal more to sustain it. How we understand ourselves in relation to our bodies is a complex matter. That sexuality is a facet of identity may well be so, but a person's sexuality might not always form a *central* part of their identity. Anyone who accepts a Freudian view of human nature might find such a claim bizarre, but not everyone is convinced by Freud. Even supposing that sexuality is important to identity this will not, by itself show that reproductive labour is likewise central such that contract pregnancy involves alienation of the self. The idea that women's sexuality *must* be connected to reproductive capacities is an idea which many would want to deny. Likewise, it may be that reproduction need not be thought of as involving sexuality. In any case it does not yet follow that because something is an aspect of identity, even an important aspect, that involving it in a money transaction is to alienate or corrupt it. Consider again my artist/jeweller. His creative skill is most certainly central to his identity, yet it is not obvious that in exercising his creative capacity for money he corrupts his talent or alienates his self. Indeed, one might say that it is through the exercise of his skill and the sale of the artifacts he produces that he is able to fulfil himself. Now, I do not want to suggest that contract pregnancy is also a way of fulfilling the self, though it might be. The point is that the identity argument does not seem to work against contract pregnancy unless it can be argued that reproductive labour is more fundamental to the self than other aspects of one's identity, or unless it depends upon a more general argument to the effect that no features of the self can ever be engaged in a commercial enterprise without it amounting to selling the self. What will be needed to sustain this line of argument is a background political theory which provides a general account of labour and the self.

The arguments I have considered here have largely been concerned with claims about the way in which women's reproductive labour might be alienated by both sisterly surrogacy and contract pregnancy. I have not considered those arguments which claim that what is wrong with such practices is that they alienate the rights of the child. I might say briefly that it seems to me that such practices no more alienate the rights of children than do fostering, adoption, and child-minding. Indeed, such practices might be thought to raise fewer problems about the rights of children than does abortion. Certainly it is difficult to see how someone who is persuaded by the affective argument, as it is put by Elizabeth Anderson, could also accept abortion, since one might think it even more damaging to the relationship which she sets so much store by. This is not a knock down argument against her view of surrogacy, of course, but it is as well to be clear about the implications of such a view. Likewise, I would argue that the arguments offered in the well-known paper by Judith Jarvis Thomson defending abortion, in which the women's bodies are seen as analogous as houses which may be rented out as the woman sees fit, would just as easily support a practice of commercial surrogacy. It may also be that extending Thomson's arguments in this way will bring out aspects of the view which are unwelcome. One might think, for instance that her way of characterising the relation between a woman and her body leads to just the kind of commodification which Anderson and others show to be objectionable.

There is just one more argument which I want to mention, though I shall not discuss it in any great detail. I have so far paid little attention to what might be called the prevailing conditions and the context in which surrogacy in general might go on. This has been intentional, but here is an argument which brings that background into focus and it is connected to that more interesting question which I mentioned at the beginning of my discussion : the whole issue of infertility. There are some things which we pay people to do, which involve a high degree of altruism. Some of these, like fostering children and tending the sick, I have already mentioned. There are no doubt many others. There are also things which we pay people to do which involve a high degree of risk. I do not say that altruism is all that is involved; there may also be some satisfactions which are not simply to do with the monetary reward, or with the sense of being virtuous. The work might be interesting, exciting or sometimes even fun. What ever is the case, we must think of these jobs involving something which we are genuinely justified in asking people to do, even though it may involve risk or sacrifice. If pregnancy can be seen as a service then it must be one which addresses a serious need, one which justifies the kind of commitment involved. Those who like Warnock think that surrogacy is utterly unacceptable unless as a response to infertility, and not even then, presuppose that infertility is a serious problem. It is not obvious that this is so. I do not mean that those who are infertile do not see it as such but it does not follow from that they are right to do so. What makes it serious is a whole background of assumptions about children, women and the family which need to be examined. My final stab at an objection to surrogacy is that as a practice, as a publicly sanctioned response to infertility, it serves only to encourage a view of women which does indeed make reproductive labour central to their identity. This perpetuates the idea that the core of a woman's life still is in the home, and we all know what that unfortunate movement leads to. Contra Lady Bracknell, I am inclined to the view that a handbag, or the technological equivalent, if it enables us to dispense with that idea of women's lives, would be not be such a bad thing after all.

Derek Morgan

Hope of Deliverance? The Metamorphosis of Surrogacy[1]

1. The Surrogacy Close

Surrogacy trespassed upon the reproductive redevelopment in 1985 with the announcement that a British woman was to give birth to a child with the intention that it should be brought up by another woman and her husband in their native America. Kim Cotton was to be paid for this labour, and an agency run by another (American) woman was to receive a fee for negotiating the contract. The world as we had known it was about to come to an end; the debates which accompanied the passage of the hastily drafted Surrogacy Arrangements Act 1985 were replete with the language of moral panic and outrage. The Bill passed smoothly through its legislative process with almost universal blessing. Surrogacy and surrogate mothers[2] were condemned as 'sick, as is any form of womb leasing'[3]; 'totally immoral'[4]; 'repugnant'[5]; 'the sale of children'[6]; 'trafficking in human beings'[7]; 'this extremely distasteful matter'[8]; 'a well defined evil'[9]; 'sheer effrontery'[10]; and as making 'reproduction as marketable for women as sexuality has always been

1 I am indebted to Frances Price who suggested this mode of analysis and suggested constructive criteria by which it might be carried forward. The usual caveat applies.

2 Following a remark by Miriam David to me to this effect in correspondence, I have before intimated the problems associated with the use of the term 'surrogate mother' when, in truth, the surrogate is a surrogate for maternity, not motherhood; see 'Surrogacy: An Introductory Essay' in Robert Lee and Derek Morgan, (eds.), *Birthrights: Law and Ethics at the Beginnings of Life*, (London, Routledge, 1989), pp. 55–84, at pp. 56–60. It is fair to say that these views have not passed without criticism. The descriptions full and partial surrogacy which have more recently entered the lexicons of assisted conception are really misnomers: it is not the surrogacy that is partial, it is the contribution of the commissioning couple that genetically is partial or full. The work done by the surrogate, a difficult term to which we shall return, is in both and indeed all cases, quite unique and cannot properly be subdivided according to the genesis of the gametes. Both forms of surrogacy are full, and in this sense, full time work for at least 9 months: the differences between them, if they are in any way determinative, are that in one the surrogate makes a genetic contribution to the resulting child, in the other she does not. To describe surrogacy in full and partial terms addresses the wrong sets of issue. See further, Morgan, 'A Surrogacy Issue' (forthcoming). If descriptions are to be accurate and operational, it may be better to recognise the force of the distinctions suggested by the Canadian Royal Commission between genetic-gestational and gestational; see *2 Final Report of the [Baird] Royal Commission on New Reproductive Technologies: Proceed with Care*, (Ottawa, Minister of Government Services, Canada, 1993)

3 Peter Bruinvels, *Hansard*, vol.77, col.42

4 Ian Paisley, *Hansard*, vol. 68, col. 555

5 William Benyon, *Hansard*, *ibid*, col. 582

6 Jill Knight, *ibid.*, col. 565

7 Patrick Cormack, *Hansard*, vol. 74, col. 1193

8 Roger Sims, *ibid.*, col.1189

9 Norman Fowler, *Hansard*, vol. 74, col. 1193

10 Alan Beith, *Hansard*, vol. 77, col.33

ARSP-Beiheft 57. Derek Morgan & Gillian Douglas (eds.)
Constituting Families.

historically'[11], resulting in 'widespread abhorrence.'[12] Fears were expressed for women who agreed to act as surrogates, commissioning parents, surrogate born children, family life, the 'whole of our country'[13] and 'the nation and humanity.'[14] The responsibility of Parliamentarians was clear; 'the eyes of the world will be upon us.'[15] The Bill was heralded because it would 'preserve family life, stabilise society and do away with this unnatural and unfortunate practice which has sickened so many decent and family-loving people'[16] and 'rightly outlaw the hell and wickedness which exists in America.'[17] Surrogacy, or at least its fully commercialised variant, was not welcome.

In fact, the 1985 Bill had more modest aims than those proclaimed for it. And life, perhaps eccentrically, progressed much as usual. An attempt was made in the House of Lords later in 1985 to expand the criminal prohibitions of the Act to render all manifestations and aspects of surrogacy unlawful, but this failed. Surrogacy became not quite as invisible as it had been hitherto,[18] but it functioned as a more or less acceptable subterranean reproductive alternative for some couples. Indeed, the anecdotal evidence available in the UK suggests that there is an increase in the numbers of people embarking on a surrogacy arrangement; Blyth reports communications from COTS, the self help group, which would suggest 98 recent or ongoing arrangements within the past few years; with 55 out of 57 surrogacy arrangements resulting in live births that have been regarded as a satisfactory outcome.[19]

Although it does not necessarily demand the most technologically sophisticated contribution to conception, nor is it presently thought to be the statistically most significant response to problems of fertility, surrogacy at least temporarily emerged at the eye of the storm over the 'reproduction revolution,' and became the whipping post for the moral backlash against the brave new world of technological rationality and scientific finality. Philosopher Roger Scruton demanded that surrogacy be seen as the revision of moral perceptions; the bond between the mother and child was severed from the experience of incarnation, it was '... demystified, made clear, intelligible, scientific.' Where, for a moment, our jurisprudence appeared poised on the brink of an evolutionary surge,[20] surrogacy thereafter slipped into the corridors of indifference of which the public policy agenda is constructed.

11 Michael Meacher, *Hansard*, vol. 68, col. 537
12 Michael Meacher, *Hansard*, vol. 77, col. 28
13 Ann Winterton, *Hansard*, vol. 68, col. 577
14 John Ward, *ibid.*, col. 578
15 William Cash, *ibid.*, col. 575
16 Peter Bruinvels, *Hansard*, vol. 77, col. 43. There is little evidence that these empirical claims have been fulfilled.
17 Harry Greenaway, *ibid.*, col. 45
18 There have been various attempts to chart the history of surrogacy arrangements in the UK in the twentieth century; see, for example my essay, 'Surrogacy: An Introductory Essay' in Robert Lee and Derek Morgan, (eds)., *Birthrights: Law and Ethics at the Beginnings of Life*, (London, Routledge, 1989, pp.55–84), but the reported prevalence has remained small; a variety of reasons could be given for this.
19 Eric Blyth, 'Section 30 – The Acceptable Face of Surrogacy' *Journal of Social Welfare and Family Law*, 1993, 249 at p.258
20 Bernard Dickens, 'Surrogate Motherhood: Legal and Legislative Issues' in A Milunsky and G J Annas, (eds) *Genetics and the Law III* (1986) pp3–5

The remainder of this essay is in two parts. In the first, I make some general observations on the changes, medical, social and legal which have attended the development of surrogacy in the last ten years. In the second, I attempt some responses to the powerful objections raised to surrogacy in Sandra Marshall's chapter, 'Whose Child is it Anyway?'

2. From Common to Uncommon: The Metamorphosis of Surrogacy

Since 1985, surrogacy has undergone a metamorphosis. More accurately, several forms of metamorphosis; from the sexual to the medical, from the private and invisible to the public and intermittently visible; from the altruistic to the commercial and back again; and from the approbated and controversial to the accepted and clinically mediated. The medicalisation of surrogacy can be charted through two strands, the responses of professional bodies, such as the British Medical Association, and, first, developments in technology itself. In parallel with this is the remarkable turn around which has occurred in the legal approach to surrogacy. These three developments need consideration; together they represent the enclosure of surrogacy from the common wealth to the private purse.

i) Technology Transfers

Two inter related themes of change are evident in the developments within the *practice* of surrogacy. While initially both appear legally and ethically to empower the 'intending' parents in important ways, they do not in themselves address more profound implications, and the empowerment may be more apparent than real. These changes are i) that from asymmetric to symmetric involvement and ii) that from surrogate 'mother' to surrogate 'gestator'.

Surrogacy can be seen as a form of 'collaborative conception'[21], which focuses attention on all those people involved. The idea of 'contracting with consenting collaborators' for the purposes of procreation allows for asymmetric and symmetric involvement. Thus in asymmetric surrogacy cases a pre-conception plan enables a man to declare a 'contractual' intent to take custody of a child to whom he will be linked genetically. There is asymmetry between the 'intending' social parents; the man contracts for the surrogate's services (without the mediation of another woman) and the woman (his wife/partner) awaits the outcome. The surrogate collaborates in the conception, with or without medical assistance, in the gestation and delivery. Perhaps more controversially, it has been suggested that here is the 'proper' sense in which we can speak of the surrogate, not just for maternity, but also in place of the woman with whom the man intends to raise the child. Debates about the status of the child bearer as surrogate or 'true' mother lose some force; nobody would deny that she is the child's genetic mother, but she is acting as a surrogate for another in this one sense.

21 John Robertson, 'Embryos, Families and Procreative Liberty: The Legal Structure of the New Reproduction' *Southern California Law Review*, 59, 1986, 939–1041

The medical profession has to be involved in 'collaborative conception' which involves symmetry between the intending social parents. Here the man and the woman (facilitated by clinicians) collaborate to enable the woman's fertilised egg to be transferred to a woman who has agreed to attempt to become pregnant using their genetic material. The total medicalisation of surrogacy which this implies (the difference between the two types of surrogacy are neatly illustrated in the experiences of Kim Cotton and her retelling of them[22]) may have profound consequences. Edgar Page, in an early article[23], where he attempted to distinguish between what I have called symmetrical and asymmetrical surrogacy, foreshadowed this question.

Page's argument was this:

> When the woman who gestates the child receives the embryo by donation, she has a strong claim to the child *because* the embryo was donated to her. But surely if the embryo transferred to her uterus was *not* donated to her, her claim to the child would not be the same, especially if those who supplied the embryo did so on the explicit understanding that the resulting child would be *returned* to them and if they would not have supplied the embryo otherwise.[24]

Notice the important limitation to Page's arguments; for he suggests that in the second case the claim to the embryo (and hence I take it to the succeeding child if born) is not the *same* as in the first case. He concludes from this that the woman has no claim at all. With the first part of his argument I am inclined to agree, but it does not follow because the claim is not the same that it should not produce the same result. This depends upon a different move than Page acknowledges. Of course, it is true that there are cases of the surrogate who changes her mind and who has been horrendously pursued through the legal and media systems. But the question here might be thought to be as much concerned with the allocation of risk of the surrogate reneging on the contract as on the enforcement of a contract of personal services. I return to this point.

However, the importance which might be attached to Page's distinction must not be overlooked, for it has persuaded at least one court in the United States that the genetic link in 'gestational surrogacy' is sufficiently important that the wishes of the surrogate to retain the child after birth should be set aside. In *Calvert* v *Johnson*, Anna Johnson agreed to in vitro fertilisation with the sperm and egg from Mark and Crispina Calvert. Midway through the pregnancy, she decided that she wanted to keep the resulting child, and the Calverts sought custody. When the child was five weeks old California Court

22 Cf Cotton, *Baby Cotton: For Love and Money* (London, Dorling Kindersley1985) and Cotton, *Second Time Around: the full story of my second surrogate pregnancy*, (London, Kim Cotton, 1992).

23 *Journal of Applied Philosophy*, 2, 1985, 162, reprinted in Brenda Almond and Donald Hill (eds), *Applied Philosophy: Morals and Metaphysics in Contemporary Debate* (London, Routledge, 1991), pp272–83

24 *Ibid* 163. As Jennifer Trusted points out (*J Applied Philosophy*, 2, 1985, 331) the view that such donation should be accompanied by legal forfeit of rights is better supported by analogy with donation of other living bodily tissues; such as kidneys. But after donation in these and closely related gametes cases, the donor has done her or his part; to adapt Marshall, they have done their work. In any case of surrogacy this is not the case. And in this way, I do not think that the analogy of donation, or spare parts gets us any further; there is, if you like, no further to go. There is no appropriate analogy for the work that a woman does in pregnancy. Thus the analogy between the souffle and surrogacy is simply implausible; the child is not a souffle, the gametes are more than eggs and milk and to try to treat them as the same – or analogous – is what we may call a recipe for disaster.

Judge Parslow decided that the Calverts should keep the child; he likened Johnson's role to that of a foster mother who cares for a child for a period when the 'true parents' are unable to. He decided also that the surrogacy contract between the parties was legal and enforceable.[25] The California Supreme Court upheld this result.

Where facilitation, (or in the case of Marion Ploch[26]) maintenance of pregnancy takes place only with the intervention of clinicians, it is in the public domain. This influences views about the options available. When women and men in their quest for a pregnancy (or their intent to secure a grandchild) seek medical assistance, there is a pressing need to explore not only the ways in which they make their choices.

In the absence of any body of knowledge or any concerted attempt to appraise the possible social implications or the complexity of the relationships involved, decisions have to be made by clinicians on pragmatic grounds. Not only in relation to the terms and conditions of clinical practice, but also about the criteria which are to be met before 'treatment services' are provided or a surrogate recruited. Some clinicians claim that they legitimately have discretion: that such matters call for their professional judgment. Some also act, in effect, as 'guarantors' in IVF surrogacy arrangements.[27]

ii) Ethical Evolution: the views of the BMA

The British Medical Association originally vacillated in its view; a 1984 statement cautioned that '... the Council ... considers that it is unethical for a doctor to become involved in techniques and procedures leading to surrogate motherhood' while the Annual Representative Meeting the following year '... agree[s] with the principle of surrogate births in selected cases with careful controls.' A BMA Board of Science *Surrogate Motherhood* Report in 1987 advised that the '... interests of childless couples were outweighed by legitimate social considerations opposing surrogacy', which provoked the 1987 Annual Representative Meeting to conclude that 'This meeting advises that, until ARM has agreed appropriate ethical safeguards and controls, doctors should not participate in any surrogacy agreement.' Thereafter, the BMA *Report of the Working Party on Human Infertility Services* (1988) concluded that '... it would not be possible or desirable to seek to prevent all involvement of doctors in surrogacy arrangements especially as the government does not intend to make the practice illegal.' And in its most recent report, *Surrogacy: Ethical Considerations*[28], the British Medical Association opines that surrogacy should be an option of last resort, in which the interests of the child should be paramount.

The BMA's recommendations provide that while the welfare of the child is to be the paramount consideration, surrogacy should only be used 'where the commissioning couple suffers from infertility due to a medically recognised disorder, and where all other

25 On appeal, see *Johnson* v *Calvert* 851 P. 2d 776 (1993), the California Supremeenforced the contract based on the parties' *intentions*.

26 *Independent on Sunday* 1 November 1992; *Sunday Telegraph* 22 October 1992, a brain-dead woman maintained on a mechanical ventilator for the supposed benefit of her 19 week old fetus.

27 *Surrogacy indeed, is now being kept under review by the HFEA and the Department of Health*

28 BMA, London, 1990, following the report of a committee chaired by Sir Callum McNaughton

appropriate means for enabling them to have a child have been tried, and failed.'[29] Any doctor contemplating taking part in the initiation of a surrogate pregnancy has ethical obligations, according to the BMA, to all the members of the 'respective households and families – including, as the most important, the child or children who would not be conceived but for the doctor's intervention.'[30] The acquisition of surrogacy by the medical profession is almost complete.

And the profession does not intend that its sanction should be bounteously distributed; only women who have partners and who have already had one child or more should be considered as potential surrogates. This is important, so that the surrogate has some experience of pregnancy and labour and has 'ideally' the support of a partner. Finally, they suggest that it is 'inadvisable for the commissioning couple and the surrogate to be aware of each other's identity.'[31] While these recommendations are couched in the language of caution, it is not difficult to appreciate the effect of this careful endorsement from one of the country's leading bodies charged with reflecting and guiding the views of medical practitioners. They assist in making the case for 'medicalised versions of surrogacy' which have been increasingly insistent.[32] It is difficult to overestimate the importance of the medical endorsement of particular techniques, such that 'the process of asserting the moral superiority of medicalised over non-medicalised forms of surrogacy and of medical over non-medical reasons for resorting to surrogacy' has gathered pace.[33] This has attracted the apparent sanction of the Human Fertilisation and Embryology Authority, which has declared that 'the application of assisted conception techniques to initiate a surrogate pregnancy should only be considered where it is physically impossible or highly undesirable for medical reasons for the commissioning mother to carry the child.'[34]

As the view within the BMA was undergoing modification, so too the general public attitude towards surrogacy. This has perhaps its best expression in the enactment of section 30 of the Human Fertilisation & Embryology Act 1990, which provides limited circumstances in which a 'parental order' in respect of gamete donors can be sought. Even though section 30 introduces only a partial attempt to bring surrogacy within a regulatory framework, it is perhaps the most remarkable manifestation of the metamorphosis thesis being sketched here.

iii) regulating reproduction: changing the template

Section 30 was a late amendment to the 1990 Bill, and, it has been claimed, has the effect of reducing 'parenthood to its constituent parts.' It recognises that 'combined with recent developments in clinical technology, genetic, gestational, nurturing and legal parenthood

29 The British Medical Association, *Medical Ethics Today: Its Practice and Philosophy*, (London, BMJ Publishing Group, 1993), p.122
30 BMA, *op. cit.*, n.18, p.122
31 *Ibid*
32 Blyth, *op. cit.*, at p.257
33 *Ibid*
34 HFEA Annual Report 1992, para. 3.17

may be performed by a variety of adults.'[35] The MP who was largely responsible for securing the introduction of the section, Michael Jopling, did so following specific concerns which had been raised with him by a couple who lived in his constituency. The clause on which the section is based was introduced following a well publicised case of *Cumbria CC* v X.[36] The effect of this local affair was to complete the first metamorphosis of surrogacy, from being cast at the eye of the storm which the whirlwind of publicity had generated in the mid 1980s, to its reception in the harbours of reproductive regulation only five years later.

Jopling's constituents had been challenged by their local social services department when they applied formally to adopt twin children who had been living with them since their birth following a 'full' surrogacy arrangement. They were the children's genetic parents, but the Social Services Department argued that they should fulfil the full legal criteria for adoption before the children were allowed to remain with them. In a very clever, but plaintiff letter to *The Times*, their solicitor urged their case;

My client, the genetic mother, would appear to have no legal rights whatsoever in her own children. On the contrary, her husband, the genetic father, would have the right to apply under the guardianship legislation to have himself recognised as the father of illegitimate children and no doubt, custody, if he required; a truly anomalous situation in these days of the equality of the sexes. Parliament appears to be proposing to perpetuate a definition of motherhood which flies in the face of present genetic knowledge and medical technology ... Surely, genetic mothers, at the very least, should be accorded the same rights and privileges as genetic fathers?'[37]

Clearly, there are number of assumptions and controversial arguments which could be joined here, but the straightforward question is a relatively simple one; should surrogacy arrangements, generally disfavoured by the legislation,[38] be given this apparent encouragement, even in the marginal case? And in an extraordinary procedural manoeuvre, Jopling succeeded in having the legislation amended so that it could apply retrospectively to the benefit of couples such as his constituents. However, a technical drafting flaw has rendered the implementation of this provision more complex and circumspect than first intended. It is provided in s.30(2) that 'the husband and the wife must apply for the order within six months of the birth of the child' or, in what may be called the Jopling amendment 'in the case of a child born before the coming into force of this Act, within six months of such coming into force.' The intended effect of that provision is to make retrospective the application of the provisions of the section, as long as the 'parents' of any surrogate born child (however long ago the birth took place) apply to the court for recognition as the child's legal parents within the specified six months. Unfortunately, different sections of the Act are to be brought into force on different days, such that there is no one date which could be identified as the apposite date. This has led the Department of Health into correspondence with representatives of the self help group

35 Blyth, *op. cit.*, p.248

36 *The Times* 25 June 1990 and *Re W, The Guardian* 30 October 1990; see *Family Law* [1990] 118 and 232 and Derek Morgan and Robert Lee, *Blackstone's Guide to the Human Fertilisation and Embryology Act 1990*, (London, Blackstone, 1991) pp153–54

37 D B Forrest, *The Times*, 28 February, 1990. See *Re W (Minors)(Surrogacy)* (1991) *Fam Law* 180

38 Indeed, in section 36 of the Human Fertilisation & Embryology Act 1990, surrogacy contracts are specifically made unenforceable; there had before this been some doubt about either their enforceability, and especially, the recovery of any monies paid under an unenforceable contract.

COTS – Childlessness Overcome Through Surrogacy – as to the most appropriate manner in which the retrospective provisions could be activated, and the possible best guess as to the number of children who may be affected by its operation.

The section demonstrates according to Johnathon Montgomery 'the worst features of a legislative system which allows anecdotal evidence to determine the shape of reform.'[39] The preceding sections of status provisions (ss.27–29) while containing their own difficulties, (such as removing 'choice' in determining who should be treated as a parent) seek to enshrine 'a uniform set of principles' in which priority is given to those 'whose link with the child derives from the birth, either directly or through partnership with the woman who gives birth.'

Thus, section 27 provides that if a woman is implanted with an embryo or sperm and eggs which do not contain her genetic material, she will nevertheless be treated as the legal mother of the child she consequently bears. And that where a married woman, or an unmarried woman who receives treatment with a man, conceives a child following assisted conception with semen of a stranger to the marriage, her husband and not that man, will be treated as the legal father of the child, unless her husband did not consent to the insemination. 'The legal definition of fatherhood is made to serve social ends: encouraging the use of licensed facilities' – because these results will only follow where a licensed clinic is involved.[40]

However, if a woman hands the child she has conceived by assistance to a married couple in consequence of a surrogacy agreement, a court may – if the conditions of section 30 are met – convert the couple into the child's legal parents. Although the surrogacy agreement is itself legally unenforceable under section 36, a court sanctioning the arrangement (which it may find difficult to resist) will confer full legal recognition on the social parenthood. Eekelaar concludes that section 30 is 'One of the most remarkable recognitions of social parenthood ...'[41]

In contrast with the attempt to enshrine some principled thought to domestic arrangements in the earlier sections, section 30 'seeks to describe as narrowly as possible the circumstances of the particular case which had arisen without concern for the principles which it enshrines. It adopts all the possible types of parental link (ie., genetic, social, consensual and marital) save the gestational link.'[42] Where a woman has undertaken a pregnancy on behalf of another couple who were either i) both that child's genetic parents (full surrogacy) or ii) where one of that couple is the child's genetic parent, having donated an egg or sperm, they may both apply for an order to be recognised as the child's legal parents.[43] The section can be used wherever the procedures for effecting a surrogacy arrangement were agreed.

Although Eric Blyth has appropriately called section 30 'the acceptable face of surrogacy', the legislative fiat is not to be granted to all and sundry on the surrogacy stage.[44] In order for the section to be applied, the applicants must be married and show

39 Montgomery, *Modern Law Review* ,54, 1991, at 520

40 Eekelaar, 'Parenthood, Social Engineering and Rights', Chapter 6, above

41 *Ibid*

42 Montgomery, *op. cit.*, 520

43 For an early attempt to make distinctions based on the genetic makeup of the resultant child see Edgar Page, 'Donation, Surrogacy and Adoption' *Journal of Applied Philosophy*, 2, 1985 pp.161-72

44 Eric Blyth, 'Section 30 – The Acceptable Face of Surrogacy' *Journal of Social Welfare and Family*

that the child's home is with the applicants. It is unclear why there should be no provision permitting stable unmarried couples to apply; a court will only make an order if it will promote the welfare of the child; if there is reason to deny recognition to an unmarried couple's claim it can be done in the interests of the child, not as the result of prejudice.[45] The husband, or wife, or both them, must be domiciled in the UK, the Channel Islands or the Isle of Man and both must be at least 18 years old. In addition, the court has to be satisfied that no money or other benefit has changed hands in consideration of the making of the parental order, the agreement to relinquish the child to the applicants, the handing over of the child or the making of arrangements prior to the making of the parental order. The child's father (where he is not her husband) and the 'surrogate mother' must freely agree to the making of the order and the court must be satisfied that the agreement is freely and unconditionally given with full understanding of what is involved. A dispensation may be made in respect of this requirement if the father or the 'surrogate mother' cannot be found or is incapable of giving consent. Similarly, the court may dispense with the prohibition on payments where it so authorises, or where the payment amounts only to 'reasonable expenses' made to the 'surrogate mother.' Finally, the section introduces what might be called a minimum period of reflection for the birth mother; hence, a woman's agreement to the transfer of the child to the applicant parents is ineffective if given within six weeks of the birth.

II Marshalling Arguments

In a short piece which I published in the *Journal of Law and Society* in 1985 I examined the making of the Surrogacy Arrangements Act 1985. I prefaced that by recalling the celebrated article by Elizabeth Landes and Richard Posner in which they articulated perceived defects in the regulatory control of adoptions in the United States.[46] Briefly, their thesis was that the shortage of babies for adoption promoted an illegal trade in babies and young children, and indeed international events in Romania and Croatia might be thought in part to bear that out. It was their highly tentative argument that the development of a market for babies might overcome some of these problems. The article drew a stinging response from Rob Pritchard, who, while acknowledging some potential benefits which a market system could afford, identified three types of objection; misconceptions in the argument of Landes and Posner, market failure problems, and objections in principle.[47] He complained that 'the mere description has a ring of parody about it.' The incongruity of market notions and babies jarred, he said, because '... the special value which we attribute to children depends in part on the fact that they cannot be traded.'

Of course, we could respond that most people derive a net positive utility from living and that the circumstances of birth only partly compromise that benefit, whatever the

Law, 1993, 249–60. As he there comments, 'in combination with section 13 and the Code of Practice section 30 demands an explicit conformity in lifestyle and family form for those who wish to achieve parenthood by surrogacy.' at p.255

45 Montgomery, *op. cit.*, p.526

46 'The Economics of the Baby Shortage' *Leg. Stud.*, 7, 1978, 323

47 'A Market for Babies' *Univ Toronto L J* 24, 1984, 341

nature of arguments about identity. And yet this is the burden of the argument which Marshall first seeks to promote; the question of identity is one of two important arguments which she deploys against surrogacy. The other, to which I return, is that of commodification and alienation of reproductive labour.

i) On Identity

In essence, Marshall's first objection to surrogacy I take to be a reflection on the proper nature and scope of family, and the way in which parents act as a gateway to assumption of a full identity in society. Her reflection on Lady Bracknell's advice to Mr Worthing addresses 'those who do not know their parents, who lack, like Mr Worthing, a family [and] who often speak of wishing to find their parents, in order to know who they themselves are; to become proper selves, so to speak.' This is challenged by developments in embryology and in vitro fertilisation which will lead, if they have not already done so, 'to a different concept of the parenthood and consequently of family.' Note that Marshall addresses her concerns not to 'the family' but of 'family', of who one's relations are; or whom one conceives them to be.

As I have attempted to show with the extended discussion of section 30 of the Human Fertilisation Act, it not so much that a redefinition is under way, it is that one is very firmly in place. Here, again, we confront the boundaries of language and experience; so much here do we lack a vocabulary for 'explaining to a child that egg, sperm, or embryo donation form part of its inheritance'[48] that we may wonder about the acquisition of identity. Although this is not an argument which I can fully pursue here, it seems to me to rest on a distinction between the social definition of one's origins and some other, presently less clearly defined notion about full civil personhood. I do not wish to deny the importance of philosophical discussions about persons and identity, about selves and being; but so far as I know, being born is a precondition for engaging in that debate. The extent to which 'genetic bewilderment' affects the presentation of self in everyday life is a contested one, but arguments about genetic origins seem to me to be intimately related to notions of the 'natural family' and appeal to the 'natural order of things' which are themselves an attempt to legitimate and reinforce a specific form of structure and specific relationships of authority and dependence.[49]

48 Katherine O'Donovan, 'What Shall We Tell the Children? Reflections on Children's Perspectives and the Reproduction Revolution' in Robert Lee and Derek Morgan, (eds)., *Birthrights: Law and Ethics at the Beginnings of Life*, (London, Routledge, 1989) at p.96. Of course, in many senses we all have sperm and egg as a part of our inheritance; O'Donovan's point is nicely captured, however, in some of the recent objections which have been voiced in relation to the Human Fertilisation and Embryology Authority's Consultation Paper, *Donated Ovarian Tissue in Embryo Research and Assisted Conception*, (London, HFEA, 1994). Responding to the canvassed possibility that eggs might be recovered for use in assisted conception programmes from aborted female fetuses, one line of argument has been that any child subsequently born would be produced from a 'mother' who had never lived; this introduces a new and startling form of motherhood, not one in which the presumption *mater est quam gestatio demonstrat* is shaken, but one which harkens back to a prior genetic possibility.

49 For an earlier attempt to work through some of these notions see Morgan, 'Making Motherhood Male' *Journal of Law and Society*, 12, 1985, 219 at 225, and the discussion of these points by O'Donovan, *op. cit.*, n.48, esp. at pp.100–02

ii) On Exploitation

Although this is not explored fully in her essay, Marshall raises important questions about the nature of infertility. I cannot treat this here either, but what is of note is the purpose for which she wants to address this; 'I might go as far to say' writes Marshall,

> that the really interesting questions are not so much the ones about surrogacy but the ones which we need to see as part of the background to surrogacy: in particular, the question about what sort of problem we take infertility to be, such that biotechnology seems a suitable way of dealing with it. ... there is no reason that I can see why surrogacy should be limited to the alleviation of infertility; this is to say that I can see no reason why infertility should be taken as the only serious reason.[50]

Of course, this is in response to the Warnock Committee's exhortation that surrogacy arrangements entered into on the grounds of convenience alone are 'totally ethically unacceptable. Even in compelling medical circumstances the danger of exploitation of one human being by another appears to the majority of us to far outweigh the potential benefits in almost every case.'[51] As Marshall in her commentary on this passage makes clear, it is possible that one or more of three different objections is being raised; i) that surrogacy is itself exploitative; ii) that in some circumstances it might be; iii) commercial surrogacy is necessarily exploitative.

This provides the introduction for Marshall's strongest concerns; that surrogacy contributes to the alienation of women's reproductive labour, is exploitative and discriminatory, and thus offends those values which essays in this collection have been seeking to explore and defend. The burden of her argument is that 'contract pregnancy corrupts or distorts women's reproductive labour in such a way as to alienate that labour.' A powerful, polemical version of this argument about reproductive labour has been presented by Andrea Dworkin – calling surrogacy 'reproductive prostitution.' Recall that in her provocative essay, *Right Wing Women*, Dworkin fashions and deploys the notion of 'sexual intelligence' as a counterweight to moral and creative intelligence. This concept she brings to bear on surrogacy as a critical challenge to its principles and practices. Dworkin expresses sexual intelligence as a human capacity for discerning, manifesting and constructing sexual integrity.[52] Its cornerstone is the honest possession of one's own body, 'not one that has already been cut into parts and fetishised.'[53]

This is a strong and arresting image, and it is to this that sexual intelligence is to set the limits; it announces values that are meaningful to the whole person and personality and it challenges 'the shallow, predestined sexuality men have counterfeited for women.'[54] Its commodification, being sold on the market, is necessarily anathema to sexual intelligence, a direct affront to its intrinsic need to confront the world in self-defined, self-defining terms.

50 'Whose Child is it Anyway?', Chapter 10, above

51 *Warnock*, Cmnd 9314 (1984)

52 Andrea Dworkin, *Right Wing Women: The Politics of Domesticated Females* (London, Womwn's Press, 1983) pp181–94

53 *Ibid* p54

54 *Ibid* p56

For Marshall, the application of economic norms;

i) requires the surrogate mother to repress whatever parental love she feels for the child (notice the interesting use of language here – not fetus but child) (and thus alienates her (reproductive) labour);
ii) denies the legitimacy of the surrogate's evolving perspective of her own pregnancy (and thus degrades her) and
iii) leaves the surrogate open to exploitation in taking advantage of her non-commercial motivations.

As Freeman has suggested, properly read these objections focus on the claim that surrogacy exploits because it involves 'a transaction in which one party is as a result of circumstances (such as poverty, unemployment) subjected to the demands of another more powerful party.'[55] Exploitation thus takes the form of coercing one person into doing something which otherwise she would not have done because she has less power than the exploiter, and when the exploiter uses his advantage of power to force her to do as he wishes. Thus the surrogate's basic claims to liberty and equality are being undermined.

This theme of exploitation is taken up by Martha Field, who objects that while some suggest that it is patronising to raise such an argument, this misconstrues the argument. It does not, she suggests, entail the view that women (or those who contemplate surrogacy contracts) are weak, rather that 'there are certain subject matters that are so important and so deeply personal that we as a society do not want the state to intervene to bind people – men *or* women – by their previous promises. ... Society also has an interest in keeping certain contracts outside of the market economy – and the transfer of children is one of them. Sometimes this objection is called an objection to commodifying children – to treating them as objects subject to barter and exchange.'[56] Of course, as Field herself readily recognises, this is an argument not so much about exploitation but about commodification; 'an advantage of simple non-enforcement, in comparison with criminalisation of surrogacy arrangements, is that it does respect a right of women to do with as they wish with their bodies.'[57]

I want to respond here only to the third of Marshall's arguments as she effectively deals with the limitations of the first two. In acting as the legislature has done and providing that surrogacy contracts are unenforceable[58] it has opted for a compromise on whether surrogacy is demeaning or liberating – perhaps permissive would be more neutral here – for women. It allows women to enter into reproductive pre-conception contracts, to be paid for the work they do, and does not dictate what work women may and may not be allowed to do. As Field strongly argues, 'non-enforcement allows women to enter into these arrangements and to go through with them on whatever terms they

55 Freeman, 'Is Surrogacy Exploitative?' in Sheila McLean (ed), *Legal Issues in Human Reproduction* (Aldershot, Gower, 1989), 164 at 168

56 'Surrogate Motherhood' in John Eekelaar and Petar Sarcevic (eds.), *Parenthood in Modern Society: Legal and Social Issues for the Twenty First Century*, (Dordrecht, Martinus Nijhoff, 1993), p.223 at p.225

57 *Ibid*, p.226

58 Human Fertilisation & Embryology Act 1990 s. 36 inserting s1A in the Surrogacy Arrangements Act 1985; 'No surrogacy arrangement is enforceable by or against any of the persons making it.'

choose ... All non-enforcement does is to protect the woman who herself decides that she does not want to go through with the arrangement after all.'[59] Indeed, it might in this way be thought to empower surrogates; in that they can if they wish hold out the possibility of reneging on the contract deal.[60]

It may be objected that there are downsides to this, both to the surrogate and to the commissioning couple. As far as the surrogate is concerned, it may raise the transactions costs of the deal, and have the effect of causing couples more carefully to 'screen' each prospective surrogate mother for the genuineness of her expressed willingness to hand over the child following birth. The result of this more accentuate screening will likely be that fewer women will decide that they could part with the child or, again, to bargain a higher price for their agreement.[61] The effect of this may not be as sure as supposed:

> ... such screening is bound to be costly and of limited efficacy, which means that the benefits of surrogate motherhood will be reduced to both sides of the transaction. The surrogate mother, for example, will receive a lower price because her performance is uncertain. So in the long run surrogate mothers will lose, not gain, from a rule designed to strengthen their bargaining position by allowing them to repudiate their contracts.[62]

If seeking to achieve a balance between liberating and protective aspects of surrogacy regulation is the desired goal this seems to me to be an acceptable price to pay in respect of regulation.

As far as the couple are concerned, there are hold-out risks that non-enforceability raises; but whether we think this is much as it should be, it brings pre-conception contracts much in line with other contracts for personal services. Oddly, much of the debate about enforcement has proceeded as though we would be creating a startling precedent in refusing to enforce such agreements, but this is far from the case; in very few circumstances indeed would a British court require the performance of any such contract or even one closely related to it.[63]

We know little of i) the number of women who would regard themselves as exploited because of their involvement in surrogacy; ii) whether surrogacy does *necessarily* entail an infringement of any basic rights of the surrogate; iii) whether in cases where the surrogate changes her mind and wishes to keep the baby the decision which is *then* taken 'in the best interests of the child' produces or reinforces any feelings – well founded or otherwise – of exploitation which the surrogate might express. The evidence which would be necessary to sustain a charge of exploitation is not readily available.

Most surrogates already have children of their own (and there may be concern at the emotional costs on these children) and few are poor, in the sense of needing the money, as opposed to needing more money. Indeed, it might be thought that one of the concerns

59 Field, *op. cit.*, p.227

60 This is the view argued by Richard Posner in *Sex and Reason* (Cambridge, Mass., Harvard University Press, 1992) p422, and John Harris, *Wonderwoman and Superman*, (Oxford, Oxford University Press, 1992) p121–27. See also Freeman *op. cit.*, at pp166–78

61 See Posner at p422

62 *Ibid*

63 Field at p.225 gives some good examples of other contracts which are simply not enforced; for the general attitude of contemporary British law to private, consensual acts which for some hold repugnance as against public policy see the House of Lords discussion in *R* v *Brown* [1993] 2 All ER 75 and the antecedent case of *Attorney General's Reference (No. 6) (1980)* [1981] QB 715

which motivated the couple would be a concern for the health and welfare of any future child which might not necessarily be secured in an environment of poverty and destitution. This is not, of course, an argument of celebration of destitution and poverty; but an observation which challenges at least some of the assumptions commonly made in respect of exploitation.

There is of course, an alternative way of telling this story, and it is most neatly captured by the challenge issued by Marcel Proust in the first book of *Things of Remembrance Past*, and which may be effectively translated as surrogacy and the question of the immobility of conception:

> Perhaps the immobility of the things that surround us is forced upon them by our conviction that they are themselves and not anything else, by the immobility of our conception of them.[64]

The version of surrogacy receiving current endorsement is one that has been colonised by both medicine, social work and law.[65] In this way it frustrates the aspiration expressed by Michael Freeman in 1986[66] that 'surrogacy presents us with an opportunity to challenge unacceptable features of medical and social work imperialism' and the hopes that surrogacy could become a dominant non-technological form of altruism and self-help between women.[67] The framework of section 30, in so far as it formally legitimates claims to parenthood by the genetic parent(s) of surrogate-born children may exercise ' ... an important symbolic impact on the acceptability of surrogacy as a form of family creation. With hindsight it may come to be seen as the acceptable face of surrogacy.'[68]

It may be that this is the more unacceptable form of expropriation and exploitation involved in modern surrogacy, one in which the state and its satellites captures and controls any hope of deliverance which collaborative conception arrangements may offer. Reproductive technology has become the bureau de change of the moral economy. Surrogacy, in confronting our notions of self and self-conception, challenges the way in which we respond to the re-evaluation of the currency of personhood which we have allowed technology to force upon us. The response will help us to understand the sort of people we say we are and want to become. Issues such as childbirth, child rearing and child care are more easily seen and identified today as raising core issues of social justice. But I remain puzzled whether the way in which children are conceived will, without more, have such a dramatic impact on us, compared with say arrangements we make for childcare, work and leisure, that the objections to surrogacy *on this level* have decisive force.

64 Marcel Proust, 1 *Things of Remembrance Past*, (trans. C K Scott-Moncrieff and Terence Kilmartin, Harmonsworth, Penguin, 1983 ed. p.6)

65 Blyth, *op. cit.*, p. 258

66 'After Warnock – W(h)ither the Law?' *Current Legal Problems*, 39, 1986, 33–55

67 Juliette Zipper and Selma Sevenhuijsen in 'Surrogacy: Feminist Notions of Motherhood Reconsidered' in Michelle Stanworth, (ed.), *Reproductive Technologies: Gender, Motherhood and Medicine*, Cambridge, Polity Press, 1988

68 Blyth, *op. cit.*, at 258